Women and Marriage
in Kpelle Society

CAROLINE H. BLEDSOE

Women and Marriage in Kpelle Society

STANFORD UNIVERSITY PRESS
STANFORD, CALIFORNIA
1980

Stanford University Press
Stanford, California

© 1980 *by the Board of Trustees of the*
Leland Stanford Junior University

Printed in the United States of America
ISBN 0-8047-1019-8
LC 78-66170

Published with the assistance of the
Andrew W. Mellon Foundation

PREFACE

This book examines the ways in which economic and political opportunities for men and women influence marriage patterns among the Kpelle of Liberia. To protect those who might not want themselves used as examples, I have changed the names of all the people I discuss in Fuama Chiefdom and have slightly altered the circumstances of anecdotes that might reveal someone's identity.

This study, a revision of my Ph.D. dissertation for Stanford University, has profited from the encouragement and assistance of many people. I must first thank those in Liberia who made it possible. I am of course indebted to the people of Fuama Chiefdom, who bore my inquiries and faux pas with patience and humor. Mrs. Bertha B. Azango and Dr. Melvin J. Mason, the successive presidents of the Liberian Research Association, were especially helpful in arranging my research visa. Many government officials provided me with research clearance and valuable administrative assistance. Among them are Minister of Foreign Affairs Cecil Dennis; Minister E. Jonathan Goodridge of the Ministry of Local Government, Urban Reconstruction, and Rural Development; Senators Boto Barclay (retired) and Byron Traub; Superintendent Harry A. Greaves of Bong County; Commissioner Charles V. Dormeyan of Salala District; Paramount Chief Ernest K. Barclay of Fuama Chiefdom; and Clan Chiefs Luke D. Pope of Dobli Clan and Dogba Worlorseah of Lorla Clan. I also want to thank my assistants, particularly Paul K. Ricks, who did a superb job during the short time we worked together. At the University of Liberia, J. Blamo was kind enough to arrange library privileges for me. And I am grateful to Jeannette Carter, Jane Martin, and Zamba Liberty for their hospitality and encouragement.

Though they strictly forbade me to thank them here, Roger Simmons and Emmy Simmons deserve special thanks anyway, for providing my husband and me with unbounded hospitality and clever insights into our work whenever we stayed in Monrovia. Bill Bailey, the luckless Peace Corps volunteer I descended on when I first arrived in Liberia, was good enough to let my husband and me stay with him in Haindii. He bore our intrusions uncomplainingly, with unfailing kindness.

During the various stages of preparation of this manuscript, I benefited from the interest shown by the following people, and from their criticism: Harry Basehart, Phil Bock, John Comaroff, George Dalton, Pat Draper, John Gay, Judy Gay, Penn Handwerker, Svend Holsoe, Igor Kopytoff, Louise Lamphere, Carol Hoffer MacCormack, Arthur Wolf, and Margery Wolf. William Welmers and Bill Murphy helped polish the orthography of some key Kpelle words and phrases, George Collier and Penn Handwerker helped with the statistics, and Wanda Conger and Lois Vermilia-Weslowski helped edit and proofread the manuscript. At Stanford Press, Bill Carver and Peter Kahn have given support throughout the writing and revising process, and Andrea Dimino has done a fine editing job.

I am grateful for the guidance of my dissertation committee: Francesca Cancian, James Gibbs (whose own work among the Kpelle parallels mine), and Bernard Siegel. Jane Collier, my principal adviser, deserves special thanks for her hours of reading and editing drafts of proposals, papers, and dissertation and book chapters.

The National Science Foundation, the National Institute of General Medical Sciences, and the Stanford Committee on African Studies sponsored my fieldwork and the writing of my dissertation, and the University of New Mexico Research Allocation Committee provided funds for revising the dissertation. Albert Swingle gave me permission to quote from his field notes, and the *Journal of Anthropological Research* gave me permission to use ideas and quotes from my 1976 article "Women's Marital Strategies Among the Kpelle of Liberia" (32: 372–89).

Finally, I must thank Bill Murphy, my husband, who did fieldwork with me and spent many hours helping edit and revise the dissertation and book. Many of the ideas set forth here must be attributed to him, but we exchanged so many ideas that I can no longer remember who thought of what.

C.H.B.

CONTENTS

TABLES

A NOTE ON PRONUNCIATION

Transcriptions of Kpelle words in this book follow the standard orthography worked out by William Welmers (1962, 1971). Except in the case of proper names, I have included marks that indicate tonal quality or nasalization for the sake of accuracy. Two paired consonants pronounced as single consonants in Kpelle, and five special symbols with their approximate English equivalents, are explained below:

kp   these two letters are pronounced as one consonant in Kpelle, with a sound approximating the "kp" in "crackpot" said quickly

gb   another single consonant in Kpelle, with a sound approximating the "gb" in "tugboat" said quickly

ɓ   this can be approximated by pronouncing the letter "b" implosively, like a cork popping out of a bottle

ɣ   this sound, produced in the back of the throat, is similar to the "ch" in the German word "ach," but is said with less friction

ŋ   this sound is similar to the "n" in the word "sing"

ɛ   this sound is similar to the "e" in the word "get"

ɔ   this sound is similar to the first syllable of the word "awful"

Women and Marriage
in Kpelle Society

CHAPTER 1

Introduction

In examining what marriage means to rural African women, we are confronted by an apparent contradiction. On the one hand, ethnographers have observed that African legal systems commonly give rights in women's productive and reproductive services to fathers, husbands, brothers, and other male relatives. On the other hand, major deviations from these legal norms occur: in some societies, for example the Nuer (Gough 1971), over half the women of marriageable age are not under any man's legal control. To explain this breach between norms and reality, we might hypothesize that women resent the system that subordinates them to men and try to evade its obligations. Yet many African women are just as conservative as men in trying to preserve the institutions that give control of women's services to men and older women. During my fieldwork among the Kpelle of Liberia, I heard bitter complaints from older women about the breakdown of marriage and filial obligation (see also Gibbs 1960, 1963).

As this book will show, Kpelle women do not see this difference between norms and practices as a contradiction. Rather, they see both norms and practices as readily reconcilable aspects of a more general "wealth-in-people" system, which binds people to their superiors in ties of marriage, clientship, and filial obligation (see Chapter 3). I will argue that all people, men as well as women, try to sever their own ties with superiors when possible, but try to keep subordinates bound to them in ties of obligation.[1]

---

1. It is beyond the scope of this book to do a cross-cultural survey that documents the patterns I discuss for the Kpelle in a systematic and exhaustive way throughout West Africa or Africa as a whole. Many ethnographers have mentioned

Rural African women's economic roles are closely related to their marital options and constraints. Both J. Goody and Huntington have criticized Boserup's (1970) argument that because of their dominant roles in production, African women are traditionally highly independent, mobile, and able to accumulate wealth and status on their own. Goody (1973:46) downplays the importance of African women's contribution to agriculture, viewing the overall system of socioeconomic stratification as the most important factor in assessing patterns of marriage, inheritance, and female status. Huntington (1975) even questions the extent to which women control their roles in production. She claims that in fact men dominate both traditional female farming systems and modern markets, and make these institutions serve their own interests. The main vehicle for this economic subordination of women is marriage. As Huntington (1975: 1007) notes, the status of women in rural African societies generally bears little relation to the amount of food they produce, because their efforts eventually line their husbands' pockets: "In many of these African societies, women's farming is the source of whatever wealth there is, and, despite women's rights in land tenure, men control women and women's production through their subordination in marriage, much as peasants are the traditionally subordinated producers of wealth for landbased aristocrats." Clearing the way for a new model of African women's status, Huntington (1975: 1011) argues that we "must take into account the past and present economic structure of the societies. Such a model would include . . . all that is summed up in the phrase 'the traditional role of women' and . . . the opportunity structure each particular attempt at modernization creates for the women in those societies."

This study provides such a model, linking female productive and sexual services to opportunity structures in traditional and modern contexts of Kpelle society.[2] I argue that because Kpelle women and

similar patterns of stratification and marriage in their descriptions of other African societies; I draw attention to some of these parallels to show that the Kpelle case is not an isolated one. My own study will hopefully stimulate a refinement of the wealth-in-people concept as it applies—or does not apply—to other African societies. I hope it will also stimulate discussions of variations in African social stratification patterns, and of the conditions under which particular patterns emerge.

2. My use of the word "model" in this book does not imply a mathematical construct with predictive power, but rather a general analytical framework. Although I

marriage are the political and economic tools of men in the traditional system, women as a group find it hard to advance in the wider society. However, they view their children—especially the older ones—along with other members of domestic groups, as resources rather than impediments: as people whose labor will lighten their burdens and offer them security in their old age. Hence, women in traditional contexts *can* achieve some degree of independence as they grow older, by using the services of the young.[3]

Modernization has provided new opportunities for Kpelle women to acquire independence and prestige. Where cash cropping is possible or wage labor opportunities are available, women can remain unmarried because cash from marketing or from wage-earning lovers allows them to hire farm labor, pay house taxes, and buy household necessities themselves, a pattern noted as well by studies in other parts of Africa.[4] But even these women still want their children to support them, and to marry spouses who will contribute to their support. In this way Kpelle women achieve the maximum freedom to make their own decisions, but still hold on to the security of the traditional ideal.

Recent studies of women's lives have sometimes lumped women into a single homogeneous group, perhaps seeking to demonstrate female solidarity and camaraderie in the face of male oppression. But women are people who occupy a number of status positions, many of which they share with men. For the Kpelle, the most sig-

---

have set up the comparison in terms of modern and traditional areas, the terminology may imply a false dichotomy for three reasons. First, the term "traditional" does not imply a timeless, untouched society. Outside influences have had considerable impact on African institutions for centuries. Second, the two kinds of economic and political organization I discuss in Chapters 4 and 5 do not imply a dual organization in which both systems operate autonomously. National institutions influence those in the hinterland and vice versa. (See, for example, Wolf 1957, J. Goody 1967, and Meillassoux 1972 on the important relations between modern and traditional sectors.) Third, the terms "modern" and "traditional" are of course relative. Haindii and Dobli Island, the modern towns, are not fully modernized even by Liberian standards, but they do have more access to modern transportation, markets, and jobs than Digei, which relies more on subsistence agriculture.

3. Obviously some women are also "young people," and some men are also "older people." For the sake of verbal facility, I hope the reader will indulge my occasional references to "women and the young," "men and older people," and so on.

4. This study deals in part with marital instability, but treats it as a manifestation of a larger process of change. I am not trying to explain why Kpelle marriage is more or less stable than marriage in other African societies; I am merely looking at marriage patterns within Kpelle society, and their relationship to larger changes in the society as a whole.

nificant status positions other than sex are age, lineage membership, possession of children, residence (modern versus traditional areas), and wealth. Kpelle women may find it in their interests to unite with other women at times, but they may just as easily find it in their interests to unite with male agnates against rival lineages, or with other old people against power plays by young upstarts. Moreover, women who have older children or wealth or who live in a modern area may take more risks than women with more limited means of support. To analyze the ways Kpelle women and men use all available resources to their own advantage, especially in conjugal and domestic situations, is the primary aim of this book.

I did most of the research for this study during five weeks in the summer of 1973 and eleven months in 1974. In 1978 I returned to my field site for a brief visit to check some details and catch up on some case histories. I began learning the Kpelle language before leaving for the field, using the excellent tapes and grammar prepared by William Welmers. When I got to Liberia I continued Kpelle lessons with native speakers, but found I still had to rely on interpreters for interviews, especially with women, few of whom had continued their education long enough to learn English, the national language taught in public schools.

I lived in Haindii, the headquarters of Fuama Chiefdom, in a house with my husband, who was also doing anthropological fieldwork, and a Peace Corps volunteer who taught at the local school. Most of my work was conducted there. I frequently visited the town of Dobli Island, just across the St. Paul River, and once every two months in 1974 I spent five or six days in Digei, a small town 25 miles up-country by footpath. To visit Digei, my husband and I and our assistants chartered a Piper Cub plane in Monrovia, and landed on the airstrip built by the Lutheran mission. We rented one room in a zinc-roofed house, cooked on a gas burner, and ate local rice and canned food we brought from Monrovia. When we left Digei, we walked seven miles with our equipment and bedding to Kelebe, a small town at the end of a new unpaved road, and rode back to Haindii by taxi, the most common means of public transportation.

Since I was going to be conversing with women much of the time,

I needed a female assistant, so I hired a woman about eighteen years old. She had completed the eighth grade and spoke English very well. Her knowledge of the people in the community was valuable, but I soon found that for several reasons she was not a good interpreter or diplomatic mediator for me. My status was rather low in the first place because I was a female, and lower yet because I was young and childless. Having a female assistant even younger than I did not help. Not only did men of status consider her far beneath them, but many women were impatient with her as well; like many young women in Haindii she had lovers, so married women did not trust her with their husbands and did not speak freely with her. Hence, I began a search for an additional assistant.

My second assistant, a man of about thirty-five, had a high school education. He commanded good salaries from his employers, mostly other anthropologists, and used his earnings to support his wife and children, whom he brought with him to Haindii, and to dress well. All these attributes gave him status among the people we worked with and also seemed to confer more status on me. Although he was a stranger to the community, he was not seen as a threat, since he had no competing loyalties and no stake in local political maneuvers. Thanks to his patience, humor, and tact, even normally reticent women opened up readily to him, and I owe many of my best interviews to his skill. As it turned out, I had an ideal pair of assistants. I kept the young woman to work with census data and to provide information on local events and people, and I benefited from the man's status and diplomacy.

My basic purpose was to compare Kpelle marriage patterns in two areas of Fuama Chiefdom, one modern and one traditional. Haindii and Dobli Island, the modern towns, had good transportation, jobs, and markets; Digei, the traditional town, was in a more remote area. I spent most of my time on a census of all the inhabitants of the three towns, a total population of 1,302 residents in 1974. The census was conducted primarily through informants. At first I tried going from house to house or inviting people to my house to record information. But when I checked the information given me by suspicious residents with that of several close informants, many discrepancies appeared. This happened primarily for two reasons. One was that the Kpelle regard information as a highly valuable resource, and guard it closely. The other was that marital status, my central focus, proved to be a particularly touchy and ambiguous topic. Women consistently tried to construe it to their own advantage to avoid antagonizing men to whom they were not legally "turned over" (married).[5] These women knew their partners would be angry with them for telling me they were not married, because other men might learn of this and would lose their fear of adultery fines. Even my closest friend told me at first that she was married, describing the occasion of her marriage at great length— where it was performed, who came, what was said, and so on. Only later did she confess that she was not really married. Thus I decided my time would be more economically spent using anonymous informants. Though I often questioned residents directly when I knew them well enough, I used several informants for census data on everyone in all three towns, and I cross-checked the data many times. This method undoubtedly excluded some people and yielded some incorrect information, especially in Haindii and Dobli Island, which had more mobile populations, but I feel that I obtained greater accuracy this way than by relying exclusively on the residents themselves.

Though the census, household, and economic data were collected over a period of eight or nine months, I naturally thought of more variables to collect as my ideas on marriage progressed. So I asked my informants to try to remember what each resident's status with respect to all items had been in January 1974, when the initial census was taken. Imprecise and incomplete as these data may be, they were important for the kinds of associations I was interested in.

The census contained information on sex, age category (I used twelve categories by which the Kpelle classify people), town of residence, number of children, and economic enterprises. In addition, I collected data on house ownership, household composition, and features of the house (zinc or thatch roof, cement or mud coating, number and kind of auxiliary buildings known as "kitchens," and

5. I will adopt the convention of using double quotes to indicate Liberian English or idiomatic expressions. Single quotes around words or phrases indicate translations or translation glosses.

so on). For Haindii and Dobli Island I gathered information on the history of each house—who built it and how the present owner acquired it. Because my main interest was marriage, I carefully collected information on people's current marital status, number of spouses (for men), current spouses' residences, number of previous marriages, and whether previous marriages ended in death or divorce.

Though the statistics in Chapter 5 help to substantiate the arguments advanced, the case studies, especially those in Chapter 5, convey more vividly my point that conjugal relationships and social identities (cf. Goffman 1959 and Goodenough 1966) are much more fluid than Westerners suspect. We assume that kin and marital categories are clear-cut and unambiguous: for example, a woman is either married or not married. Kpelle marital status, however, is more accurately seen as a process that gradually transfers a woman from her kin to a man and his kin. Thus marital status is not ascertainable from appearance or clothing, as it is in many societies. Nor are people always certain about their own marital status, as Comaroff and Roberts (1977) have shown for the Kgatla. Even the cognitive categories "married" and "unmarried" are not clear-cut. For example, the word for 'woman,' nɛnî, is also the word for 'wife,' and the word for 'man,' surɔ̀ŋ, is also the word for 'husband.' (See Comaroff & Roberts 1977: 113.) Chapter 4 explains how I tried to impose order on Kpelle conjugal categories for purposes of comparing the modern and traditional villages.

Not only is marital status often unclear, but people can play upon gradations in status to achieve certain ends. It is common knowledge that genealogies may be fudged in any society—invented or denied as the occasion warrants. But I was unprepared for the kinds of marital manipulation I witnessed among the Kpelle, particularly in Haindii and Dobli Island. Men, for example, usually insist that women with whom they are living have been "turned over" to them, but they may swear that troublesome wives are only girlfriends whom they can discard with no legal penalties. Married women, on the other hand, may try to prove they were not "turned over" to poor men or men they have come to dislike, but may try to hold on to wealthy men even though they are not yet "turned over" to them. Similarly, mothers may manipulate the social identity of their children's fathers in order to leave men they do not like or to get support from wealthy men. Women may also manipulate their own social identity to keep possibilities open for support from lovers. Married women, for example, may present themselves as single to acquire extra support, or to help their husbands gain wealth by suing their lovers for adultery. Single women may present themselves as married to keep different lovers from getting jealous of each other. Single women may also use different names with each of their lovers, to keep them ignorant of each other.

When brought to court, cases involving disputes over marital status invariably end in a tangle of contradictory testimonies from numerous witnesses. Whether attempts to restructure social reality are successful depends, of course, on the personal influence of particular actors, as well as on social and economic support for their efforts. Given the sometimes hopelessly ensnarled disposition of legal rights in women, as well as the changing definitions that actors try to impose in different situations, I hope the reader will understand why taking a census and recording marital statuses, biological fathers, and even names was such a long and painful, though fascinating, process. Despite seeming confusions, actors' attempts to formalize or change marital reality are consistent with the generalization that Kpelle people try to escape obligations to superiors who want to control them, but try to keep docile subordinates bound to them. (Comaroff & Roberts 1977 provide a helpful discussion of the logic behind the apparent manipulation chaos.)

Manipulation of marital status is, of course, not confined to modern areas such as Haindii and Dobli Island. People in traditional areas also misrepresent their marital status, and they do it for the same reasons: to gain wealth or political power. But this manipulation becomes intensified in changing areas such as Haindii and Dobli Island simply because new options, particularly for women, are developing so rapidly. So although such manipulations are common in all Kpelle areas, their prevalence in the modern area signifies that people there are taking advantage of new economic opportunities to restructure limiting relationships.

During the last two months of my stay I administered a domestic organization questionnaire to a sample of 44 women in Haindii and 35 women in Digei, with the help of my male assistant. To choose the sample of women, I categorized household types, calculated the percentage of each type in both towns, and figured the proportion of women from each type that I would need to make the sample representative. Finally, I chose houses as randomly as possible within each type and interviewed only one woman from each house I chose. I asked a few general census questions but devoted most of the questionnaire to the organization of domestic activities such as cooking, child care, housekeeping, farming, and the acquisition of food, shelter, clothes, and money. In addition, I asked women whether they would rather be married or single, and why.

Because I was interested in women's business enterprises, I also interviewed women in the towns outside of Bong Mine, a German-run mining concession seven miles from Haindii. I picked this area because it was convenient and because it had many shops and market stalls. I administered a market questionnaire to sixteen women to find out why they had taken up marketing and how it related to their marital status. I administered another questionnaire to ten women in the same area who were not engaged in marketing, to find out why not.

My arguments about Kpelle men's and women's marital strategies are based heavily on inferences from my census and questionnaire data. In addition, I learned a considerable amount about marriage strategies and values from folktales and proverbs, from observing ritual activities, from listening to court cases, and from tapping sources of local gossip. Only a few close friends would talk to me about their own future marriage strategies—the best kind of evidence for a study of people's strategies—but I often succeeded in getting people to tell me their thoughts about hypothetical situations and dilemmas of my devising. This tactic often reminded informants of stories of actual cases. I also drew pictures of people performing various tasks and asked informants to comment on the probable marital situations of the people portrayed.

Marriage was a topic very much on the minds of nearly all Kpelle men and women. Men worried about how to control adulterous wives, and women worried about how to escape dependence on adulterous husbands or how to pry them loose from their girl-friends. Needless to say, my male assistant learned a great deal about women's goals and strategies. People knew he was earning a good salary, so even for the short time he was working for me he was a prime target for women seeking lovers with money. He told me he was leaving the project a much wiser man, able to penetrate the tricks of some of the wiliest women in Haindii.

My discussion of marriage in this book tends to stress individual actors. Though this may accentuate the self-seeking side of the people described, I do not mean to imply that the Kpelle I knew acted only out of mercenary or self-interested motives. Indeed, people do things for many different reasons, especially in the context of such complex relations as marriage and the family. In most cases, however, I was careful to have my interpretations verified whenever possible by the people involved or informants who told me about them. Thus, although the responsibility for choosing one interpretation over another must rest with me alone, I believe my choices would generally find favor with my more analytical informants.

A similar problem of emphasis emerges in the discussion of kin relations. People tend to talk about close kin ties in terms of morality and altruism rather than self-interest. Beidelman puts the anthropologist's problem of dealing with kin ties into helpful perspective (1971: 59–60):

This is not, of course, intended to suggest that Kaguru [in Tanzania] do not feel deep ties of affection and loyalty between kin, for they do. However, enormous pressures are put upon such ties, and intense competition occurs within the field of primary kin relations precisely because kinship is so deeply important since it provides the basic avenue to broader economic, social, and political security. In any society where kinship is this important, we may be sure that it is a sphere not only of intense sentiment and moral obligations but also, at least potentially, of bitter competition and feelings of betrayal and enmity.

Similarly, regarding marriage arrangements, Beidelman remarks that "all this discussion of social manipulation and potential tensions does not mean that many Kaguru marriages are not happy affairs with considerable affection. But marriages are not usually contracted with these feelings as the primary goals or motives, and other factors encourage what Kaguru claim is a fairly high divorce rate." (*Ibid.*, pp. 61–62.)

These observations apply very well to the Kpelle cases I discuss. Most Kpelle feel a great deal of affection for their spouses and close kin, yet larger issues of social advancement as well as basic subsistence force them to think of the people close to them in pragmatic as well as moral terms. Thus, although my focus on pragmatic motives necessarily slights the other side of the picture, I believe it is not misplaced.

Chapter 2 is a brief description of the geography and history of Liberia and Fuama Chiefdom. Chapter 3 examines the "wealth-in-people" system, the basis of the traditional Kpelle economy as well as many other traditional African economies. The chapter shows that extensive agriculture, combined with military needs and personal patronage, has produced a stratified socioeconomic system based on the control of labor and political patronage. In Chapter 4 I locate women and marriage in the Kpelle wealth-in-people system, arguing that legal control of women's production and reproduction enables men to control the labor and allegiance of other men. Because they are the tools of men, most women in traditional areas have few alternatives to marriage. Older women with grown children are better off in this regard. If they seek to divorce an intolerable husband, or not to remarry after a husband's death, they can usually call on their children for support.

Changes in marriage patterns in Fuama Chiefdom are analyzed in Chapter 5. Statistics and case studies comparing the traditional and modern areas support the argument that many women in the modern area are using cash from outside resources to marry later, divorce more frequently, and remarry less often than they would in traditional areas. Even women who break up their marriage in this way, however, demand continued filial support as they grow older and press their children to marry hard-working spouses. Similarly, young men try to avoid onerous brideservice but reinvest in the traditional control of women when they can. I conclude that men's and women's goals in both the traditional and modern systems are surprisingly alike: both seek to escape debts and obligations to superiors when possible, but keep dependents tied firmly to them. Chapter 6 examines some implications of the study for our understanding of African marriage, women's roles in society, and modernization.

CHAPTER 2

Liberia and Fuama
Chiefdom

LIBERIA

Liberia has an area of 43,000 square miles, mostly equatorial
rain forest, and an Atlantic coastline of some 350 miles (see Map
1).[1] The 1974 census showed a population of just over 1.5 million.
From Monrovia, the capital, and Buchanan, the country's two major ports, millions of tons of raw materials—principally iron ore,
rubber, and timber—are exported annually to the United States and
Europe.

Six major rivers flow from the northern regions of Liberia to the
Atlantic on the south. None of the rivers is suitable for long-dis-
tance transportation because of waterfalls, rapids, rocks, and shift-
ing banks. The Liberian government, with the aid of foreign loans,
has constructed some paved and unpaved roads linking coastal
towns with those in the interior. But many parts of the country, especially the eastern interior, still cannot be reached by motor vehicle, and small airplanes provide the only fast way into such areas. A
vast network of footpaths connects the villages in the interior.

Liberia has two major seasons. The dry season begins in October
or November and lasts until May or June. During that time the tem-

1. Much of my information on physical and climatological features is from
Schulze (1973).

MAP I. *Liberia, showing the location of Fuama Chiefdom.*

perature rarely reaches 90° F in Monrovia, but because of the high humidity and intense equatorial sun the air is hot and enervating to a visitor from a more temperate climate. Cars traveling on unpaved roads deposit thick red clouds of dust on the tropical foliage, an image that provided the title for John Gay's novel *Red Dust on the Green Leaves* (1973). When the rainy season begins, the temperature in Monrovia occasionally drops to about 70° F. Towns along the coast receive the heaviest rainfall, up to 200 inches per year; places farther up-country receive less.

History

The earliest known history of what is now Liberia dates from sometime after A.D. 1000 with the arrival of two tribal groups from the north and east: one group, consisting of Kwa speakers, was the ancestor of the modern Bassa and perhaps Belle tribes; the other, which spoke West Atlantic, was the ancestor of the modern Gola and Kissi (Kup 1960, Person 1961). Dapper, a seventeenth-century Dutch geographer, reported that before the seventeenth century the interior of Sierra Leone and Liberia was still populated only sparsely by these groups, who most likely practiced hunting and gathering.[2] Later arrivals, the De and Vai peoples, controlled coastal trading stations. Two major events influenced Liberian history during this period. First, there was a dramatic increase in warfare and migration in the western Sudan. The formation of powerful states in this area and the desire of Mandingo and Fulani rulers to control northern trade routes during the fourteenth to sixteenth centuries caused a number of fringe Mande populations, including the Kpelle, to migrate southward into the coastal rain forests. There they made war on, or formed confederacies with, the hunting and gathering groups they encountered as well as with other Mande.

These early wars and migrations were intensified by a second major event: the advent of European traders to the Guinea coast in the

2. Unless otherwise noted, the analysis presented in this section follows d'Azevedo's (1959, 1962b) excellent reconstruction of the history of what he terms the Central West Atlantic region of Africa: southern Sierra Leone and western Liberia.

fifteenth century. Ottoman control of North Africa and the eastern Mediterranean seaports had forced these traders (first the Portuguese and later the Spanish, British, Dutch, and French) to seek alternative routes to West Africa. At first European traders exchanged such things as salt, cloth, and guns for gold, cloth, dyes, hides, livestock, and pepper. But as the demand for labor grew in the Americas, the slave trade expanded and soon became the most lucrative of all. D'Azevedo describes its effect on the people of the Central West Atlantic region (1959: 55–56):

> The early warfare and disturbances created by the pressure of new populations in the interior regions . . . [were] now replaced by active competition and warfare directed to the control of trade . . . routes to the sea. As these routes were most frequently along the major rivers, the present day distribution of many of the larger tribes can be explained by their coastward expansion along these lines of control. The "Hondo" area of Western Liberia . . . very soon became the center of intensive Mandingo activity, and was actually an extension of the trade routes from Musardu. The resulting great confederacy of Kondo (or Bopolu) in the late eighteenth century was based essentially upon a commerce involving the exchange of Western Sudanic trade products for slaves, which were, in turn, sent to the coast via De and Vai middlemen. The wars of this region became more a matter of slave-procuring than a juggling for lands or advantageous position.

Because the Liberia–Ivory Coast area was not as densely populated as areas farther north and south along the coast, the slave trade there did not get fully under way until well into the eighteenth century, when more people had moved in and trade routes had been established. Nevertheless, the sharp increase in the slave trade in this region "created enormous sources of wealth, and the access to gunpowder, small arms and cannon provided a basis for a new kind of warfare and unprecedented concentrations of power. The old trade routes along the St. Paul, Loffa, and Mano rivers in Liberia and Sierra Leone became the great thoroughfares of the slave traffic." (*Ibid.*, p. 59.)[3] The new wealth from the slave trade made the

3. Although it was devastating in many ways, the European descent on the Guinea coast did not in itself cause major changes in social structure. Instead, it spurred competing tribes and factions to greater aggression and sharpened the lines of stratification (d'Azevedo 1959, Rodney 1970).

coastal groups (the Vai and De) the most powerful in the region, leaving groups in the interior such as the Gola and Kpelle to wage war among themselves for the control of trade routes leading to the coast (see also Holsoe 1974).

These intertribal wars, which lasted well into the twentieth century, had profound effects on people's lives. Before outside intervention brought an end to most warfare, people in Liberia needed powerful patrons with large bands of warriors to avoid capture or harm. Oral and written histories are filled with descriptions of fortresses, weapons, battle strategies, and spoils of war in what was to become Fuama Chiefdom, as well as the rest of the Central West Atlantic region. The dangers of these times came across vividly in the following narrative, based on a conversation with two old Kpelle men:[4]

Once there was a big town right on the top of a big hill by Gumbeta. No town could beat them because they had a fence around the town and lived on the top of the hill. They said that even women could defend the town because it had big stones tied near the path. Whenever an attack would come, they would just cut the vines and the stones would fall down and kill all the people. But if someone from the town had his wife taken from him by the townspeople, he would leave and go to their enemies and tell them how they could beat the town. The town was surrounded by one row of sticks in the ground. But in one place there [were] only stones on the ground and the sticks could not be put in the ground. They were only tied up with vines. So the people cut a secret path to the place, cut down the vines and the sticks fell, and they captured the town. When a town was captured the chief and the soldiers were killed and all the rest were taken in slavery. . . . If two towns were at war, three or four of the best warriors would go to the farms of their enemy and capture the men. They would jump on them and say, "If you shout I'll cut off your head," and then take them to the town as slaves. . . .

This is how the war was fought at night. The sia-nùui [pathmaker] would come in town and "love" with some woman at night and she would take rice to him during the day by pretending she was going to the waterside for water, with the rice in the bucket. And then she would secretly go off in the bush with the rice. The man would ask the woman to help him

4. The conversation was recorded in the 1966–68 field notes of Pastor Albert Swingle, a Lutheran missionary stationed in a Kpelle chiefdom adjacent to Fuama. I have corrected various slips of the pen in these rough field notes.

destroy the town, and if she would, he would give her ten slaves to work for her. The help the woman would give would be to tell him where the warriors would be stationed so he could put the path someplace else. Sometimes he would put a few warriors on the main path to distract the townspeople. When the town was defeated, the townspeople would give a chicken and beg the victors, saying: "You men have passed us [won] and we beg you." . . . The woman who sold her town would then be killed by the victors, who cut off her head, saying, "What you have done to your own town, you will also do to us, and so we will cut off your head." This would help to reconcile the two towns. Of course, if her townspeople found out what she did, they would also kill her. . . .

When people [were] killed, the victors didn't even bother to bury their dead. They just threw them back into the bush for the animals to eat. The victors would take some captives back and present them to the chief [ko-kàloŋ] to show that they were successful. So he would thank the warriors and give them some slaves. The woman who lost her husband would cry when she was told that he had been left in the war [a lɛɛ goi sù]. They would tell her to shut up and then she would take a new husband.

During the eighteenth, nineteenth, and early twentieth centuries, the main purpose of warfare was to gain wealth and power by capturing land and trade items, and by capturing and selling slaves. The only chance most people had of avoiding enslavement was to align themselves with powerful chiefs, and to switch when possible from a less powerful patron to a more powerful one. As a result, d'Azevedo (1959: 51) notes, "The alliances of war and peace never involved politically unified tribal entities, but rather particular families, kingdoms, or other relatively autonomous units which formed inter- and intra-tribal systems of varying degrees of importance and stability." Because groups in the area shifted ethnic affiliations when politically expedient, ethnic labels such as Kpelle or Gola should not be interpreted as markers of long-standing cultural or linguistic homogeneity. (See d'Azevedo 1971 for an excellent discussion of such shifts.) Nor indeed, as we shall see, were family genealogies always as accurate as people like to claim.[5]

5. Though the Kpelle may represent an extreme case of ethnic, political, and kinship flexibility, descriptions of many other African societies reveal similar processes. See, for example, Gough 1971. Horton (1972) also helps to shed light on Kpelle history in his discussion of West African "stateless" societies.

The arrival of a new group of migrants in the nineteenth century was to have profound implications for the fluid nature of tribal confederacies. In 1822 the first ship of freed American slaves arrived at Cape Mesurado, now Monrovia. Sent by the American Colonization Society, these people fought off sickness and hostile tribal groups, and established other colonies along the coast. Responding to Britain's attempts to acquire more territory for neighboring Sierra Leone, the Americo-Liberian settlers declared themselves a nation with territorial sovereignty in 1847. By 1879, when the last large group had arrived from the United States, the settlers numbered 15,000, including several contingents from Barbados. Soon after its formation, the new government began to engage in coastal trade, tax the indigenous peoples, and recruit them for farm work. Government leaders also imposed new administrative boundaries on territories that many different tribal groups had previously disputed. The new administrative units linked ethnic groups and territories in a way previously unknown, altering traditional balances of power and inhibiting traditional tendencies to form heterogeneous federations. As a result, groups began to crystallize into much more inflexible ethnic units, producing in large part the "tribalism" that worries Liberian leaders today (d'Azevedo 1971). Policies of national integration have discouraged the formal distinction between Americo-Liberians and tribal peoples. For example, unlike the 1962 Liberian census, the 1974 census does not break down the population into ethnic groups. Nevertheless, the settlers' descendants continue to dominate political life, although tribe members have begun to move into some positions of importance.

Government and the National Economy

The formal structure of the Liberian government resembles that of the United States. The president, head of the executive branch, is elected for an eight-year term and is eligible for succeeding four-year terms. The judicial branch is headed by nine Supreme Court justices, who are appointed for life by the president. Members of the legislature are elected by popular vote from their local districts;[6] senators serve six-year terms, representatives four-year terms. There are two senators and one representative for approximately every ten thousand people in each of the nine counties. Further administrative divisions, in decreasing order of size, are districts, chiefdoms, clans, towns, and quarters, all headed by officials ultimately responsible to the central government.

Liberia is what economists variously call a developing, underdeveloped, or peripheral nation (Myrdal 1957, Adelman 1961, Wallerstein 1974). Foreign companies control much of Liberian industry. The country cannot raise enough rice, its staple food, to feed its population, and must therefore import large quantities. As we have seen, relatively few motor roads have been built, and these are unevenly distributed throughout the country. Liberia also has a shortage of skilled labor. The 1962 census revealed that only 3.4 percent of the population (including expatriates) were employed in skilled professional, technical, administrative, or clerical jobs. Finally, there is a large gap between rich and poor. Clower et al. (1966) estimate that in 1960 at least 90 percent of gross domestic money income was received by less than 5 percent of all people with money income.

Despite its problems, however, Liberia has experienced a tremendous growth in production and income in recent years. One index of this growth is the federal budget, which increased from $33.2 million in 1960 to $83 million in 1973.[7] Another is gross domestic money income, which more than quadrupled from $35.8 million in 1950 to $154.7 million in 1960 (Clower et al. 1966: 24). The main impetus for this phenomenal growth came from President William V. S. Tubman's Open Door Policy. Noting the success of the Firestone rubber plantations established in Liberia in the 1920's, Tub-

6. As Liebenow (1969) and Lowenkopf (1976) point out, however, the Liberian government operates differently in practice than on paper. Anyone desiring high office in Liberia must attain it through patronage networks created by the small elite class who are members of the True Whig Party, the only political party in Liberia. Moreover, as head of the party, the president controls the political and economic machinery necessary to keep him in office indefinitely. President Tubman, for example, served 27 years until his death in 1971.

7. *African Research Bulletin* 10, no. 3: 2688 (1973). Liberian dollars are equal to U.S. dollars.

man initiated the policy when he came to office in 1944. Under this policy, which has continued in the succeeding administration of William R. Tolbert (1971–), foreign businesses are allowed to establish "concessions" in Liberia. They are given generous tax and rental terms and access to cheap contract labor. With other encouragements, such as a nonrevolutionary political environment and few strikes (Liebenow 1969), Liberia's foreign concessions have multiplied and flourished. The largest are the rubber and iron ore concessions. Liberia now exports more iron than any other country on the African continent. Together the iron and rubber industries employed well over half the wage-earning population in 1962 (Schulze 1973: 153).[8]

Although the Open Door Policy has brought benefits to many people, lower-class Liberians find it hard to compete with big businesses because they have little capital and are therefore poor risks for business loans. This accounts in large part for the dearth of Liberians owning retail stores throughout the country and for the large number of foreign merchants. In recent years elite Liberians, who formerly preferred legal and administrative pursuits, have been entering the business world on a large scale, leaving those with little capital far behind.

Most of the Open Door Policy's effects on people in the interior have been indirect, though no less profound. In order to bring economic growth to Liberia's hinterland, the government needed the labor and cooperation of the tribal peoples of these areas, who formerly had little contact with the national sector. Several programs were initiated to assimilate the tribal peoples. One of the first such programs was building roads to link the hinterland with Monrovia. Tubman encouraged foreign concessions to build roads not only to their main sites in the interior but also to outlying support areas. The road to Bong Mine, for example, was built after a German

8. Average per capita incomes have risen and more people have wage jobs, but Dalton (1965) and Clower et al. (1966) argue that Liberia has grown without concomitantly developing its industrial infrastructure. Furthermore, although Liberia is trying to diversify its economic base, reliance on a few raw materials leaves the country vulnerable to the price fluctuations of the international economy—a problem common to other African nations (Bretton 1974).

mining company signed a concession agreement with the Liberian government. Soon after, the company built the road to Haindii because of its ideal location for piping water from the St. Paul River to Bong Mine.

To the credit of the national administration, these new roads have had beneficial effects on the people in the interior. Easier transportation by taxi and truck has allowed people to migrate to Monrovia and other cities to work for wages, thereby escaping sometimes oppressive patron-client relationships that indentured them to their tribal superiors. Roads have also enabled people to take their crops to coastal cities to sell and to bring food (imported rice, dried and frozen fish, and so on) and other goods back to the interior. Finally, roads have made schools and hospitals more accessible. But the roads have also created difficulties. Heavy migration has brought Monrovia problems common to other big cities: unemployment, slums, pollution, and periodic shortages of food and water. In the interior, easy transportation has encouraged wealthy people, many of tribal origin, to buy land near the roads to plant cash crops. This practice is beginning to create land shortages for people who continue to plant subsistence crops. More seriously, a new system of land ownership is depriving tribal people of free subsistence production. People already work hard to produce staples for themselves and some of their urban relatives; requiring legal deeds to land will make their lives even more difficult.

Establishing a national school system was a second way of developing ties with hinterland peoples. Education in Liberia, at first supported almost entirely by American missions, had been restricted mainly to coastal children. Only after the Second World War, apparently in conjunction with assimilation policies, did the missions send more teachers to the interior (Liebenow 1969: 102–3). Similarly, before the advent of foreign concessions in Liberia, little technical or administrative training was available to tribal youth. Needing skilled workers, the concessions opened schools to train tribal children as well as the children of the elite.

Inherent in these new educational opportunities, of course, was the possibility of political competition from a new tribal elite seeking participation in the national government. Rather than deny educated tribal people political mobility, Tubman wisely began to appoint some to high office and allowed them to join the True Whig Party. This policy solidified the loyalty of many tribal people by allowing them to advance in a structure that formerly excluded them. It provided better opportunities for individual tribal members, but in effect the same political structure remained: a small rich class—with some new members—on top, a large poor class below.

Changes in tribal government were a third way of developing ties between the interior and the capital. Before the early twentieth century, groups such as the Kpelle had been organized under strong warriors who led them to battle and protected them from invaders. Such a man (kɔi-nàmu—'war leader') might owe political allegiance to a 'landowner' (lɔi-nâmu) in the area, but there were few formal political relations among groups. Hence, serious disputes were settled by war.

The national government instituted policies that brought peace to the hinterland and opened new channels of communication with the tribal peoples. It also secured their labor and loyalty by acquiring the support of tribal leaders. The government extended its administrative control over the interior by creating a system of indirect rule and a formal hierarchy of chiefs. Under the direction of higher officials in Monrovia, paramount chiefs supervised chiefdoms. Clans (territorial units, not kinship groups) were administered by clan chiefs, towns by town chiefs, and quarters (subdivisions of towns) by quarter chiefs. However, the indigenous political system was not visibly altered at first. Traditional leaders were often appointed paramount or clan chiefs of their areas, especially if they were friendly to members of the national government. Other traditional leaders assumed lesser positions.

Though tribal leaders actually strengthened their power over their followers by allying with the national government, they have become increasingly dependent on their ties to it. For example, the Liberian government has begun to issue the paramount chiefs and clan chiefs a monthly salary, at the same time forbidding them to tax their constituents for this purpose. Though chiefs still find ways to extract economic support from their followers, this new salary links them more closely to the government in Monrovia and allows them to be less responsive to their traditional clients.

Even more important than the institution of salaries, however, is the government's ability to depose elected officials, including tribal chiefs. Superior officials may remove chiefs from office for insubordination, or reinstate them on promise of good behavior. A chief must tread softly, for he risks losing not only the extra riches his position can bring him but his position itself, with its accompanying salary and prestige.

The new system of indirect rule also brought on centralization through tax collection. Though some taxes had been instituted previously, Tubman's administration added a tax of $16 per house (later reduced by Tolbert to $10) and made tribal chiefs responsible for tax collection. To pay these taxes, tribal people have had to become more dependent on commercial ties with the outside world (Cole et al. 1971). People who formerly raised their own crops and bartered for other goods now have to obtain cash by selling produce and migrating to work for wages. Furthermore, people who cannot pay their taxes become more dependent on chiefs, who can ensure reelection by helping their constituents pay or evade taxes.

The government instituted a new court system as well, to bring disputes—and revenues—into centralized channels. Chiefs were authorized to conduct court cases, render verdicts, and collect fees. The government is supposed to collect $7.50 for cases in a clan chief's court and $15.00 for those in a paramount chief's court. Chiefs may also impose additional fines on those found guilty. But because few tribal people have much ready cash, a chief sometimes demands only part of the total fine he claims is justified, leaving the guilty party indebted to him for lowering it. Since the fine does not cover the basic government court fee, he neglects to record the case and "eats" the money himself. At the same time he benefits from the indentured labor of those who are compelled to work off their court debts. As a result people are more dependent on chiefs, who are in turn more dependent on the central government's authority to collect court fines.

FUAMA CHIEFDOM

The Kpelle belong to the Mande-speaking group of the Niger-Congo family of languages (Greenberg 1966). Relatively late arrivals to Liberia, they reached what is now upper Bong County just before A.D. 1600. Thereafter some Kpelle groups migrated southwest along the St. Paul and St. John rivers in search of farmland, salt, trade with the coast, and refuge from other expanding groups. Though they did not settle on the coast, the Kpelle conquered the De groups of the coastal region, and forced them to pay tribute in coastal trade goods. Only in recent times have some Kpelle people reached Monrovia, seeking jobs. About half their population now lives in Guinea to the north, and the rest live in Liberia: some 106,000, according to the 1962 Liberian census, the last to report individual tribal affiliations.

The Kpelle are traditionally slash-and-burn rice farmers. They are often noted in the anthropological literature for their secret Poro and Sande societies, religious-political organizations that initiate almost every boy and girl, respectively, into their membership. Though the Kpelle say that their inheritance and descent are patrilineal, my data from three towns reveal that in most cases this is not so. Polygynous marriage is permitted, and bridewealth, brideservice, or both are desired by the woman's parents. Men prefer virilocal postmarital residence, but the wife's parents' desire for brideservice often forces a nonwealthy husband to settle permanently in their community.

Like other contemporary tribal groups, the Kpelle have paramount, clan, town, and quarter chiefs. Formerly political leaders remained in power until death or public clamor or insurrection removed them. With increased centralization, chiefs now face the election process every four years or so. However, incumbents are rarely unseated in elections because they tend to become entrenched in power—and because voting is not secret.

In addition to the political offices formalized by the Liberian government, the Kpelle still have traditional leaders whose wealth and power surpass even that of paramount chiefs and traditionally

TABLE 1. _Population of Fuama Chiefdom by clans_

Clan	Males		Females		Total population	
	1974	1962	1974	1962	1974	1962
Dobli	1,781	1,466	1,827	1,477	3,608	2,943
Lorla	951	988	1,046	1,149	1,997	2,137
Yarbayon	1,748	967	1,781	1,015	3,529	1,982
Zarwiakomu	8,829	1,050	7,432	777	16,261	1,827
Zulo Hills	375	349	393	380	768	729
TOTAL	13,684	4,820	12,479	4,798	26,163	9,618

SOURCE: Adapted from the 1962 _Liberian Census of Population: Area Report for Central Province_, Table 1; and the 1974 _Census of Population and Housing, Population Bulletin No. 2_, Table 1 (02), Bong County.

TABLE 2. _Population of Haindii, Dobli Island, and Digei_

Town	Males		Females		Total population	
	1974	1962	1974	1962	1974	1962
Haindii	227	205	282	177	509	382
Dobli Island	165	192	200	234	365	426
Digei	203	169	225	229	428	398
TOTAL	595	566	707	640	1,302	1,206

powerful secret society leaders. Such a leader is called a 'landowner' (lɔi-nâmu) and is usually a descendant of tribal leaders who settled the area. Landowners have the right to allocate land to newcomers, mediate important disputes, and make decisions affecting the whole community. Dumu, described later in this chapter, was the landowner of the area where I worked.

The Population of Fuama Chiefdom

Fuama Chiefdom, where I did my fieldwork, is in the western corner of Bong County, about 70 miles north of Monrovia by road (see Map 1, p. 14). Table 1 shows the population of Fuama Chiefdom by clans, as reported in the 1974 and 1962 government censuses. In both censuses women outnumbered men in most clans, probably because of male migration to wage labor centers, though different mortality rates for males and females may also be a factor. Zarwiakomu Clan had more men than women because it covers a large part of the Bong Iron Mine concession area. The huge population increase of Zarwiakomu from 1962 to 1974 can be attributed to the growth of Bong Mine.

Table 2 compares my 1974 census of Haindii, Dobli Island, and Digei with the 1962 government census.[9] Both my 1974 figures and the 1962 figures show more females than males in the three towns, again revealing the effects of male migration to wage labor areas. The one exception is the 1962 count in Haindii. According to informants, Bong Mine established a factory on the St. Paul River in Haindii in the late 1950's to make cement blocks for the mine. Because men from up-country came to work in the factory, men in Haindii temporarily outnumbered women. Later the factory was dismantled and most of the workers left.

Another notable feature of Table 2 is that Haindii and Digei have grown in population, whereas Dobli Island has diminished. I attribute this partly to what people increasingly see as the inconvenience of crossing the river, and partly to the aging of Dumu, the man who has controlled Dobli Island for the last 40 or so years, and his inability to control or watch over the residents as before.

Dumu and the History of Fuama Chiefdom

The history of Dumu's family, closely linked with that of Fuama Chiefdom, typifies the histories of other West African groups that waged war and jockeyed for favorable geographical position. Though this lineage claimed Gola ancestry, the groups they aligned with were predominantly Kpelle. Dumu's father Kalo and his paternal grandfather Mata were the original landowners of the area, the leaders who established settlements and defended their lands from hostile neighboring groups. Making his way south, Mata settled in Kɔni Kao ŋa, a town in the north central part of what is now called Fuama Chiefdom. To obtain a more defensible position, a group of settlers, including Mata's son Kalo, moved farther south to the only

9. Government census figures for 1974 for the three towns were unavailable to me. Any comparisons between the two sets of figures must be considered approximate, since the boundaries used by the government in 1962 almost certainly differed from the ones I used in 1974. This is especially true for Haindii, which is spread out over a large area.

hill in the area and established the town of Zulotaa ("Zulo's town") or Zulo Hill. Once settled, Kalo, who had become a renowned warrior and chief, began receiving complaints from local people traveling to White Plains, a market area about forty miles to the south. Mandingo traders and chiefs, who had also come from the north and had recently settled near the present location of Haindii, were robbing traders of their goods and capturing members of their parties as slaves. Deciding to gain a more strategic location from which he could ward off these attacks—and perhaps attack trading parties himself—Kalo pushed farther south with a group of followers and established an outpost on an island in the middle of the St. Paul River. This was a perfect location for seeking refuge from enemies, since few people could swim. From this island, Kalo subdued neighboring rivals, opened the trade routes for his followers, and attracted more dependents seeking protection. Kalo's clients paid for this protection with slaves and wives, which Kalo redistributed to other men to cement their allegiance.

Kalo's son Dumu, who was born around 1900, later assumed his father's role of patron for the people of Fuama Chiefdom, acting as a mediator for them with the outside world. His father took him to Monrovia at about the age of six, and for some fourteen years he lived in the house of an important national leader. The wardship system is common among Liberian tribes, and all three parties in this case used it to their advantage. Kalo used Dumu's wardship to establish an alliance with the kwi ("civilized") people in Monrovia, who could help him subdue tribal competitors seeking to capture his territory. The national leader and his successors used their ties with Kalo and Dumu to pacify troublesome groups. And Dumu used his wardship to boost his political status in both the modern world and his native home, since a contemporary tribal man's success often rests on his education and connections with the "civilized" world.

Some years after his father's death, Dumu returned to Dobli Island and consolidated his tribal power by surveying and defining the boundaries of Fuama Chiefdom, which he claimed as his domain. By securing President Tubman's validation of his claim to the land, he subdued his rivals and ended years of warfare among tribal groups in the area. He settled on the island, taking on in succession the main political offices created by the national government for tribal districts: he became the paramount chief of Fuama, then a member of the national House of Representatives, and finally a senator from the Central Province (this was before Liberia was divided into counties). With prodding from his mother, Dumu began to collect tribal clients. (See Chapter 3 for a fuller discussion of clientship.) In return for his mediation in dealings with the outside world he received numerous wives, whom he used to consolidate his economic and political power.

Dumu was at the height of his power from the 1940's to the 1960's, and in the 1970's people still appeared from any part of the chiefdom at least once a day to ask Dumu to solve a palaver. Though people seeking large fines usually took their cases to formal courts, Dumu still settled marriage, divorce, land, and witchcraft matters. He also heard complaints about the outside world, such as exorbitant court fees and taxes, and often rectified injustices. Frequently he gave money to people for trips to the hospital or school fees. Even those who migrated to urban areas came back for his help. Consequently, many Fuama people remained loyal to Dumu. However, two factors were diminishing his control over Fuama Chiefdom. First, he was growing old and sick. People were becoming wary of staking their futures on his patronage, because his death would crumble the personal network he had created. Those of his followers with no economic or political footholds in the modern world would be vulnerable to officials in the new bureaucracy, who derived their power from the top and consequently had fewer personal obligations to constituents.

Second, though Dumu was quite wealthy, he could not provide all the cash or services his dependents needed. The outside world was bringing new economic opportunities and demands to people who formerly relied on their patrons' networks for goods and services they did not produce. Many left their patrons or sent their children to school in the outside world. On the one hand, new economic opportunities were giving these people a way to escape dependence on their traditional patrons. On the other, people who left their traditional lands became more dependent on a reliable cash income and more vulnerable to mistreatment by bureaucrats with no personal interest in their welfare.

The Agricultural Economy of Fuama Chiefdom

To understand the effects of economic change on the people of Fuama Chiefdom, we must examine some of the chiefdom's basic resources and subsistence activities. Like most of the rest of Liberia, Fuama Chiefdom has reddish brown laterite soils. Though more suitable for agriculture than the rocky lithosils of Liberia's hills or the sandy soils of the coastal plains, laterites are highly vulnerable to leaching, in which important plant nutrients such as nitrogen are washed away. After one or two crops, fertilizer must be added for further planting. Where land is plentiful, the predominant mode of agriculture is slash-and-burn: leaving a plot fallow after one or two years and cutting and burning the vegetation on another plot that has itself been left fallow for several years.

Typologies set forth by Boserup (1965) for worldwide agricultural systems and by Morgan and Pugh (1969) for West Africa provide a general model for understanding changes in land use in Fuama Chiefdom. These typologies posit a rough continuum from "extensive" (slash-and-burn) to "intensive" agriculture (using plows, irrigation, fertilizer, short fallows, and so on). In general, land use shifts from extensive agriculture in most of the northern and central parts of Fuama Chiefdom to more intensive farming in the extreme southern part near Bong Mine. According to informants and my own observations, most of Fuama Chiefdom's land is fertile enough to support its population by traditional extensive agriculture. Fallows range from ten to twenty-five years; land near Digei, for example, may have lain fallow as much as twenty years, long enough to regenerate climax vegetation (stable populations of tall trees and other plants). Because people are continually cultivating new plots, however, the land near Digei is rarely virgin, and settlements may be a two-hour walk from farm sites.

The fallow period shortens as one moves south into the more inhabited area around Haindii and Dobli Island, but even here land is seldom used more than once every ten years. In this system, vegetation is allowed to regenerate to the tall tree stage, but no climax vegetation is present. People are beginning to complain that the land is growing less fertile, necessitating the cultivation of larger areas and the abandonment of some farms after only one rice harvest. But during my 1973–74 fieldwork people had adequate farmland for their needs.

Rice, the staple crop of the chiefdom, is usually cultivated in plots of two to four acres. The cultivation of upland rice follows an annual cycle. At the end of the dry season, men "brush" away small trees and bush and then cut down the larger trees. After a month of drying, the felled vegetation is burned. When the rains begin (May to June), women plant the rice. They throw the seed on the ground and "scratch" the soil with short-handled hoes, covering the seeds and removing weeds at the same time. While the rice is in the seedling stage, everyone, including children, helps to drive birds away with slings and rocks, and men often spend the night on the farm to keep "groundhogs" (cane rats) from eating rice shoots. Women continually weed the young rice plants. In September or October, when the rice is ripe, it is cut, tied in bundles, and put in rice "kitchens," small buildings that may serve for cooking and lounging as well as for storing rice. Women usually perform these harvesting operations, though men sometimes help. Women hull some of the rice with mortars and pestles to eat immediately. The rest is smoked to discourage insects and mildew.

Women work almost continually on rice farms. Their main tasks, planting, weeding, and harvesting, are long and arduous. Van Santen (1974: 24) reports that these chores take about two-thirds of the total time required to grow a rice crop. In addition, women must cook for their families while the men are working, and they spend more time driving birds away than men do. I heard no reports of men who did all the work on their farms. Single men farmed with friends or relatives in groups that included women. On the other hand, I did hear a few reports of women who did all the farm work with the help of their children, including brushing, tree felling, and burning. Most of these women were said to live farther east in Jokwele Chiefdom. Though women spend more time farming than men, they also spend more time on such auxiliary activities as making oil, growing vegetables, catching fish, and raising poultry, and they assume the greatest responsibility for feeding the family. Also, any cash that women earn from selling surplus produce is supposed to benefit their families, paying for clothes, medicine, school fees, and so on. (In reality, of course, when women use their cash earnings to begin a market business, they sometimes want to acquire independence from a constricting marriage as well.) At any rate, men find it easier to use the money from their surplus produce for a wider range of purposes.

Cassava (manioc) is another Kpelle staple, second only to rice in importance. Its leaves can be picked and eaten as a nutritious vegetable any time after the plant begins to grow. Since the starchy roots can remain in the ground for up to two years before rotting, they can be used when the much-preferred rice becomes scarce, usually midway through the rainy ("hungry") season. Cassava can be interspersed with rice, or, because it requires fewer nutrients, can be planted in a harvested rice field. Growing cassava requires little labor. After men clear the plot, women and children plant, tend, and harvest the crop. Both farm and village women grow vegetables and fruits, notably peppers, eggplants, pumpkins, greens, beans, okra, tomatoes, onions, "bitterballs" (a very bitter vegetable resembling a small green eggplant), plantains, mangoes, avocados, bananas, corn, cucumbers, pineapples, and papayas.

Kpelle women cook with palm oil, which people prefer to imported vegetable oils. The small red fruits of the oil palm ("palm nuts") are gathered by men and boys, who climb to the tops of the trees and cut bunches of fruit. (Most oil palm trees grow wild, and unless they are on someone's farm, they can be harvested by anyone.) The fruit is picked from the stem, washed, boiled, and pounded with pestles in large bins to loosen the flesh, which is then washed and strained to remove fibers and seeds (see Photograph 1). The solution is then boiled again to make the oil rise to the top, and the oil is scooped out and put in containers. After lying in the sun, the seeds are cracked open to extract the kernels, which can be used to make another kind of vegetable oil. Surplus kernels were sold to Haindii traders for seven cents a pound while I was there.

Women spend more time than men making palm oil. Though cut-

1. A woman strains fibers from crushed palm nuts in preparing palm oil.

ting the palm nuts is the job of men and older boys, women usually process the oil and crack the seeds. Van Santen (1974: 37) estimates that it takes a man one day to cut 24 bunches of palm nuts, enough to make about ten gallons of oil (13.5 percent of the work), whereas it takes four or five women one day to process this much oil, and two women one day to crack the palm seeds (86.5 percent of the work). I noticed, however, that women in Haindii often paid or coerced younger people to pound the nuts and crack the seeds for them, so they spent less time at the task than the women Van Santen observed.

There is an increasing market for palm oil, because people working for wages have little time to make their own oil, and many live in areas that no longer have wild oil palms. People in Haindii are particularly well located to sell their oil. Every week on market day traders from Bong Mine come in taxis to Haindii to buy oil, which they sell at the mine or relay to Monrovia. While I was in Haindii, the price of oil reached as much as $3.50 a gallon in the rainy season, when it was dangerous to climb trees to cut the fruit. Women in Haindii and nearby areas take advantage of these opportunities, making profits that lessen their dependence on their husbands for pocket money. Many pay boys to cut the nuts for them and process five gallons of oil at a time, keeping a gallon or two for their consumption and selling the rest.

Like many other Liberians, the people of Fuama Chiefdom get a good deal of their protein from fish. The Mesurado Group, a consortium of companies controlled largely by interests in Monrovia, ships large quantities of saltwater fish to markets up-country. People who live near the rivers, however, such as those in Haindii and Dobli Island, usually catch their own fish. Women and children catch most of the small fish, crayfish, and crabs used for domestic consumption. In the dry season, when the St. Paul River is down, women use traps to catch crayfish, which they cook for their families or sell to German workers from Bong Mine, who make special trips to Haindii to buy them (they are considered a delicacy by Africans as well as Europeans). Women can sell crayfish to Germans for as much as eight or nine cents apiece, often earning more than a dollar a day at the height of the season. Children are encouraged to fish for the family's meals—boys with hooks and lines, and girls, like their mothers, with nets. (See Photograph 2.) Boys, however, are more independent from the family than girls, often selling larger fish in the village to make their own money. People farther away from rivers depend heavily on meat and poultry. Chickens and guinea fowls, accounting for a large part of domestically produced protein, are raised by women. In addition, men engage in hunting and trapping, and well-off farmers raise goats.

This description is essentially the way things were in Haindii, Dobli Island, and Digei in 1974. Even at that time things were changing in the most southerly regions of the chiefdom near Bong Mine, where land used for subsistence farming was being increasingly bought up by entrepreneurs for cash crops such as rubber, oranges, and coffee, with the result that subsistence land might be allowed to lie fallow only three or four years and was accordingly losing its fertility. By 1978, when I revisited Haindii, similar changes were occurring there. The population had grown, rice was not growing well in the exhausted soil near town, and many people were relying on imported rice or were moving up-country during the farming season. I noticed many more vegetable gardens planted near houses. The cash economy had spread rapidly, bringing with it increasing economic hardship.

A Journey Through Fuama Chiefdom

A traveler through the chiefdom can see ample signs of both the old subsistence patterns and the new economic opportunities. The southernmost part of the chiefdom is about 50 miles from Monrovia; travelers can drive on a paved road north from the capital. Just beyond Monrovia the road is lined with large, modern, air-conditioned houses (watched constantly by a guard or two) belonging to wealthy Liberians, most of Americo-Liberian descent. Interspersed with these are the houses of foreigners who work in business, government, or church missions. Farther along the road, houses belonging to tribal people can be seen, most of which are

2. *A young woman weaves a fishing net.*

of wattle-and-daub construction (a layer of poles covered with mud and a thin layer of cement) and are topped by a corrugated tin ("zinc") roof. Older houses may have thatch roofs. Many people walk along the road with heavy loads on their heads. Women often carry a double load: a bundle on their head and a child on their back.

After a rise from the coastal plain, a dense curtain of tall trees and bush (which Graham Greene, in his 1936 memoir *Journey Without Maps,* describes as "hectic green") begins to enclose the highway. Before the 1950's only wild vegetation would have been visible. Now rows of tall, bent rubber trees have replaced much of the wild bush along the road, and men in worn working clothes may be seen tapping the rubber. The Firestone Rubber Company has a large plantation just off the main road, employing many Liberians to tap and process rubber to ship to the United States. Many Liberians also grow rubber independently, which they sell to Firestone. Fields of citrus trees, cocoa, coffee, and sugar cane also line the road, taking up acreage formerly used for subsistence farming, especially along the roads and near towns.

At a town called Kakata a wide gravel road built by Bong Mine turns off the paved road to the left. Along this road one can usually see a Volkswagen or a Mercedes-Benz with one or two Europeans or upper-class Liberians inside. Small Toyota or Datsun taxis with loads of up to seven Liberians also pass every few minutes. The Bong Mine concession, about twenty miles (or 60 cents by taxi) from Kakata, lies just inside the unmarked boundary of Fuama Chiefdom (Map 2).[10] The trees suddenly clear away, leaving iron-rich Bong Mountain visible in the distance to the right of the road. Shaved bare of trees, one side of the mountain resembles a row of steps, with right-angle chunks removed by dynamite and bull-dozers. Next to the mountain lie the housing and administrative areas of the concession. The housing areas form distinct hierarchical patterns. Houses of "staff" personnel (mostly highly paid Ger-

10. Map 2, showing Fuama Chiefdom, is compiled from three maps, all differing from one another in some respects. It should be regarded as schematic rather than authoritative.

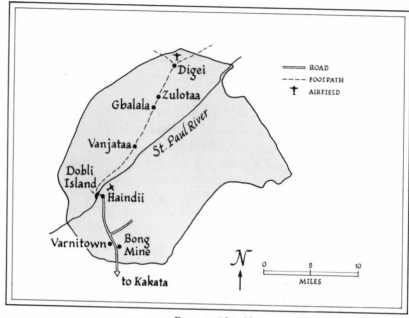

MAP 2. *Fuama Chiefdom.*

mans) cluster at the tops of wooded hills, far from the main road, whereas the houses of most "workers" (Liberians) lie near the main road on bare, level ground.

Bong Mine attracts young men to work for money—most residents are immigrants—and it attracts people who live off the young men who make the money. To the left of the road is Varnitown, a settlement of closely packed wattle-and-daub houses and shops. Workers and their hangers-on live here. A string of Lebanese-owned stores lines the left side of the road, selling goods from the United States, Europe, Lebanon, and the People's Republic of China. Store owners buy locally grown produce such as coffee beans and palm kernels to sell abroad. Almost every African house along this road operates some kind of small business as well, usually with a woman in charge. Some houses have built-in shops of goods to sell, such as bottles of palm oil, peppers, Maggi bouillon cubes, candy, salt, sugar, cigarettes, and lengths of trade ("lappa") cloth. Other houses have smaller "table markets," arrays of goods in jars and bottles for sale on porches or small wooden platforms. At the big market along the road, a hub of activity every morning, women buy and sell produce and other foods and food products.

Every two weeks on payday the Bong Mine road becomes a mass of colors and people. Itinerant traders set up their wares, small boys peddle fried bread and drinking water, and relatives come down from the bush to visit their kinsmen and ask for money. The streets also fill with girls in brightly colored dresses, seeking money and clothes from their boyfriends. Itinerant prostitutes, hard to distinguish in appearance—or purpose—from visiting girlfriends, also arrive in great numbers on payday, lodging with friends at their clients' expense.

At the end of the Bong Mine–Varnitown area stands the courthouse of the paramount chief of Fuama Chiefdom. Although Haindii is the official headquarters of the chiefdom, the current paramount chief moved his court to Bong Mine. The litigation business there is lucrative: people have more money to be fined in "palavers" (disputes) over women and property. Especially on payday the chief does a thriving business.[11]

Along the seven-mile road from Bong Mine to Haindii are rubber groves and small villages of perhaps eight houses whose inhabitants tap the rubber. Upland rice farms appear frequently. About six miles from Bong Mine, Dobli Island Public School (so named because the school used to be on Dobli Island), a modest cement building, can be seen on the right. At the beginning of the 1974 school year, 230 pupils were registered, from primer (kindergarten) through the ninth grade, following the American system. That year the school employed six African teachers and a Peace Corps volunteer. Because few tribal people see much use in educating daughters, most of the pupils were boys, though several girls had advanced to the eighth and ninth grades.

11. This was the case when I was doing my fieldwork; subsequently the chief was ordered to move his headquarters back to Haindii.

3. *Haindii.*

Haindii is about a mile from the school. (See Photograph 3.) Most houses in Haindii line the motor roads, giving the town a spacious appearance compared with the compactness of towns away from roads. The first houses are those of Siafataa ('Siafa's town'), a quarter headed by an old trader and medicine man from another tribal group, the Mandingoes. About an eighth of a mile from Siafataa, the main road to Haindii forms a T with a road that extends the length of the town. Two stores are located at this crossroads. One is owned by a rich Lebanese man in Bong Mine and run by a less wealthy Lebanese man and his wife; the other is a slightly smaller store owned by a Mandingo man. As in Bong Mine, the local people sell palm kernels, cocoa beans, and coffee beans to these stores for cash or credit.[12]

12. During my visit to Haindii in 1978 I noticed a flurry of building activity in this part of town. Because Haindii had recently been made the headquarters of newly

To the right (east) of the crossroads is a swamp rice demonstration project, run with government aid by a Grebo man, a member of a group from the southeastern part of Liberia. Few Haindii farmers have expressed an interest in intensively cultivated swamp rice because it must be fertilized, an expensive proposition for most. Furthermore, people see the Grebo man working much harder than they do on their slash-and-burn plots. The road branches again at a part of town called Gbomotolipolu. At the end of the road is an airfield built by Germans who work for Bong Mine and fly small planes for recreation. The left fork in Gbomotolipolu brings the visitor to the pump station that pipes water from the St. Paul River to Bong Mine. About fifteen men living in Haindii and Dobli Island are employed by Bong Mine; some work at the pump station, and others commute to the mine by taxi or on foot.

The road to the west from the main crossroads leads to the oldest part of Haindii, which is located at the top of a hill. Here stands one of several small shops in town owned by Liberians. In this shop a battery-powered record player blares West African highlife tunes or American hits for a group of teenagers and young children dancing on the porch. Across the road from the "nightclub," as my husband and I called it, is the market area, where as many as 3,000 people come every Tuesday to trade and socialize. Next to the market is the Dobli clan chief's courthouse, which sees a healthy business on market day, when people who have traveled from remote areas to trade at the market can be summoned into court and sued.

North of the market area lies the St. Paul River. In pools beside the river women fish with large homespun nets. People traveling through or visiting Dobli Island climb into the community canoe and paddle about 75 yards to the island's shore. The town of Dobli Island is about a quarter of a mile from the shore. (See Photograph 4.) Since transportation of goods to Dobli Island only involves crossing the river, there are several shops and table markets there,

---

created Fuama District, workers were constructing a house for the district commissioner, an official guest house for important visitors, a soldiers' barrack, and a large maternity clinic.

4. *Dobli Island.*

as in Haindii. Because of the ease of transporting goods and people, residents of Dobli Island and Haindii theoretically have equal access to wage jobs and cash; for this reason I classify both places as modern towns. (However, even though traders do not view the river as a problem, many people dread crossing it.)

Some of the most salient features of Dobli Island are associated with Dumu's residence there. To the east is Dumu's compound. In contrast to the small wattle-and-daub houses in Haindii and in the town of Dobli Island, Dumu's large house is built of cement blocks and has glass windows. Inside the house are modern curtains and furniture. Behind the house are several smaller buildings for Dumu's wives and remaining clients. The most distinctive feature of Dumu's house is its large, shaded cement porch with perhaps a dozen strong wooden chairs—in contrast to the sagging rattan chairs most houses have. On this porch Dumu hears palavers and deals with his clients.

More evidence of Dumu's power and influence can be seen in the town of Dobli Island itself. In the middle of town stands a large, tin-roofed structure, built on his orders for funerals, receptions for important visitors, and some secret society rituals. Next to this structure, several of Dumu's sleek cows often lounge, chewing their cuds. In the past they roamed the island freely, and would lie down on people's porches to avoid the hot sun. When Dumu heard that people were beating his cows to move them from their porches, he threatened to leave the island, taking his cows and his patronage. Now, unlike other porches in Liberia, most Dobli Island porches have fences and gates.

The path leading to towns farther north begins on the far bank of the St. Paul River, on the other side of Dobli Island from Haindii. Digei, the third town I studied, is a 25-mile walk from Dobli Island. People usually make this trip in two days. On the way are several old towns important to the history of Fuama Chiefdom. As we have seen, Zulotaa, a town in Zulo Hills Clan, perches on top of a hill overlooking a broad, flat landscape. Settled in the mid-nineteenth century by Dumu's ancestors, it was chosen for military advantages in the days of warfare. Several famous old warriors such as Mata, Dumu's paternal grandfather, are buried there. On the way to Digei are many upland rice farms, as in the Haindii–Dobli Island area. But there are no rubber groves and few other cash crops because it is uneconomical to carry heavy produce 25 miles to market along a narrow, unpaved path.

Digei (in Lorla Clan) is laid out like most towns in the interior with no motor road. (See Photograph 5.) The houses, built close together in a circular area, form a bewildering maze of alleys and walls to a stranger. This was a strategic device in the past, when inhabitants tried to confuse invading enemies.[13] A third of the

13. It took me a week to learn the way back to my own house from the opposite side of town, less than 150 yards away. More than once I was rescued by giggling children as I wandered haphazardly through tiny alleys.

5. *Digei.*

houses have "zinc" roofs; the rest are thatched. A few gardens
surround the town, but quickly give way to the bush. Interspersed
with the gardens are several woven rattan "fences" (kpaŋ), behind
which the business of various tribal societies is conducted. Digei has
a Poro fence for the men's secret society—actually some distance
from town, to the southeast—and a Sande fence for the women's
society, as well as fences for subsidiary horn, snake, and spirit
societies.

In addition to three small shops, Digei has half a dozen small
table markets, several of which appeared after we arrived with gifts
of tobacco, which was promptly shredded to sell as snuff. Digei's
shops are smaller than those in Haindii and Dobli Island, and they
do not buy local farm products. People seeking cash for palm ker-

nels or other products must carry them to distant markets. Clearly, cash is harder to obtain in areas not connected by roads.

Digei has three "quarters," a division characteristic of large traditional towns. Most quarter residents are closely related by blood or marriage. One Digei quarter is headed by an old, powerful landowner whose father is said to have founded Digei. Another quarter is headed by the landowner's son-in-law, the current chief of Lorla Clan. The third quarter consists of another old family, now related by marriage to the other two. Digei has a government-built medical clinic and a two-room schoolhouse for children in primer through fourth grade. Only about 2 percent of the pupils were girls in 1974, none in the third or fourth grades. About an eighth of a mile from town lies the airfield built by the Lutheran mission and used to fly a nurse to the clinic once a month.

This chapter has outlined some of the basic features of four towns in Fuama Chiefdom: Bong Mine, Haindii, Dobli Island, and Digei. We have seen that women may earn cash through marketing, but that they concentrate on subsistence production where land is available—in Haindii, Dobli Island, and Digei. Women in these rural areas are valuable to men as agricultural laborers and producers of children who also contribute to subsistence. Men help with subsistence production, and they are more active than women in cash cropping and wage labor. Men in the southern part of Fuama Chiefdom (Haindii, Dobli Island, and Bong Mine) have the most opportunities to earn cash because they can work for the iron mining company. People in these towns have also benefited from the road built by the mine, which enables them to engage in marketing. Digei, 25 miles into the bush, has better subsistence resources but fewer opportunities to earn cash. The absence of a motor road discourages large-scale cash cropping. Furthermore, young men migrating to other areas for work must stay away for long periods of time, spending money where they work and bringing less home. The following chapters will show how these factors are related to larger patterns of political and economic control, and to patterns of marriage and domestic groups.

CHAPTER 3

Wealth in People

SOCIAL PROCESSES AND KPELLE STRATIFICATION

There is some initial utility in using broad categories such as "patrilineal," "acephalous," or "chieftaincy" to differentiate traditional African societies. However, these labels tend to obscure rather than illuminate the complex and dynamic nature of people's political, kinship, and ethnic ties (see also Leach 1961). Among the Kpelle, for example, it is usually taken for granted that the most powerful man in the community—or his "front"—will become the paramount chief, or whatever title the modern system provides for him. Hence, the title is little more than a label for extant power relations. Rather than ask what roles and power the paramount chief has by virtue of his position, therefore, it is more useful to ask how he acquired prominence in the first place. In a similar vein, the distribution of political and economic power in a given area can shape social definitions of kinship. Everyone is quick to point out close kin ties to important leaders in the area, whether or not these ties can be documented, whereas deposed leaders quickly lose kin. Only by examining such social processes and transactions can we understand concretely how people acquire and use power. Furthermore, as Barth (1967: 661–62) argues, an approach based on social process is essential for an understanding of social change:

Our contributions as social anthropologists must lie in providing such primary materials for understanding the processes of change. . . . If this means that we must recast our very description of social systems in order to accommodate these data from the events of change, that makes our task more difficult but also more interesting. . . . The reason for the social anthropologist's impasse when he tries to add change to his traditional description of social systems is found in the basic characteristics of the descriptive concepts we habitually use. . . . We then construct a system composed of such formal features, and characterize the whole system as one "with" dowry, or "with" cross-cousin marriage, or "with" ambilocal residence.

Since the 1960's some African ethnographers have emphasized the importance of social processes. Van Velsen (1964: 6), for example, notices that Tonga leadership "is acquired . . . not so much through formal, constitutional channels but rather through skilful manipulation of personal relationships (which are generally expressed in terms of kinship) within an elastic framework of formal values." Van Velsen sees social action as the manipulation of formal roles and statuses in the pursuit of specific goals. The present study adopts this approach, but focuses as well on the importance of social fictions for particular ends. As we have seen, kin ties to powerful leaders are often fictionalized, and kin ties that are ambiguous, such as fatherhood, can be claimed or denied as the occasion warrants. Such processes as the creation of social fictions draw attention to the fact that there are at least two facets to social institutions—ideal formal rules (e.g., "patriliny") and behavioral reality—that may or may not resemble each other. To settle for categorizing Kpelle society as "patrilineal with brideservice and bridewealth" or as an "acephalous polity" is to ignore the differences between rules and people's behavior. Moreover, a narrow focus on categories discourages an examination of how people's acts create and change institutions such as marriage. Therefore, this chapter goes beyond standard typological phrases used to describe social systems, focusing instead on economic and political factors that underlie people's marital choices. An analysis of these factors will provide a basis for understanding the institutions of Kpelle marriage in a period of rapid change.

Issues pertaining to women and marriage in African societies are inextricably bound up in political and economic issues in the wider society. Indeed, I am arguing that the control of women is central to the Kpelle system of stratification, as well as that of many other African societies. Kpelle stratification is based primarily on the production of economic surpluses to attract dependents. Political allegiance, another important ingredient, is rooted both in the history of West African warfare and migration described in the last chapter and in present-day needs for political protection. Labor and allegiance are critical to people's economic subsistence as well as to their political and economic advancement. Wealth and security rest on the control of others.[1]

This system, which I refer to as the wealth-in-people system, is formalized in the legal notion of rights in people; that is, Kpelle legal rules allocate rights in someone's labor, reproduction, and property to a group or to another person. In Kpelle society, men and the old have legal rights in women and children, and they use rights in women not only to reproduce and to gain labor for supporting their immediate families, but also to lure young men into ties of debt and obligation. As Chapters 4 and 5 demonstrate, women do not always cooperate with the ambitions of elders and men; nevertheless the political, economic, and legal bases of the system must be examined in order to understand men's and women's options and constraints. The wealth-in-people model developed here is, of course, not an original concept. With all the variation in African societies, a general wealth-in-people model still seems to be one of the most persistent themes of African ethnography. Therefore, although my primary interest lies in the Kpelle of Fuama Chiefdom, my discussion of the theoretical issues pertaining to the wealth-in-people system will include examples from other parts of Africa and from Melanesia.[2]

1. See Nieboer (1900) for an early hypothesis relating slavery to the availability of land in Sierra Leone. Since then various authors have noted that controlling dependents is necessary to status and security in Sub-Saharan Africa as a whole (Mair 1953, Fallers 1964, J. Goody 1971) as well as in specific areas in West Africa (Little 1951, Terray 1972, Hopkins 1973), East Africa (Fallers 1964; Schneider 1968, 1970), Central Africa (Reyburn 1959), and Southern Africa (Gluckman 1941, Mitchell 1949, Barnes 1951).

2. In my discussion of the economic and political bases of the Kpelle wealth-in-people system, later in the chapter, I do not imply that plentiful land, labor shortage,

This chapter will first trace the development of the concept of legal rights in people, and will then explore the relation between this aspect of African law and extensive agriculture. Finally, I will show how traditional Kpelle institutions function in terms of the wealth-in-people model. These institutions, which include filiation, wardship, slavery, pawnship, and secret societies, may all be seen as means of controlling the labor and allegiance of people—particularly of young men. The discussion of the wealth-in-people concept will provide a framework for my examination of Kpelle marriage and the control of women in the following chapters.

LEGAL RIGHTS IN PEOPLE

In any society the rights that people have in the services and persons of others are tremendously important. According to Kopytoff and Miers (1977: 7), "Such rights, usually mutual but seldom equal, exist in almost all social relationships." Sir Henry Maine, a nineteenth-century English jurist, helped lay the legal groundwork for subsequent British studies of rights, duties, and authority in African societies. Maine (1910) saw all primitive societies as corporations of kin groups bound together by a system of rights and duties. Discussing what he called the *Patria Potestas* (primitive patriarchal family), Maine argued that law gave formal justification to the natural order of things: the strong over the weak and men over women. A man controlled his family's property, corporal punishment, marriages, divorces, free or slave status, and so on (1910: 114). These rights, however, were balanced by a series of obliga-

---

warfare, and so on are inevitably the bases of other African stratification systems. As Kopytoff and Miers (1977) have stated, facile correlations along these lines are often wrong. These authors note that Nieboer's (1900) theory that land surpluses lead to slavery (as means of increasing agricultural production) is contradicted by evidence from the Sena of Mozambique, who had a low population density, but very mild forms of slavery, compared with other groups. Similarly, Handwerker (1977) shows that polygyny, another characteristic of the wealth-in-people system, increases among many urban dwellers after they become securely established—a pattern opposite of what we might expect. Therefore, for the present purposes, I will just say that the wealth-in-people system is typical of much of Sub-Saharan Africa.

tions to the wider kin group, prohibiting a man from squandering family resources (1910: 120).

The status of females, according to Maine, was perhaps the most important aspect of the Law of Persons generated by the *Patria Potestas*. Daughters were bound even closer to the authority of the primitive patriarchal family than sons, who could eventually become heads of families themselves. Mothers were incapable of inheriting property or passing on agnatic descent or authority to their children. Only with the advent of more modern jurisprudence were women released from the authority of their natal descent group. However, they were by no means freed from male supervision: their husbands assumed rights over their persons and properties in much the same way their fathers had. In ancient Rome, in fact, women were transferred to the *Patria Potestas* of their husbands (1910: 128).

British anthropologists applied Maine's notions of rights and obligations to African societies. Combining the legalistic approach of Maine with the sociology of Durkheim (which posited social solidarity and social sentiment as primary values), Radcliffe-Brown (1952) contended that social sentiment and solidarity gave rise to moral and legal rights and obligations that bound individuals to the social order and created mechanisms for mediating conflicts. Noting that family relationships were the cornerstone of social organization in African societies, Radcliffe-Brown sought to identify the principles of organization by which kinship relations were extended to a wide range of people. He found that people's legal ties were formed according to principles of generation, sex, exogamy, and the unity of the sibling group, and that the ties could be consanguineal, affinal, or fictive. Marriage, for example, is a legal transfer of rights in people and property that creates ties of alliance through exogamy and generates the legal perpetuation of descent through socially sanctioned ties. A husband and his kin, said Radcliffe-Brown (1950: 50), acquire certain rights in the wife. They may acquire rights *in personam*, her labor and domestic duties, and rights *in rem*, indemnity for outsiders' sexual transgressions with her. In a patrilineal society, a husband and his kin also acquire rights in the children a wife bears. These rights, or course, are balanced by certain duties and obligations toward the woman (economic provisions) and her kin group (recompense for taking her).

It is also important to note that economic conditions help to generate the legal aspects of the traditional African wealth-in-people system. Gluckman (1965) discusses the connection between legal rights and obligations and property, which provides a useful framework for the present analysis. He argues that defined statuses or status relations are created through transfers of property. Thus, property is important not merely for its material value but also as a way to symbolize relationships between people. For example,

The rules for distribution of the marriage-cattle ... show how a chattel, like land, may be subject to a cluster of rights held by different persons in terms of their relationship within the network of kinship ties. In fact their rights to claim on the marriage-cattle define their kinship relationships to the central parties. If they are not given their shares, this denies their kinship: hence they state they did not know of the marriage. The law of property is again intricately intertwined with the law of status. It means that to understand the holding of property, we must investigate the system of status relationships; and to describe the system of status relationships, we must deal constantly with relations to property. (Gluckman 1965: 74)

Such a conception of property has significant implications for an analysis of women and marriage in Africa. A wife, in Gluckman's view, is not merely property for which bridewealth or brideservice is paid: she also symbolizes the relationship between her natal and affinal kin. Furthermore, Gluckman contends that rights in women acquired at marriage are particularly important in attracting a following and in securing material wealth. These rights in people give access to the goods that people produce. Wealth in material goods may then be converted into relationships that bring rights in people, and so on:

... the means to prestige and power are ... restricted in tribal societies. On the whole, they reduce to acquiring dependants for oneself, so that one can be a "big man." It is possible to beget one's own dependants: this is one basis for polygyny.... An additional wife in an agricultural tribe is no burden since she and her children are supported by her own cultivations;

and she helps produce something of a surplus in good seasons with which her husband can entertain others. (Gluckman 1965: 86–87)

Meillassoux (1964) and Terray (1969) also examine the relations between production and social structure in African lineage-based societies. In the Guro society of the Ivory Coast, Meillassoux notes, land is ample for the needs of the community. Rights in land are owned by corporate lineages and are distributed by older people to the entire lineage. J. Goody (1971) uses this economic framework to analyze patterns of stratification resulting from extensive farming systems. He argues that because land is relatively available in less modernized areas of Africa, land holdings do not stratify the population as they do in Europe and much of Asia. Wealth and social standing rest not on the amount of land a person owns, as in Eurasia, but rather on the number of people he or she can muster for farm work (see also Fallers 1964, Hopkins 1973: 35). With some qualifications, this general pattern does seem to hold in rural areas of Africa.

At this point it is necessary to clarify the way in which the term "social stratification" is used in this book. Although Fallers (1973) has objected to the "layer cake" implications of the word "stratification," especially as it applies to Africa, I will use the word in the broad sense to mean social inequality or ranking (see Cancian 1976). I discuss stratification or inequality in social relationships (such as patron-client, old-young, husband-wife) in order to show that Kpelle society is not a homogenous whole. (It must be noted, however, that although there is inequality within African groups, there is usually more mobility and less differentiation than in European class systems and Indian castes. See also La Fontaine 1962, J. Goody 1971.)

Although ascribed family status is not as crucial for political success among the Kpelle as it is among more rigid class and caste societies, a person's chances of political success are strongly shaped by the nature of his or her ties with powerful lineages. Land may be plentiful, but it is not freely available to anyone who comes along and wants to farm it. People must seek the permission of the local landowners, who claim rights in the land by virtue of their ancestors' original settlement of the area. Older members of these lineages[3] distribute farming privileges to loyal family members and to "latecomer" families who were driven out of their former territories by warfare or by the relative scarcity of resources. Latecomers normally maintain rights in the land they have farmed even while the land is lying fallow, and they need not request permission to farm the same plot again. But this does not guarantee them permanent security. If they fall out of favor with landowner patrons or if resources become tight, latecomers may lose their rights in the land they farm. There is, then, some mobility in the system, but one's position by virtue of birth plays a large part in determining one's status.

Kpelle elders wield even more important kinds of control, however. Through marriage mediation and through the all-powerful men's and women's secret societies, elders in traditional areas gain power over all the women and children in their territory. They control strangers and lower-status people through clientship, wardship, pawnship, and slavery (especially in times past). Labor requirements, coupled with the need for political support, help explain why legal rights in the services and persons of others are so important for African groups such as the Kpelle. Because wealth, status, and security lie in people, many political processes and relationships pertain directly to attracting and holding on to followers.[4] Status in most Kpelle areas is based on labor and allegiance rather than on wealth in privately owned goods or land. In a labor-based system, a political leader needs male and female followers. Men are needed as farm laborers, political clients, and warriors (more in the

3. One Kpelle term for "landowner," lɔi-ɓêla, literally 'land people,' can also be glossed as "elders." In this study the word "elders" will refer only to older members of landowning families.

4. Although the Liberian government tried to solidify a previously existing hierarchical system of tribal chiefs, Kpelle leadership continues to resemble Melanesian big-man political organization in several ways; not all Kpelle leaders, however, are comparable to Melanesian big men. See Sahlins 1963 for an analysis of Melanesian big-man politics. Studies ranging from Sierra Leone (Little 1967, Howard 1972) and Liberia (d'Azevedo 1971) in West Africa, to Uganda in East Africa (Vincent 1971) have characterized some African leaders as big men (see also Gluckman 1965).

past than today). Women raise crops and livestock and bear children who can contribute to domestic production; they also manu-
facture many of the products used in domestic groups, and take on
the time-consuming task of processing food.

The control of Kpelle women and children is considered relatively unproblematic because of their inferior legal status. But because legal rights in men are difficult to acquire, the control of adult
males is less assured. Furthermore, land is not scarce, so there is
little to keep disgruntled men from deserting political leaders, taking their kinspeople, and moving elsewhere (Nieboer 1900, Douglas 1963, Meillassoux 1964, J. Goody 1971, Stauder 1972). Since
wealth and social mobility often depend on an ability to escape subordination (Dorjahn & Tholley 1959), men have strong reasons for
avoiding social control.

Nevertheless, people in Kpelle society find it necessary to have
patrons. The importance of having a patron is often misunderstood
by newcomers to Liberia. Peace Corps volunteers teaching in local
schools complain of negligence and corruption among the local
teachers, who practice extortion on apparently helpless students.
However, an insightful volunteer named Ted told me that his students were deriving more benefits from a tyrannical patron than he
had thought. For example, a Kpelle colleague of his, Teacher Andrews, was often harsh and capricious with his students. So Ted
was surprised at first when students criticized him for failing to act
as Teacher Andrews did: Andrews took their sides in palavers with
other teachers, ignored their absences, and even raised their test
scores on occasion. "But I've begun to notice," said Ted, "that
Teacher Andrews uses the role of sponsor in a more political way
than I do, making the students indebted to him for standing up for
them. Even though they hate his brutality, they have more respect
for him than for me. I won't play that patron role because I'm an
outsider and have no stake in the on-going affairs of the community
like the other teachers do."

Though subordinates are vulnerable to powerful people, they
know how to play high-status people off against each other to their
own advantage, and they make sure that they have someone to sup-

port them in exchange for political allegiance. Here again Ted had some insights: "I don't feel sorry anymore for the [little guy] in this culture," he said, "because there is always someone 'behind him' [standing up for him]. I used to feel sorry for Wua, the cook who was dismissed from her job at the school so the principal could put his own wife in. Then I realized that Wua's lover is the most powerful man in the area, and he can stand up for her very well. In fact she was reinstated almost as soon as she was fired."

There are several reasons why people cannot remain without patrons. In traditional West Africa, those who lack the protection of a powerful patron are vulnerable on many fronts: they may be denied access to farmland or women, or fined on fabricated charges, and in former times they or their families might be pawned or sold into slavery to repay debts, or even killed. Rattray (1929: 33) forcefully describes the tenuous position of "masterless" people: "It will have been observed that a condition of voluntary servitude was, in a very literal sense, the heritage of every Ashanti; it formed the basis of his social system. In West Africa it was the masterless men and women who ran the imminent danger of having what we should term 'their freedom' turned into involuntary bondage of a much more drastic nature." This point has been echoed by many who write about African political organization. Kopytoff and Miers (1977), for example, insist that no one in traditional Africa is "free" in the sense of owing no obligation. Everyone is indebted to others to a greater or lesser extent. And d'Azevedo (1962a) aptly describes Gola social relations as a hierarchical series of patrons and clients: every adult is a patron to lesser people, but a client to a more powerful person.

For the Kpelle, political success rests not only on a person's ascribed position, but also on his ability to create relationships of obligation and dependency with subordinates. Such relationships often take the form of legal debts. In any case, they give a person "leverage on others' production" (Sahlins 1963: 292). Because time is required to cultivate these relationships, political success is usually the reward of old age—especially for men. The most important way in which elders lure and hold on to young men is by the careful accumulation and deployment of women, as Chapter 4 will demonstrate. Before examining the specific roles of women and marriage in the wealth-in-people scheme, however, this chapter will outline several other institutions that subordinate outsiders to aristocrats, women to men, and youths to elders.

RELATIONS OF SUBORDINATION AND CLIENTSHIP

Central to the problems of advancement and social control in African societies are economic exchanges, which can variously be called allotments, gifts, debts, or payments for services or loyalty, depending on what aspect of the relationship the speaker chooses to stress (Collier 1971). In Kpelle society, where farm labor and political alliances are the key to economic and political success, the importance of economic transactions is clear. Though the specifics of these transactions vary with the context and participants, they all may be used to bind people to one another, or to symbolize those bonds. Since we can assume that people are anxious to define these transactions in ways that will benefit them the most, we will examine several institutions in which people use economic transactions to gain advancement and control. Transactions between people of equal status may be defined as allotments: that which is one's due. But transactions between social unequals are frequently defined as gifts or as payments for services and political loyalty: "The most demeaning transaction . . . occurs when a superior gives a large sum of money, or a woman, to an inferior without demanding a specific return. When a chief agrees to 'forget' a large fine, or a rich man gives a surplus wife to a follower, the inferior is trapped into the position of being a client. Loyalty and services will be forever expected of him" (Collier 1971: 7). The irony of the gift, of course, is that a debt is created, and that the expected return is often worth more than the original gift.

One of the most common ways in which debts are created actually costs the superior nothing. During my fieldwork I heard of several court cases in which chiefs trumped up exorbitant charges against defendants and subsequently acquired farm labor by dismissing the charges. One such case involved Charlie, a young man in Haindii whom I knew quite well. Charlie had a reputation for drinking, laziness, and palavers, much to the despair of his family. One night he and a friend were seen attempting to steal a bag of cement from a local store, and the next day one of the chiefs sent some men to arrest them. Both escaped, but Charlie returned to town a few days later, protesting his innocence.

At Charlie's court hearing, the chief jumped to his feet and shouted that Charlie had "abused" (cursed) the chief's men and had run away from the law. Therefore, he would be incarcerated on the spot. Charlie tried to convince the chief to hold a small, private hearing at which he promised to prove himself innocent of the charge of abusing the chief's messengers. But the chief refused to grant the request until Charlie paid a $25 fine to the court. Two days later I learned that the chief offered to let Charlie work off the fine by clearing some of the chief's land for a rice farm. Despite the fact that the reputed abuses were leveled against the messengers— and that someone else's bag of cement had been threatened—the chief managed to redefine Charlie's offense as one against himself and the dignity of the court: an offense that Charlie could atone for by working on the chief's farm.

Transactions among social unequals may encompass kin as well as nonkin relations. Young men seeking bridewealth funds, for example, try to define these as their due patrimony. But their older male kin are equally determined to define bridewealth as a debt that the younger men must repay with labor and loyalty.[5] The problem of defining the nature of economic transactions brings up a perhaps even more fundamental problem: the distinction between kin and nonkin. One confusion in the anthropological literature, for example, arises from an overly restrictive definition of the word "cli-

---

5. The assertion that fathers and sons try to define transactions between them in different ways is supported by an anecdote that Goody (1962: 206) relates about the patrilineal LoWiili of Ghana. A father had given three agnatic relatives some money for bridewealth, saying that he did not expect repayment because the men belonged to his lineage. When his financial accounts were scrutinized at his death, however, his son tried unsuccessfully to define the money as loans. Although Goody uses the anecdote to stress corporate ownership of wealth and property within a lineage, the son's action may reveal an unwillingness or an inability to maintain the patron role his father played, and an attempt to cash in, instead, on the money.

ent." Authors such as Mair (1961: 315) claim that clientship does not overlap with kinship, but is created by acts of deliberate choice among unrelated individuals. However, in Kpelle society kinspeople do enter into relations that are best described as patron-client relations.[6] Moreover, as noted earlier, clientship is not completely voluntary: people need the protection of a patron, and they also need rights in land and women, although the choice of a patron is up to them (Maquet 1961; see also Asad 1972). Rather than make a false distinction, at least for the Kpelle, between voluntary and involuntary subordinates, or between kin and nonkin, I will use a very general definition of a Kpelle client: a male subordinate. (Women who control legal rights in themselves may also be considered clients.)

The problem of separating kin from nonkin emerges on a more general level as well. In Africa, access to valued resources such as land, livestock, and labor is usually acquired through lineage systems. Since kinship is so important in allocating rights in land, labor, and reproduction, people are anxious to claim kin ties with powerful families or individuals, making it difficult to determine precise genealogical links in contemporary communities. As we have seen, the extreme flexibility of kin ties in the Central West Atlantic region has been attributed primarily to warfare and disjunctive migration (d'Azevedo 1962a, Horton 1972). Because kin categories have been fictionalized so often for political purposes, and because actual kinship relations often make little difference in hierarchical relations, I have made little attempt to separate kin from nonkin.[7] The fuzziness of these boundaries will become apparent as we examine relations of subordination and obligation among people of different statuses.

6. In the Kpelle language there are several expressions that refer to patron-client relations: ínúu kété, 'your big person' (patron); gaa íyééi mù, 'he is under your hand' (client); and íyééi ŋá núu, 'person in your hand' (client).

7. As Kopytoff and Miers (1977) note, kinship organization may be considered a continuum from full kin membership to outsider status ("marginality"). In many traditional African societies, outsiders—slaves as well as clients, pawns, and wards—begin incorporating themselves and their offspring into the dominant group as soon as they are acquired.

Filiation

Perhaps the most important female function in the eyes of most Africans is childbearing. Among the Kpelle, for example, the main purpose of Sande rituals is to confer fertility on young female initiates. Only women who have borne a child or two may assume the prestigious role of assisting in deliveries, and mothers of several children are highly esteemed. Sterility is a source of great anguish, especially for women, and the sterility of either marriage partner provides legal grounds for divorce. Even sterile men and women, however, may take in children as wards, and men have legal rights in the children their wives bear, even if they are not the natural fathers. Consequently, few people are completely childless, even though they are biologically incapable of producing children.

There are several reasons why the Kpelle place such a high value on children. First, children are a form of social security for old age. Parents apprehensively envision the time when they will be too old to work on the farm and will need the labor of their grown children and their sons- and daughters-in-law. However, infant mortality rates are high, and surviving children may not be willing to work for their parents. The Kpelle often complain that children nowadays are ungrateful to the elders who sacrificed to raise them. Therefore, parents prefer to have as many children as possible in order to ensure the survival and future support of at least one or two.

Children are useful for older people's political endeavors as well. The labor of children increases the productivity of their parents' farm, thereby helping to attract more wives and clients upon whom a political following can be built. Young children fetch water and firewood and run errands; older children work hard raising crops. Girls are particularly useful, tending younger siblings while their busy mothers work in the house and on the farm.

Older people can also use children to establish important alliances with other families. Young boys are commonly sent as wards to unrelated families with which their fathers or male kin seek ties of friendship, economic cooperation, or political support. Daughters, on the other hand, are sometimes sent to relatives (see also E.

N. Goody 1975), but are even more valuable as bait to lure impecunious young men into long periods of brideservice, and as potential marriage partners of powerful men.

Though children contribute substantially to their parents' households they are regarded as indebted to their parents for their food and shelter. Parents often remind disobedient children of the food they have given them and the money they have spent on them. Thus children early acquire a sense of debt and duty to their parents, making them vulnerable to parental demands. As we will see, mothers try to persuade their children to live with them and to help support them, but fathers have legal authority over their offspring. And since most filial benefits accrue over time, it is usually older men who hope to gain the most from their children's labor and marriage arrangements.

Wardship

People can also gain control over the young through the institution of wardship. Though the wardship system has other aspects and functions, I am chiefly concerned here with its economic and political ramifications. (See E. N. Goody 1973, 1975 for a detailed analysis of wardship patterns among the Gonja.) When children are sent to the households of their parents' siblings or other close relatives, they are taking part in a process involving "the claims, rights, and obligations of members of an extended kin group," since the expense and effort of rearing the child is spread over more than one household (E. N. Goody 1975: 140). Like filiation, the act of rearing a ward creates a debt that the child is expected to repay (E. N. Goody 1975: 141). A barren woman in Haindii, for example, was raising three of her younger sister's sons, who tended her shop and made palm oil for her to sell. From the way the woman talked, it was clear that she looked to them to support her in her old age as well.

Wards may also be raised by nonrelatives, though fictionalization may eventually create kin ties. Wardship of this kind is usually initiated by parents or groups seeking alliance with or patronage from powerful families. Young boys in particular may be sent to political leaders to work and, it is hoped, to acquire the skills and political connections necessary to boost their social standing, as well as that of their families (see also Richards 1960: 352). In return, wards and their families incur debts of obligation to the patron who raised the ward and bestowed status on the family. However, many of the boys sent to live with powerful political leaders end up as clients with little status and large work loads in the households of their patrons (see also Grace 1975: 207). Much depends on their families' status. The leaders to whom they are sent are more inclined to favor wards from aristocratic families, thereby ensuring the goodwill and support of these families.

Wardship continues undiminished in traditional areas of Liberia as well as in more modern areas. As we have seen, the most important example of wardship in the recent history of Fuama Chiefdom was that of Dumu, raised in the Monrovia household of an important national leader.[8] In return for the advantages conferred on him, Dumu had to execute the policies of the increasingly powerful national government and help national leaders create ties of allegiance with hostile native groups. But the benefits of playing the role of broker for coastal and hinterland politics greatly outweighed the disadvantages. Dumu was able to collect women and redistribute them to dependent clients, thus gaining more wealth and power than would have been possible without the resources and backing of the national government.

Slavery

Though the term slavery conjures up images of repression for Westerners, in effect it was a form of clientship in some parts of Africa, often similar to institutions such as wardship or brideservice.[9] Because social institutions and processes similar to slavery

8. Just as Dumu took the surname of the important leader to acknowledge the man's patronage, many people quite unrelated by birth or marriage to Dumu have in turn taken this surname to acknowledge and reinforce Dumu's patronage.

9. Slavery in most areas was fairly benign, since slaves were not captured for sale but were kept as members of the household. Domestic slaves were often indistinguishable from free members of the household; they usually ate with their masters and worked no more than other members of the household. Slave children were also valued as laborers and warriors, and most of their descendants were assimilated as

still exist in Liberia, even though slavery has been officially outlawed, a discussion of Kpelle slavery (lûɛ, 'slave') is not out of
place.[10] Moreover, the word "slave" is commonly used in the schol-
arly literature, and I will continue to use it, bearing in mind this
qualification.

Slavery's similarity with other social institutions can easily be
understood in terms of the model proposed by Kopytoff and Miers
(1977), who discuss slavery in the context of corporate descent
groups controlling rights in people. By viewing African social relations as a continuum, ranging from full members of a kin group to
unassimilated "marginal" outsiders, these authors go beyond the
notion of "free" and "enslaved" as absolute dichotomies:

> In most African societies, "freedom" lay not in a withdrawal into a mean-
> ingless and dangerous autonomy but in attachment to a kin group, to a
> patron, to power—an attachment that occurred within a well-defined hier-
> archical framework. It was in this direction that the acquired outsider had
> to move if he was to reduce his initial marginality. Here, the antithesis of
> "slavery" is not "freedom" qua autonomy but rather "belonging." (Kopy-
> toff & Miers 1977: 17)

Basing my definition on this model, I will treat Kpelle slaves as "involuntary" or "acquired outsiders" (Kopytoff & Miers 1977) used
"by other people for the economic value of their labour and for the
power and prestige they bring their owners" (Grace 1975: 7).

In an analysis based on Westermann's (1921) research near Dobli
Island, Sibley and Westermann (1928) divided Kpelle society into
three main categories of people: free persons, those descended from
longtime inhabitants of the area, or "landowners," in Horton's
(1972) terminology; serfs, descendants of slaves or of people who

---

members of the dominant lineage after several generations. Descendants of slaves or
even the slaves themselves could eventually become important members of the community. Though my data on slaves in Fuama Chiefdom are scanty, I know that at
least two very important elders, one in Digei and one on Dobli Island, were slaves
when they were young.

10. Clower et al. (1966) report that de facto slavery existed as late as 1962,
when, they estimate, one-fourth of the Liberian wage-labor force was recruited
involuntarily.

had come to "landowners" seeking protection or patronage; and slaves, prisoners of war, people bound as recompense for loans, criminals, and people bought in distant areas. Unlike serfs, slaves could be sold or given away. But like free persons and serfs, they could own property and were given spouses to live with.

Slaves provided manpower for warfare and labor for agricultural production.[11] Crosby (1937) reports that slaves and wives constituted the main labor force of Mende households: women (free and slave) did the sowing and weeding, male slaves did the heavier clearing, and slave children worked alongside free children, driving birds away. Like bridewealth, brideservice, and wardship, therefore, slavery enabled leaders to build local kin groups, produce a surplus, and acquire warriors for defense.

Pawnship

Rodney (1970) reports that when slavery was profitable, political leaders along the upper Guinea coast often made their followers incur debts, forcing them to sell themselves or their families into slavery. One favorite ploy was to find someone guilty of witchcraft or adultery and set the fine so high that neither he nor his family could pay it. The whole family might then be sold into slavery to settle the debt. Similar tactics were used to acquire pawns: a leader might fine a man for adultery with a woman, particularly one for whom bridewealth had been paid, and then demand a pawn (sɛyɛ) if the fine could not be paid.

Pawnship was an institution in which members of a household (male or female) could be given by the head of the household as security for a debt or a loan. Alternatively, the debtor could pawn himself. Though some pawns worked for a certain period to repay a debt, most remained pawns for the rest of their lives. And as long as

11. As an indication of the importance of slavery in the Liberian economy, slavery paradoxically increased after the British and Americans put an embargo on the further export of slaves in the latter half of the nineteenth century. With outside markets cut out, the Gola, for example, turned their slave labor to the development of intensive agriculture: rice, cocoa, and coffee (d'Azevedo 1959: 60; see also Grace 1975: 33).

the debt remained unpaid, the pawn had to be replaced upon death
by someone else (Grace 1975: 13–14). A leader and his heirs could
thus acquire a pawn's labor indefinitely, making it difficult in many
cases to draw the line between slavery and pawnship (Grace 1975:
206–7). As noted earlier, wards often spent their lives working in
the households of their patrons, but their obligation did not extend
beyond their death.

Though the uses of the term "pawn" vary among groups, it is
clear that a desire for labor and reproductive rights was paramount
in most people's acquisition of pawns. "Redeeming" people (pawnship) was a common practice in the Fuama area. Even contemporary political leaders assert that one of the first steps in acquiring
power is to pay a man's debt for him and accept in return the labor
of the debtor or of a member of his family. Also, a chief may gain a
pawn by trying a case, fining the defendant, and then grandly agree-
ing not to throw him in jail if he will come and work for the chief.
Not surprisingly, adultery with one of the chief's wives is often the
cause—or rationale—for the fine. Thus pawns may be created in a
manner similar to slaves and clients.

Secret Societies

So far this chapter has considered economic and political transactions primarily between individuals. We have seen that institutions
such as clientship, wardship, slavery, and pawnship bind the labor
and political allegiance of the subordinate to the superior. Though I
have pointed out some of the more prominent examples of inequality, such as the inequality between latecomers and landowners and
between the old and the young, the overall pattern of stratification
is brought into sharper focus with an examination of one last
Kpelle institution: the secret society.[12] This will set the stage for the

12. Since the Liberian government has prohibited research on many secret
society functions in tribal areas, the following discussion is based on my own
observations and interviews, other scholars' analyses of secret societies, and a bit
of speculation. The discussion reveals no secrets of the societies: it represents only
what uninitiated people can know. Even so, the nature of the secrets is not as
important as the fact that they are used for political and economic purposes
(Murphy, forthcoming).

discussion of marriage in Chapter 4, which shows how male elders of aristocratic lineages use rights in women to control other men.

The Poro and Sande secret societies exist under various names in parts of West Africa, particularly in Liberia, Sierra Leone, the Ivory Coast, and Guinea. Though the Poro and Sande have analogues throughout much of Africa, they are regarded by many authors as distinctive of the Central West Atlantic region of West Africa, as well as of West Africa itself (see d'Azevedo 1962b, Gibbs 1965, and Horton 1972). These societies have fascinated and puzzled scholars for years. Contemporary interest seems to focus on the ways in which secret societies serve as cross-cutting mechanisms to balance secular political power, educate the young, and create solidarity among people of the same ethnic group or sex. However, another aspect of the Poro and Sande has by and large been overlooked: the ways in which they strengthen patterns of stratification within the larger society. This section will show how women, marriage, and the secret societies fit into a stratification framework embracing all of traditional Kpelle society. Even though all the members of the Sande are women, we will see that the Sande intensifies power differences not only between male and female members of different lineages and age groups in the wider society, but also between men and women, and between women themselves. Sande leaders' power over female initiates' sexual and domestic services can be used to gain the loyalty of young men or those from outside lineages[13] whom Kpelle elders—male and female—seek to control. Such transactions may be seen as another aspect of the wealth-in-people system.

Every Kpelle boy and girl is urged, if not forced, to join the Poro or Sande, though occasionally some children sent to government or mission schools in distant areas will avoid initiation. For periods ranging from several days to several years, initiates remain in secluded "bush schools," away from contact with non-members and

---

13. Though I will occasionally refer to "lineages" in this section, I do not mean to restrict these units to neat patrilineal groups. Because people are constantly seeking affiliation with high-status individuals and families, kinship units almost always include people affiliated by marriage, wardship, clientship, and so on.

people of the opposite sex; the age of initiation varies from about six to sixteen. Boys and girls do not enter their bush schools at the same time. When a group of boys "comes out," the men "turn the land over to the women," who can then prepare to initiate a group of girls. A complete cycle may take as long as seven years: four for the men to occupy the land and conduct their bush school, and three for the women.

On entering the bush schools, male initiates are ritually devoured by the "forest spirit" or "devil" (ŋamù) and female initiates may be devoured by its female counterpart, the zèɣele. Both sexes undergo scarification to show that they have been "eaten" by the devil. Uncircumcised boys are circumcised, and girls often undergo clitoridectomies and labiadectomies. Instruction is differentiated according to sex and family status. Boys may be instructed in tribal history, warfare, handicrafts, farming, and medicine; girls in household skills, farming, raising children, medicine, and so on. Initiates swear to keep the secrets of the societies from non-members on pain of death. When the bush school closes, they emerge from the forest and rejoin their families, whom they have not seen during the initiation period. The initiates supposedly have no connection to the uninitiated "sinners" (a Liberian English expression) who entered the bush.

Both the Poro and Sande have grades. Young initiates are lowest in status, but have more prestige than the few people in their tribal group who are not members of the secret society, for many people believe that non-initiates are ignorant of important cultural secrets. Schwab (1947: 287), for example, cites a case of a Vai man who refused to marry his betrothed until she joined the Sande, and who paid her expenses in the bush. In general, the older people are, the more status they have in a secret society, even if they do not hold office. The secret society leaders, called zóo-ŋa (plural of zóo— 'medicine person') have life-or-death authority over members.[14]

14. The heads of the Sande and Poro societies are often powerful members in both societies. Harley (1941: 12) says that the head Sande zóo, for example, was a kind of cult mother to male initiates, supervising cooking and exercising some discipline, as well as assuming custody over important ritual objects of the Poro. Harley (1941: 12) and Schwab (1947: 268) suggest that even though Sande leaders often

Anthropologists have stressed three basic functions of the Poro and Sande secret societies. I will consider the importance of each function chiefly in relation to the Sande, though the conclusions I draw can be applied to the Poro as well. One of the most commonly mentioned functions of the secret societies is to educate tribal youth. In reply to criticisms of the seeming lack of formal education in West Africa, Watkins (1943) argued that secret society "bush schools" were quite effective in passing on practical cultural knowledge to both girls and boys (see also Little 1951: 120). The main purpose of the Sande society, Watkins claimed, was to prepare "a girl to assume her place as a wife and mother attached primarily to the domestic unit in the social order" (Watkins 1943: 674). Similarly, Sibley and Westermann (1928: 234) noted that Sande girls "are taught all kinds of housework, farming, harvesting, and dancing and singing." They also noted that "the girls receive instruction in all matters pertaining to sex relations."

I contend that in reality young Sande initiates learn little more than they already knew before they entered the bush (see also Ottenberg 1973), or than they would learn at that stage of their lives if they did not become secret society members. Because girls are drafted into household, farming, and child-care duties as soon as they are physically capable, such skills are no mystery to them. Girls are also said to learn the art of poisoning food (Harley 1941: 29) to keep husbands in line, as well as the art of preparing simple herbal remedies for sickness. Few girls, however, learn more than rudimentary "medicine." Like the Poro, the Sande reportedly divides initiates into classes: commoners, chiefs' daughters, and zóos (Harley 1941: 29). Zóos are given more instruction in medicine than other girls, although if the Sande parallels the Poro in this regard, female zóos may learn most medicine outside the bush school, under the tutelage of female relatives.

Thus Sande initiates seem to be taught practical skills for sym-

---

had husbands and children in the outside world, such women were ritually considered "men," possessing legendary powers far beyond those of ordinary mortals. In the remainder of the text I will Anglicize the plural zóo-ŋa as zóos.

bolic rather than utilitarian purposes (see also Little 1949: 211, Welmers 1949: 241, Ottenberg 1973). What young initiates do learn in the bush school is absolute obedience to Sande leaders, both while they are in the bush school and in later life (see also Murphy, forthcoming). Disobedience or disrespect may be threatened with infertility or even death. This explains the seeming paradox that girls are taught to be good, obedient wives on the one hand, and how to poison troublesome husbands on the other. Girls are supposed to obey the husbands that Sande leaders give them to, but they know that their ultimate allegiance lies with these secret society leaders, who could command them to poison their husbands for serious transgressions against higher tribal authority.

Besides their educational aspects, secret societies are said to have unifying functions. For example, Welmers states that "both the pɔlɔŋ [Poro] and the sàneŋ [Sande] exist for the sake of a spirit of tribal unity and responsible respect for tribal institutions" (1949: 230). Horton (1972) concurs, arguing that secret societies can best be understood as organizations that moderate rivalries between lineages in societies where territorial unity is crucial. Secret society elders make important decisions for the community in secret, and wear masks when announcing their decisions to the public in order to appear united and unanimous. (See also Fulton 1972: 1230.) Similarly, Little's (1949: 202) early work on secret societies among the Mende of Sierra Leone describes how the societies promoted solidarity: "A general and important feature resulting from both Poro and Sande schools is the sense of comradeship imparted. Initiates obtain a feeling of participating in a national institution. The common bonds of the society unite men with men, and women with women, as fellow members over a very wide area, and to an extent which transcends all barriers of family, clan, tribe, and religion." (See also Hoffer 1972a.)

However, too much emphasis on solidarity obscures important patterns of stratification in West African secret societies. Little's subsequent work has begun to focus on Mende political leaders' use of the Poro to preserve power, rather than to equalize it. And Meillassoux (1964) and Terray (1969) have examined how secret societies help to maintain stratification based on age. They note that in traditional Guro society (Ivory Coast) land and farming tools are not privately owned, and that elders use no physical force against younger people (cf. Murphy, forthcoming). Elders maintain power by controlling both access to women and the knowledge of subsistence technology, and they use secret societies to ensure their exclusive control of all important information.

However, Meillassoux and Terray attribute too much importance to information as a basis of power. As I have argued above, initiates in the secret society "bush schools" learn little that they did not already know. Furthermore, initiates are even derided for talking about higher-level secrets, which are not rightly theirs to know (Murphy, forthcoming). Hence, information and secrets may better be viewed as ideological dressing on a rigid gerontocratic hierarchy. It does not matter what the secrets are: it is more important that the young believe that the secrets the elders protect are important, and that they have no right to know things only elders are entitled to know.

Moreover, Meillassoux and Terray do not deal adequately with the importance of landowning lineages. Only certain old people— those members of landowning lineages who achieve religious or secular office—get to learn the society's most important secrets. D'Azevedo (1959, 1962a) has written some of the most perceptive analyses of stratification to date. He maintains that uxorilocally married Gola men from low-status lineages, as well as latecomer warriors and clients, may try to usurp power from the original inhabitants or fictionalize their relationships to the high-status lineages in order to become members. To quash these threats, older members of the elite lineages use their positions as leaders in the secret societies to memorize and expose the true ancestry of newcomers and their descendants, and to select and approve secular leaders. Cloaking their self-interest in the ideal of social unity, members of the elite lineages (or a group of allied lineages) call for duty and self-sacrifice from those beneath them. Thus, secrecy and

secret societies primarily exist not to eliminate factional lineage interests, as Horton maintains, but to preserve these differences and
protect the aristocratic lineages from the threat of ambitious newcomers. In some contexts, of course, such as external threat, the
secret societies do try to unify lineages for the common good. But in
most internal affairs, the decisions defined as unanimous and beneficial to the whole society invariably benefit the aristocratic lineages
the most.

To follow up on d'Azevedo's insights, we must examine the relation of Kpelle secret societies to Kpelle political and economic organization, and the relation of secret society leadership to secular
authority. As we have seen, landowner families claim rights in certain territories and distribute farming privileges to family members
as well as latecomer families. Political leaders in the secular world
tend to be closely related to Poro and Sande leaders.[15] (It is significant that important landowner elders need not hold secular office
themselves, since they control their relatives or front men who do.)
Hence, not only do elite elders use rights in land to control lower-
status people, but they also can invoke supernatural sanctions
against those who threaten their authority.

We have seen, moreover, that during periods of military strife in
the Central West Atlantic region, political allegiance involved at-
taching oneself to a powerful patron who could offer protection
from marauding groups seeking captives and booty. Various degrees of subordination (slavery, pawnship, clientship, and so on)
were the price of safety. Though active warfare has ceased in present-day Liberia, the protection of powerful patrons is still necessary
in order to ward off unjustified taxes, fines, lawsuits, and the like.
One way in which people gain protection and possible opportunities for advancement from powerful leaders is to send their sons or
daughters to be initiated in the secret societies organized by these
leaders (see also Little 1966: 66–67; Hoffer 1972b: 161), a tactic

15. Data on the kin ties between secular and religious leaders in the chiefdom
where I worked revealed that the head secular leader, the landowner, was the -kêra
(mother's brother) to both the Sande and Poro zóos. (The Kpelle say that a -kêra has
unquestioned authority over his sister's son or daughter, who must lay down his or
her life if necessary to the -kêra.)

closely resembling wardship or clientship.[16] Initiates may then be put to work; for example, one of the main tasks Poro boys perform in bush schools is to make rice farms for the Poro leaders. Sibley and Westermann (1928: 224–25) report that Poro initiates near Dobli Island made fishnets, fish traps, baskets, thatching for houses, drums, mortars, canoes, and game boards during their seclusion. The profits from the sale of these fatten the coffers of the dominant Poro leaders (see also Harley 1941: 16; Murphy, forthcoming). Hoffer (1972a) notes similar patterns among female Bundu leaders in Sierra Leone, who benefit from the labor of initiates on their farms. I also suspect that Kpelle Sande leaders sell any surplus crafts that girls make during the course of their "education" to outsiders, keeping the profits themselves. And during important Sande rituals outside the bush, I observed that the money that the young Sande dancers collected from spectators went straight from their decorated collection gourds into the hands of older female leaders (see Photograph 6).

Poro and Sande elders not only control the production of the initiates, they also control reproduction, the most important function of the whole society. They do this in several ways. First, they bestow "new" children on the people whose children the secret society "devil" killed and ate. A careful examination of Poro and Sande symbolism reveals that people are made to believe that they depend on secret society leaders for any grown children they have. When the "devil" ritually kills and devours its initiates, parents know that their children are alive, but must pretend otherwise. During the initiation period parents must supply the bush schools with food, and they must accede to occasional demands for money and favors from the leaders while the schools are in session, as well as when the children emerge from the bush. Such economic control has led Murphy to label parents' payments to secret society elders as "ransom." If a child dies in the bush school, a broken pot or other symbol is placed

16. Little (1966: 66–67) observes that the King of Quoja, a seventeenth-century confederacy in southern Sierra Leone and western Liberia, began a bush school for boys in the territory he had conquered in order to cement local support. Little speculates that the king bound their allegiance with oaths of obedience, and sent them back as a secret police force to control unrest in their native territories.

6. *A young woman turns over money to a Sande leader.*

by the parents' door; but they must not grieve when they see it, for the child is supposed to have died on entering the bush. When the initiates come out of the bush, a midwife of high rank in the Sande society often accompanies them, symbolizing the birth of new people (Gay 1973). The initiates and their families act as though they did not recognize each other. Thus, people regain their children supposedly through the beneficence of the aristocratic elders, who mediate between fearsome supernatural powers and ordinary mortals. Indeed, I suspect that uncooperative parents are less likely than others to get their children back safely. Since children are the most important source of labor, political support, and old-age security for most people, the elders wield formidable power.

Aristocratic lineages also control women's reproductive functions more directly. Through the agency of the secret society "devil," the sister of the men's "devil," women are ritually invested with fertility and therefore eligibility for marriage (Sibley & Westermann 1928: 232; and Schwab 1947: 287). (The fact that the women's "devil" is the sister is significant in symbolizing the kin relations between Poro and Sande leaders.) Furthermore, these lineages usually produce the most important midwives, on whom women depend to deliver their babies safely.

All members of Kpelle society, especially women, fear and respect midwives, whose power stems from their exclusive knowledge of obstetrics and gynecology. Contrary to previous belief, Sande leaders hide more than they teach about reproduction, and midwives try to keep the knowledge of childbearing secret. Many girls, I am convinced, do not find out how babies are born until the very moment their own children emerge from the womb. Even women who have had children profess ignorance of how babies are formed in the womb, and of the techniques and medicines the midwife uses to facilitate birth. Women therefore believe themselves highly dependent on midwives' services and knowledge. Believing she was performing a useful medical service, a Peace Corps teacher once brought a model of an exposed female torso to class and told her female pupils how babies were conceived and delivered. When the girls reported what they had learned, the teacher was nearly expelled from town because her lesson posed such a threat to local midwives.

Midwives are paid well: a woman fears making a midwife angry by not paying her, for the midwife may threaten to make her next delivery difficult—or she may not come at all. Midwives also use women's dependence on their obstetrical services to extract private secrets from women during childbirth. If a woman is having a difficult delivery, the midwife may tell her that she will die unless she confesses her lovers' names or any crimes she has committed. Later, fearing that the midwife will expose her secrets, a woman rarely neglects to pay her. The knowledge of midwifery, like most any medicinal skill, can now be bought by any woman who has borne children and has the necessary cash. But because they do not want to die or lose their babies, women prefer to patronize the midwives whom they believe to have the most powerful medicines: those who belong to landowning lineages and occupy positions of leadership in the Sande society.

Finally, landowning lineages play a large role in controlling the most basic resource in the wealth-in-people system: the disposition of women in marriage. This control is particularly noticeable when the young female initiates emerge from the Sande bush. In former days girls often stayed in the bush schools for three years, and could be married almost as soon as they came out. Since the girls were marriageable, their exit fees were paid by suitors. Alldridge (1910: 224–25) reports great rivalries among young husbands-elect of Mende Sande initiates, each seeking to outdo the others in the quantities of goods they bestowed on the secret society leadership. My own informants reported rivalries among men for the best dancers or singers or for the most beautiful girls. Conversely, girls and their families vie for suitors wealthy enough to "bring them out of the bush" in style, by contributing bright new clothes for the girls and generous gifts for the leaders who initiated them.

Nowadays men wanting wives still have to pay exit fees for older marriageable girls. But because of public schools and other commitments, girls in more modern areas rarely stay long in the bush school, so that few girls are ready to marry when they come out.

(See Photograph 7.) Hence, it is more often their parents who must pay both the entrance fee and the exit fee. A taxi driver I knew told me that he had been ordered to pay twenty dollars apiece to bring his two daughters out of a Sande bush school run by high-status Vai immigrants. It is significant that parents as well as suitors of older girls still must go through dominant lineage members to regain these marriageable girls, and both must show obedience and loyalty to the ruling lineage.

Although the production and reproductive capacities of Sande initiates clearly benefit secret society aristocrats, we must note that girls and their parents rarely protest. In fact, parents sometimes compete with each other to enroll their daughters in the bush schools run by the most important political leaders. Such behavior makes sense in terms of the wealth-in-people system: the secret society, like clientship or wardship, can be seen as an institution in which low-status people attach themselves to powerful lineages through their children, in hopes of protection or possible advancement.

As I have argued, the Kpelle secret societies may function in some ways to educate initiates and create bonds of solidarity among members. But their most important functions lie in quite the opposite direction: strengthening patterns of stratification that allow aristocratic families to control low-status people, elders to control youths, men to control women, and older high-status women to control other women. Applied to the Sande society, this proposition flies in the face of much recent women's literature that fails to view women as rational actors who may readily cast aside female unity when it is unprofitable. Hence, it bears closer scrutiny.

Female solidarity is often the most salient feature of important Sande rituals, in which members take pains to differentiate themselves from men and to accentuate their femaleness. (See Photograph 8.) But it is interesting to note that such gestures of solidarity are commonly exploited for practical gain. Hoffer (1972a, 1972b), for example, mentions a group of Bundu (the Temne equivalent for the Sande) women who used their control over initiates as well as their own formidable numbers to extract money from the fathers

7. Sande initiates sit covered with chalk for ritual purposes as well as for beauty and coolness.

8. *Sande girls dancing.*

and prospective husbands of their charges. And observations that Sande leaders manipulate young women's labor and reproductive capacities dispel the notion that the Sande society is a united, egalitarian organization of women joined in sisterhood to confront men.[17] When profits are to be made by exploiting Sande members or by uniting with Poro or secular leaders, Sande leaders readily put aside women's solidarity in favor of more lucrative coalitions.

The Kpelle Sande society must therefore be seen as a means by

17. Leadership of the local Sande society is a major route to power for a woman seeking secular political advancement. Hoffer (1972b, 1974) mentions two female paramount chiefs in nineteenth-century Sierra Leone who drew all the best local girls to the bush schools they sponsored. One of the chiefs, Madam Yoko, had come to power through her kin connections and her marriage to an important chief, as well as by strategically distributing girls initiated in her bush school to men from whom she sought political favors.

which aristocrats maintain power. Though parents may strongly influence the choice of their daughters' husbands, they often find it
advantageous as clients to bring their daughters to powerful leaders
in both the secular and sacred realms to be redistributed to other
men. In conjunction with their close relatives, the secular leaders,
Poro and Sande leaders take in these girls, invest them with fertility,
make them suffer a ritual "death," regurgitate them as new people,
and give them back to grateful families and suitors. The girls are
carefully distributed to young men, to men of non-aristocratic or
rival families, and to powerful men whose cooperation they seek. In
this way aristocrats gain followers and allies, and solidify their control over potentially dissident individuals and families. Though
powerful men usually retain ultimate control over female productive and reproductive services,[18] women play a large part in this
process, acting in concert with their male relatives (or independently, when they can) by teaching young initiates to be good wives
and to depend on Sande leadership for the rest of their lives, and by
distributing initiates to husbands.[19]

Women who become powerful secular or secret society leaders
thus achieve their status mainly by playing the "male" game of
trading rights in the women they control for political support (see
also Bledsoe 1976). Furthermore, although individual Sande leaders may eventually acquire immense wealth and power, they rarely
attain their positions without affiliation by birth or marriage to
powerful men. It is easy to see, then, why older aristocratic women
who control Sande leadership often have more to gain by promot-

18. The contention that Poro males ultimately control both Sande initiates and
Sande leaders finds support in the fact that my informants of both sexes were quick
to inform me that the men's "devil" had jurisdiction over the women's "devil" (see
also Schwab 1947: 287–88). I was also informed that Sande zóos are the ritual
wives of their male agnates who head the Poro society (see also d'Azevedo 1962a).
As obedient "wives" of Poro men, Sande women are supposed to train all the girls in
their keeping to be good wives. Finally, male as well as female zóos pounce on Sande
dancers during rituals for any misdemeanors. For these reasons I believe that Poro
elders are the ultimate recipients of many of the Sande girls' benefits.

19. Similarly, Beidelman (1971: 107–11) describes female initiation ceremonies
among the Kaguru of Tanzania as a process by which female religious leaders attempt to "cool" a girl's sexuality, teach her to obey her future husband, and invest
her with fertility to make her a desirable wife.

ing lineage or age group interests, than by siding with younger women of low-status families who have no legal rights in themselves and who are, moreover, valuable items to be manipulated in the competitive political arena. Given this perspective, it is little wonder that older Kpelle women use the young as well as other women for their own purposes, just as men do. In this wealth-in-people system their own status rests on their ability to do so.

CONCLUSION

Given the demands of traditional West African slash-and-burn agriculture, as well as the demands of warfare in the history of West Africa, political leaders have been anxious to acquire followers—especially male followers. Older, more established leaders try to win the support of other men, who are both dangerous as potential rivals and necessary as farm laborers and political followers. Some of the main tools older aristocrats use to gain the labor and allegiance of other people are clientship, wardship, pawnship, slavery, and secret societies. It is interesting to note that the main fly in the ointment of such a system is often the impatience of young men, who are denied wives and power unless they show obedience over a long period of time. Young men are in a bind: either they indebt themselves to older people in order to acquire women, or they forgo the chances for advancement that marriage and the control of women bring. The same principles of gerontocracy among the Lele of Zaïre have been well expressed by Douglas:

The Lele redressed the balance between the generations by the way they distributed the things they valued. Entry to cults was by fee and restricted to married men. As the age of marriage was late, this automatically reserved positions of esteem to older men and lined their pockets with the fees of new entrants. Polygyny created a scarcity of marriageable girls; marriage fees were also high. So for the first step on the social ladder, marriage, a man had to go to his wealthy seniors and solicit their aid. *Often a young man, receiving financial help, never touched the goods which were transferred in his name direct from one old man to another.* And the same goes for every subsequent step, since wealth was thus drawn into the control of the older married men. (1963: 4, italics mine)

Political aspirants who succeed in the wealth-in-people system depend largely on debts created by fines, loans, protection, and most importantly the transfer of women at marriage. Thus it is to women and marriage that we now turn. The next chapter examines the ways in which rights in women are used to maintain the traditional Kpelle system of stratification, which channels wealth and power up the hierarchy to political leaders and older men.

CHAPTER 4

Traditional Kpelle
Marriage

We have seen that the traditional African wealth-in-people system of stratification rewards those who gain control over labor and reproduction. The last chapter analyzed the economic and political bases of this system, showing how people who aspire to political power use various social institutions to acquire followers. However, the institution perhaps most potent in binding people has remained in the background until now: marriage. La Fontaine remarks that among the Gisu of East Africa "marriage entails an economic transaction and . . . the bonds it creates between giver and receiver of bridewealth are similar to, though more lasting than, those created by other economic transactions" (1962: 97). Here I will explain how Kpelle men, parents, and political leaders use legal rights in women to control younger men and male clients, thereby acquiring security, status, and wealth.[1]

This chapter has two purposes: to examine the legal basis of different types of Kpelle conjugal relationships, and to analyze traditional Kpelle marriage in a political and economic context. I will

1. In many rural areas throughout Africa, marriage and the control of women form the core of economic and political advancement; see Mair 1953 and J. Goody 1971. These patterns have also been noted in specific groups in southern Africa (Schapera 1940), Central Africa (Van Wing 1947, Colson 1958), East Africa (Schneider 1968, 1970), and West Africa (Forde 1941, Green 1947, Little 1951, Meillassoux 1964, Terray 1969, Hopkins 1973).

show that because young men and women need each other's labor and support, marriage in traditional society is stable, a system that effectively channels wealth and status up the social hierarchy.

LEGAL ASPECTS OF KPELLE MARRIAGE

Radcliffe-Brown (1950) provides a particularly useful delineation of African marriage as a legal transfer of rights in people and property from one lineage to another. Marriage in a patrilineal society, for example, gives a husband and his kin group various rights in a woman: the right to her domestic and sexual services and her agricultural labor, and the right to legal fatherhood of her children. In exchange, marriage gives the woman's kin group rights to bridewealth or brideservice from the groom or his kin.[2]

Rights in people, property, and labor transferred at marriage are backed by rules that provide compensation for dissatisfied parties. For example, a man or his lineage may demand the return of bridewealth if a woman wants to divorce her husband. Especially in patrilineal societies such as the Kpelle, rules ensure that a woman and her children remain the property of the lineage that paid bridewealth, even if the husband dies. Though seldom practiced, the Kpelle levirate legally transfers a widow to one of her husband's brothers or other male lineage mates as his wife. A widow may even be transferred to one of her husband's sons by another marriage, usually if she is of the same age or younger, though many of my informants regarded this dubiously, calling it a marriage between a man and his 'mother.' (All of one's father's wives are called 'mother.') Conversely, the sororate allows a widower to claim another women from his dead wife's lineage.

2. As Radcliffe-Brown (1950: 46) notes, feelings of affection between African spouses are better seen as a by-product of a conjugal relationship than as a reason for marrying. For example, the domestic organization questionnaire I administered to women in Digei and Haindii included this question: "Do you think it is better to be single or better to be married? Why?" All the women who replied to the second part of the question gave reasons pertaining to economic security, respect, or freedom. In Digei 71 percent of the women mentioned economics, as did 65 percent in Haindii. None mentioned companionship or emotional factors, as a woman in a Western society might.

Legal marriage also gives parties recourse to formal courts that can enforce sanctions on those who break marriage rules. One of the most important court sanctions allows a legally married husband or his lineage to claim an adultery fine of ten dollars from his wife's lover. A man can reinvest these adultery fines in marriage payments for still more wives for himself or wives for dependent clients. Thus, the courts that adjudicate marriage cases not only ensure justice, but they also help people advance politically.

The Kpelle distinguish two basic conjugal arrangements: marriage (see-lâa, 'to sit down') and "loving" (wéli).[3] Though it is often difficult to distinguish married people from unmarried cohabiting people, only those people whom the courts agree are married have recourse to legal sanctions if their partners mistreat or neglect them. Unmarried people have only informal kin support. Moreover, cohabiting men have no legal rights in their children, nor do they have rights to adultery payments from rival lovers of their women.

Legal Marriage

As Chapter 1 has outlined, Kpelle marriage can be seen as a continuum, or a process, as many students of Africa have called it. (For example, see Evans-Pritchard 1951, Kuper 1970, Comaroff & Roberts 1977.) Though the order of stages in the process may vary, Kpelle marriage usually consists of Sande initiation, betrothal, coresidence, "turning over" the woman to the man symbolically with a token or bridewealth, and bearing the first child or two. Indeed, the whole marriage process bears some resemblance to the gradual absorption of outsiders or "strangers" into a lineage (see Kopytoff & Miers 1977). Because marriage is a process, certain people—especially women in the modern area of Fuama Chiefdom—can manipulate their marital status, thus handing the ethnographer the difficult task of distinguishing who is married and who is not for purposes of statistical analysis. Realizing that any firm division is in some sense artificial, I settled on the "turning over" event as the

3. For further discussion of marriage arrangements and ceremonies, see Gibbs (1960, 1963) and Sibley and Westermann (1928) on the Kpelle, and Schwab (1947) on other Liberian tribes.

best indicator of the actual transfer of legal rights. Most informants agreed. (I too was asked several times if I had been turned over to my man.)

A Kpelle woman may be betrothed by her parents when she is very small, but she is officially "turned over to the man" (dí dèɛ ǹâloŋ pɔ́, 'they turn her over to the man') after puberty. A man, on the other hand, must usually wait at least until his elders agree he is mature enough to start a rice farm. (There is no specific age at which a man reaches legal majority.) People may sometimes choose their partners if they are not yet betrothed, but parents still exercise much control, creating disputes between prospective partners, denying them access to family resources, and so on. The "turning over" event usually takes place in the house of the bride's relatives. Present are the bride and groom, their parents or the parents' representatives, someone to receive a payment or token for the girl's family, and other interested friends or passersby.

Gibbs (1960, 1963) has observed that the Kpelle marriage ceremony is inconspicuous and almost clandestine. Because my research was on marriage, I tried very hard to witness a "turning over" ceremony during my fieldwork, but like Gibbs I was unsuccessful. Early ethnographers such as Sibley and Westermann (1928) reported feasts and dancing at weddings, but I was told by all informants that these customs have died out in Fuama Chiefdom.[4] In any case, Roberts (1977) shows that among the Kgatla of Botswana, such ceremonies and events associated with marriage do not confer validity on marriage. Rather, validity lies in the kinsmen's recognition and acceptance of the union. We can see a similar concern with kin acceptance in the Kpelle "turning over" ceremony itself. Older people in both families take charge of the event, and lecture the bride and groom about marital responsibilities and the importance of sexual fidelity (especially for the woman). Moreover, they remind the kinsmen of the couple of their responsibility to

4. In contrast, as Carol [Hoffer] MacCormack notes (personal communication), initiation into the Sande society overshadows not only marriage but also events that are prominent in many other African societies: defloration and the birth of the first child. Sande initiation confers eligibility for marriage, which seems more important than the occasion of marriage.

intervene in marital disputes and to see that the families are compensated should the marriage end in divorce or death. The groom must have a sponsor, or "father," to "stand for" him; the sponsor can be his real father, but need not be, especially if the groom is from a distant town. In such cases, the girl's parents may prefer that the man have a local sponsor. The sponsor of the groom gives the bride's family a token, perhaps only a small coin (kpeyaŋ-kâo nɛnî, 'cowrie shell wife'), and the woman is "turned over to the man" by her family. Arrangements for bridewealth (dâleŋ nɛnî, 'money wife') or brideservice, both of which are optional, may be finalized at this time, although actual payments of bridewealth may be protracted or even remain unpaid for the duration of the marriage.

To enhance their political and economic status, men want as many wives as possible (see also Schapera 1940, Forde 1941, Little 1951, Colson 1958). But many head wives also want junior wives in the household, not only for companionship but also for help with the chores; Little (1951) notes that in most cases the status of a junior wife is like that of a servant to the head wife. Women with political aspirations try to build their own status in the community by becoming wives. So eager are women to have junior wives that I heard of several cases in which husbands had little to do with the selection of their second wives. One man in Haindii came home one day to find that his wife—without consulting him—had brought a young girl into the house to be her junior wife. I failed to ask the details of the arrangement, but because the woman ran a profitable cane juice shop, I suspect she used her earnings to help pay the girl's bridewealth.

The Kpelle believe it is important for co-wives to get along well with each other, since they must cooperate in performing domestic tasks at home and on the farm. For this reason the first wife (nɛnî kɛ́tɛ, 'big wife') usually "approaches" a close friend or a younger sister to be her junior wife (nɛnî loŋ, 'small wife'). Gbili, a woman of about twenty-four, told me that when her husband asked her to choose a "small wife," she approved the idea and approached her best friend, Lɔpu, a recently divorced woman slightly younger than herself. The two women were inseparable as friends and coworkers. Indeed, I hypothesized that they would divorce their husband before they left each other.

A close relationship between co-wives is of course, ideal. In cases where a husband has ordered his wife to approach a girl she does not like, trouble inevitably follows. From what informants say, most second marriages not initiated or approved by the first wife fail because of economic disputes and jealousy. The first wife notes that the resources she has carefully built up (kitchen utensils, food, clothes, and the like) must be spread thinner when another wife comes in. More serious problems arise if a man tells his wife to approach a woman with whom he has been carrying on a secret affair. A married man, just like an unmarried man, must give his lover gifts of money and clothes. A wife resents sharing her "properties" with a woman whom she finds has been draining the family coffer behind her back.

In talking to informants, I was struck by a remarkable fact: in only one or two cases among all the arrangements I heard about had both marriages survived when a man ordered his first wife to approach a woman she did not like. One typical case was that of Kpana, who had been married for several years to Sam, a Dobli Island quarter chief. In 1970 Sam began "loving to" Nyɛ̃ɛ kole, a young girl who had recently come out of the Sande bush school, and he decided to marry her in 1972. Although he did not tell Kpana he had been "loving to" the girl, Kpana suspected it. Nevertheless, she "loved to" (approached) Nyɛ̃ɛ kole, saying "ŋa íwêlii ŋásurɔ̃ŋ mɛni mà" ('I love you on behalf of my husband').

Tensions quickly surfaced. Kpana began making palaver with Sam and Nyɛ̃ɛ kole, trying to drive the new wife out of the house. She snubbed Nyɛ̃ɛ kole's cooking, declaring she preferred to cook on the farm for herself and her daughter by Sam. Because she was the senior wife, she had the key to the rice kitchen, and refused to give Nyɛ̃ɛ kole rice. After seeing these efforts fail, she finally left town and went to stay with relatives. When she came back a month later, she found that her own lover's wife had died, so she and her daughter moved in with him. Sam agreed to let Kpana keep the daughter, fearing that Nyɛ̃ɛ kole would mistreat the girl.

However, co-wife arrangements in which the first wife initiates a second marriage and chooses the new wife do not always survive either. A senior wife may initiate the second marriage not to acquire labor and companionship, but to contrive grounds for divorce, trying to trump up charges of favoritism and neglect against her husband. Informants told me that this is a common trick. Kɔto, a middle-aged woman in Digei, had been married to Sale for several years but had grown dissatisfied. She wanted to divorce him but knew she would have little chance of keeping their household goods and part of the year's rice harvest if she had no justifiable reasons for divorcing. Therefore, she told Sale she wanted a "small wife." He gave her permission to find one, so she approached Bɛmɛ, a young girl who was not a close friend of hers. As soon as Bɛmɛ came into the house, Kɔto began making palaver with her and with Sale, accusing Sale of neglecting her and favoring Bɛmɛ. She brought the matter to a chief and asked for a divorce, but according to my female informant, he saw through her trick and found her at fault.

Divorce

Though the rules of legal marriage seek to bind partners permanently, divorce is common among the Kpelle. A spouse seeking a divorce brings a complaint to the people who arranged the marriage. If the plaintiff is the woman (usually the case, I found), she complains to her mother's brother or whomever gave her to the man and accepted the marriage token for her family. If her uncle cannot mollify her, they go to the man's relatives to try to settle the matter informally (pérɛ mù mɛni saa, 'house dispute'). If the man's relatives cannot dissuade her, the woman's uncle returns the marriage token, and the man's relatives formally return the woman to her family.

Nowadays a divorce is often heard in court (koti mɛni saa, 'court dispute') by a chief. A man may be found guilty of physical abuse of his wife or failure to provide her with adequate support. Women, on the other hand, may be found guilty of adultery or failure to perform domestic tasks. This does not mean that the guilt has been one-sided. A woman may try to get her husband to divorce her by refusing to cook—thereby provoking him to beat her. She then complains to the court chief that she has been mistreated, hoping that physical abuse will appear more serious than mere neglect of household duties. Conversely, a husband may withhold spending money from his wife, provoking her to neglect household duties or to seek an outside lover in defiance.

Gibb's (1960) data on the Kpelle of Panta Chiefdom showed that women were usually found at fault in formal courts of law. My observations in Haindii, though not systematic, differed. In the divorce cases I witnessed or heard about, Kpelle women fared at least as well as men in the verdicts. However, when I asked a chief whose court I observed who is usually at fault in divorce cases, he answered without hesitation, "the woman." "The 'friend' [lover] palaver," he explained, "is the only thing that spoils the native girls." Even if a woman is married to a good husband who takes care of her and gives her what she needs, the chief asserted, she will "love to" other men, thus destroying her chances for a favorable verdict. Because the chief insisted that women were almost invariably guilty, either the cases I recorded were exceptions, or the chief—a man—perceived all cases women won as exceptions.

Divorce proceedings are highly complex, involving tangled histories of relationships and property ownership. A divorce is one of the most notable social processes in which parties contest the definition of the situation. The husband's family wants everything they have given (bridewealth, gifts, expenses) to be called bridewealth so that it may be reclaimed, whereas the wife's family tries to construe the goods as gifts or loans so that they need not be returned immediately. Even clothes and household goods may be disputed.

In interviewing people about divorce, I soon found that "properties" (kɔ́lin) and rice farms, rather than emotional traumas, were the most important issues. "Properties" include material possessions such as houses, clothes, and household and farm implements. Rice farms, on the other hand, are so basic for subsistence that people often separate them from "properties." Most of the "properties" people seek are items bought or built with cash. In 1974, for example, zinc roofing for a single house cost at least $120. Hoes, cutlasses, and axes are no longer manufactured by blacksmiths in Haindii; most people buy them ready-made in stores. Plates, cups, knives, spoons, pans, buckets, and clothes are also purchased. Because all these items represent a sizable investment for subsistence farmers, whose cash income is minimal, it is no surprise that material possessions such as these are highly coveted and closely guarded.[5]

When property is to be divided in a conjugal breakup, the court chief will consider what the legal status of the conjugal arrangements is, who bought the properties, and who is at fault in the breakup. If a couple has acquired goods together during the course of a legal marriage, most informants agree that the person found at fault in the divorce loses most of the properties in the settlement, a rule that makes both sides anxious to establish innocence. Powerful or wealthy men, of course, are notably immune from this rule, often evicting troublesome wives with little but the clothes they wear. The rule is further complicated in actual court cases: those earning cash—usually men—have the most claim to the property. A woman's subsistence production is rarely considered to have earned her a share in goods bought with cash. Even a woman's market business is usually set up with her husband's capital. Her husband will certainly demand his investments back if she wants to divorce, and will claim her properties if she has no ready cash.

Despite the uncertainties of holding on to properties after a divorce, even an adulterous woman may be awarded such important items as the house, the rice farm, and all her household possessions, provided that she has custody of the children. However, one woman remarked to me that if a woman just "eats" the money and spends it foolishly, she will have nothing to fall back on when she

5. I never saw my neighbor in Haindii so upset as when the daughter of her deceased ex-husband refused to give her the two old buckets she had used when married to the man. Also, watching our Haindii garbage pile being rummaged, I quickly learned that people threw hardly anything away. In Digei the situation was even more striking; therefore I began to distribute even empty jars and tin cans as gifts. One day I rinsed out a particularly sturdy sixteen-ounce can and presented it as a cooking container to the old woman who lived next door. She was so delighted that she thanked me over and over, and sang happily to herself the rest of the day.

no longer has a husband. The best way to prepare for divorce, she confided, is to invest any cash your husband gives you while you're married in clothes, dishes, or a house. When a woman contemplating divorce receives money for household expenses from her husband, she should buy the material goods she wants and take them to her mother to keep, telling her husband they are for her mother. (Entrusting cash to a mother is less successful, said my informant, because the mother invariably "eats" some of it.) Naturally the woman should avoid telling her husband she intends to divorce him until she has all the goods she needs. Though the husband may try to reclaim the goods, they are difficult to retrieve from a determined mother-in-law.

In contrast to married couples, a cohabiting man and woman who decide to separate will keep only what they have acquired individually. The case of Sumo and Lɔpu illustrates what happens to items of value when cohabiting partners break up (taa, 'to divorce'—the same word describes the breakup of cohabiting couples as well as married couples). Sumo, a man about fifty years old, sued a girl named Lɔpu for $200 in the paramount chief's court at Bong Mine. I heard Sumo describe how he had approached Lɔpu two years before to marry him. She and her relatives agreed, probably because by local standards Sumo was quite wealthy. When the agreement was reached, Sumo began to buy lappas, head scarves, shoes, brassieres, rice, and fish for Lɔpu and her mother. Though these goods were readily accepted, Lɔpu resisted Sumo's amorous advances, and finally announced that she was pregnant by another man and wanted to marry him instead of Sumo. (Young women commonly lead on older wealthy men, while maintaining sexual liaisons with younger but poorer men.) Fearing now that she might have to pay for the items Sumo had given her and her mother, Lɔpu tried to persuade the paramount chief that they were "gifts" that need not be returned. Sumo retorted that he had bought the items with his own cash and wanted compensation for them, since Lɔpu was not his legal wife. Realizing she was trapped, Lɔpu tried to change her tack, arguing that Sumo had listed too many items and had overestimated their value. Striking a compromise, the paramount chief listed the items

Lɔpu agreed she had received and the prices Sumo said he had paid. Finally the chief announced that Lɔpu or her relatives would have to pay not the $200 demanded at first, but $66: $48 for the items Sumo had bought, $15.50 for court fees (since she lost the case), and $2.50 for the court messenger's fees, paid initially by Sumo to subpoena her.

OTHER CONJUGAL CATEGORIES

Besides legal marriage, there are other kinds of conjugal union that fall under the category of unmarried "loving" (wɛ́li). The rights and obligations that accrue to partners in these unions are not legally binding. As we have seen, properties belong to individuals, not to the couple as a unit. Families welcome children born of such unions (wɛ́li-lòŋ, literally, 'love child') and attach no stigma to them. Though both families try to claim these children, they technically belong to the mother's family if the father has paid no compensation. Thus in a sense children are a form of property that fathers must pay for and maintain if they are to be considered the legal "owners."

Although there is only one recognized category of legal marriage, the "loving" forms of conjugal union may be seen as a continuum from transient to permanent (or at least a continuum of intentions to maintain the relationship). One kind of "loving" is trial marriage or engagement. People contemplating marriage are frequently encouraged to live together (díkáa see-lâa wɛ́li sù, literally, 'they are sitting down in loving') before the woman is legally turned over to the man. Compared to the strictures of societies in Europe and Asia (J. Goody 1969, 1971), Kpelle rules for premarital sex are quite lenient.[6]

6. I suspect that this leniency is to a certain extent related to the importance of labor among the Kpelle: because children contribute to production, the Kpelle welcome children from nonlegal as well as legal unions. I also suspect that adultery is prosecuted not because of risks to family reputation, as in Europe and Asia, but because confusion may arise over the fatherhood of the children. An adulterer may try to claim the child and take it away from the legal husband of the mother. Thus adulterous women are prosecuted not so much to punish them as to reaffirm their husbands' sovereignty over their sexuality and reproductive capacity.

A trial marriage is seen as one protection against later divorce because the prospective partners get a chance to "see each other's ways" before they make a more permanent commitment. An older chief, for example, told me about his trial marriage to a young girl whose parents had sought his patronage by bringing him a wife. The chief agreed to keep her a while to "see her ways." But soon he noticed her "going between the houses" to a young man who lived nearby. The chief said nothing to the girl, but when her parents came to finalize the marriage, he told them she had been "loving to" the young man, collected $3 from her mother as an out-of-court adultery settlement, and gave the girl back to her parents. Such trial marriages not only allow partners to try each other out, but also allow men in particular to try out their potential in-laws, and vice versa. (See Comaroff & Roberts 1977.)

Besides this engagement period, there are several kinds of unmarried loving. Nɛɛ-lâa ('stable loving') refers to a long-term relationship between an unmarried man and woman who are cohabiting or having sexual relations regularly. Though there are no legal compensatory rules that apply to the creation or dissolution of nɛɛ-lâa unions, parents usually demand favors and labor from a man cohabiting with their daughter, in exchange for her domestic services. Children of such a union belong to the man if he supports them and their mothers. Because the woman has not been turned over to him fully, however, he has no legal obligation to support her. On the other hand, she has no legal obligation to remain sexually faithful to him or to share with him any property she has acquired during the relationship.

Another kind of unmarried loving is 'night loving' (kpíni wêli) or 'hidden loving' (loo wêli), a sexual affair carried on secretly. A woman's 'night loving' is not particularly condoned by her parents, who cannot ask favors from an unknown lover. Any children of the union (kpíni lóŋ, 'night child') belong to the woman and her family, unless the man identifies himself or the woman "confesses" her lover's name in order to make him pay her maintenance expenses while she is pregnant and nursing the child. Having paid the child's expenses, the father may than take his "property." If the woman is married, a child from such a union belongs to her husband, unless the lover pays her expenses plus adultery damages to her husband.

Some women "love to" many men, and seek money and gifts from all their lovers (kule too nɛni, 'promiscuous woman,' or sia sia nɛnî, 'walk-about woman'). Women with stable conjugal relationships may hold these women in disrepute, claiming that promiscuous women have no self-respect. But morals are usually less at issue than material concerns: married women say that they fear their husbands will deplete family resources by having affairs with unattached women and giving them money and fancy lappas. Despite this public condemnation of promiscuity, however, many wives privately admit that they envy the freedom and material advantages of unmarried women.

Children of women with many lovers (kpɔ̀ŋ-lòŋ, 'child of a crowd') are considered the offspring of all the men with whom their mother has had sexual relations during her pregnancy. Though welcomed by the mother's family, these children belong to no one particular man, unless one of the lovers volunteers to compensate the woman or her relatives for their expenses during pregnancy and nursing and the cost of raising the child. Parents, of course, do not want their daughters to carry on like this, because they cannot press any one man for money, favors, or labor. They urge their daughters to settle down with one man, and even bring errant daughters or their lovers to court.

Though virtually everyone marries (all the middle-aged women and all but one or two of the middle-aged men in Haindii, Dobli Island, and Digei had married at least once), people may remain single (goiēŋ) after the demise of a marriage. Most people, however, admit to—or boast of—occasional sexual affairs. Despite the fact that people distinguish many different conjugal categories, it is not easy to determine the status of relationships between particular people, even for the parties involved. As we have seen, relationships may be redefined when it is expedient for one or both partners or for their kin. Redefining a conjugal relationship is of course easier to get away with in an area such as Haindii or Dobli Island, where there is a more transient population. But people in more traditional areas such as Digei also attempt to redefine the kinds of marriages they have when it suits their interests. (See also Van Velsen 1964: 122–25 on his difficulty in distinguishing between "formal" and "informal" Tonga marriages.) Legal marriage, though manipulated as often as other categories, is somewhat easier to define. Furthermore, because legal marriage is an important tool by which men and older people solidify control over women and the young, I will be primarily concerned with two basic conjugal categories: legal marriage and all "unmarried" states.

POLITICAL AND ECONOMIC USES OF MARRIAGE IN TRADITIONAL KPELLE SOCIETY

Kpelle marriage and divorce patterns are the outcome of actors' efforts to bind or escape each other in the context of larger economic and political opportunities and constraints. In traditional Kpelle areas, where wage jobs and cash are scarce, there are few opportunities to earn a living outside the subsistence sphere. Basic subsistence and political advancement rest on the production of staple crops and vegetables, as well as occasional goods to sell for cash. Because people must exchange their own services for those of others, young men and women in traditional areas are constrained to marry legally, with all the obligations this implies. Hence, marriage in traditional areas is more stable than in modern areas where there are opportunities to subsist outside the traditional system of control. (See Chapter 5 for statistical support of this point.) Besides enabling people to acquire subsistence labor, marriage also provides the opportunity to generate food surpluses that may be used to attract political support from clients (see also Gibbs 1960, 1963). Thus, marital stability affects not only the conjugal partners themselves, but also the entire traditional system of stratification.

In analyzing specific ways in which political and economic aspirations depend on conjugal bonds, it is useful to distinguish between the control of women and that of men. Female services are fairly simple to acquire because the Kpelle legal system hands rights in women to men. The control of men, however, is more problematic. Because men legally control their own labor and reproductive powers, they must be lured into debt by other men and elders. Political leaders as well as parents seeking security therefore use rights in women to indenture the labor of clients such as young men and strangers. Because this system stratifies people on the basis of three major attributes—sex, age, and family status—the following analysis will use these criteria to examine the marital interests of men, parents, and women.

Men's Strategies

Marriage in most traditional African societies is crucial as a mark of maturity (Barnes 1951, Little 1951), and a mark of citizenship in a community (Fortes 1962). More important, a man seeking status and power must begin his political career by acquiring legal rights in women. A wife's labor repays her husband for his initial bridewealth or brideservice investments, and her subsequent services help advance his political interests. Women who have been legally turned over to their husbands are expected to (1) bear and raise children for their husbands, (2) work hard on the farm to produce food for their husbands and children, (3) perform household chores, (4) respect and help support their husbands' parents, and (5) perhaps scheme with their husbands to extract adultery fees from lovers.[7] In addition to these roles, women often pay many of the expenses formally assumed by men. Kpelle women may earn cash for their conjugal families by selling rice, vegetables, and palm oil. In traditional areas a Kpelle man must marry legally to obtain all these services from a woman. The more women he can control and distribute to men who cannot afford bridewealth, the more wealth and power he accrues. His higher standing, in turn, attracts still more people seeking his political and economic support, and the labor and women he receives from these new clients will enable him to rise in a spiral of increasing success (see also Gibbs 1960, 1963; Collier 1971).

7. Husbands may loan the money acquired as adultery fees to other men, thereby gaining control over these men; or they may agree to forgo adultery fees, thereby gaining labor and loyalty from their wife's lover for many years.

The story of a núu kέtέ ('rich man,' 'big man') in a neighboring chiefdom will serve as an excellent example of how profitable this system can be. By collecting wards, wives, and clients, this man enlarged his labor force and increased the initial power and reputation his family name had given him. People desiring his patronage brought him wives, children, and gifts, hoping to win favor. He raised the male children as wards in order to gain help in the house and on the farm, and kept some of the girls and women as his own personal wives in order to forge alliances with important neighboring chiefs to whom they were related. But he gave or loaned most of the women to young men and male clients in exchange for their labor on the farm. (Meek 1931, Little 1951, and Green 1947 note similar patterns elsewhere in West Africa.) To lure these men, he kept some of the lower-status wives in a large house called the golai (taken from the English word 'garage'). Once a man began "loving to" a woman in the golai, the big man would extract a confession from her, allow the two to cohabit, and draft the man to work on his farm. (Men who seek sexual partners in exchange for labor are called kîe-ni kɔ́lɔŋ, 'know-each-other people'—that is, men who know that they are all "loving to" a big man's wives.)

Wealthy or important strangers wishing to relocate also use ties of legal marriage to forge alliances. Protection is especially important for people hoping to set up a business enterprise, because they are vulnerable to unscrupulous local leaders who might try to extort part of their capital by threatening them or imposing fines on them. Mandingo traders are particularly noted for marrying daughters or sisters of local leaders. When Mɔmɔlu, an old Mandingo trader and 'sand-cutter' (diviner), came to Fuama Chiefdom he first stayed with Dumu, who was then the paramount chief. Announcing that he wanted to live in Haindii, he asked Dumu for his sister's daughter (a Kpelle girl, although Dumu's family was predominantly Gola) in marriage, paid bridewealth for her, and took her as his senior wife. Though he subsequently married several Mandingo women, ordinarily considered more prestigious than Kpelle women, he kept Dumu's relative as his senior wife.

Men's access to women depends in large part on age. Most men begin their marital careers in debt to older people, through either bridewealth or brideservice.[8] As they grow older they try to overcome these debts by indenturing other men. Accordingly, three classes of men can be defined in terms of their access to women: wife borrowers, wife keepers, and wife lenders (Gibbs 1965: 214).

Wife borrowers are men who fail to overcome their debts to patrons or patrons' relatives, and so they remain clients who must borrow women from rich men. They have no rights to adultery damages should these women take lovers, nor do they have legal rights in their children. A man in this class may be a stranger to the community or a fugitive from justice, with no relatives to lend him money or back his credit. Because outsiders are regarded with great suspicion, such a man must have a responsible person to "stand for" him, in much the same way a suitor needs a "father" to "stand for" him. He must indenture himself to a local big man, who becomes his "stranger father" (ŋɔ́ya lee, literally, 'stranger mother') and requires loyalty and farm labor in return for political protection, economic assistance, and a woman's sexual services. Other wife borrowers are young men from low-class lineages who, lacking bridewealth, agree to perform brideservice for big men who give them wives. Although this arrangement involves uxorilocal residence, which is generally regarded as onerous, some families view the arrangement "as a means of establishing advantageous connections with higher status groups through out-marrying males" (d'Azevedo 1962a: 507). Men who make this move often desire to return as prodigals to their own lineages at a later period in life. Poverty and incomplete bridewealth prevent most low-status men from accomplishing this feat of social mobility and escaping the control of their male in-laws, but these men may redefine their goal as the "eventual assimilation into the new group by genealogical fiction and pronouncement of its elders" (d'Azevedo 1962a: 507). Fictionalization alters their genealogies to create links with key

8. Bridewealth and brideservice are a boon to older people, but a sore affliction to young men, who must allow themselves to be subjugated in order to get married. This pattern has also been noted by Hunter (1936) for the Pondo of South Africa, Douglas (1963) for the Lele of Zaire, Harris (1962) for the Taita of Kenya, and Mair (1953) for the continent as a whole.

ancestors in the aristocratic lineage. Though loyal uxorilocally married men usually do not attain sufficient status for membership in the dominant lineage, their descendants may achieve enough success in war or in politics to press for fictionalization.[9] Hence, in many "patrilineal" systems such as the Kpelle, the strict rule of agnatic descent is broken down by brideservice, uxorilocal marriage, and clientship. (Patterns such as this have also been noted by Gough 1971 for the Nuer, and by Horton 1972 for West Africa as a whole.)

Most Kpelle men eventually become wife keepers: men who have repaid most of their marriage debts or have otherwise established autonomy from creditors. In return for full legal rights in his wife (usually only one) and children, such a man must also pay for clothes, small food items, house taxes, school fees, and medical bills, often for his wife's family as well as for his conjugal family. He is more than amply compensated, however, by his wife's labor and by the economic contributions of his children.

A wife lender is a man who uses rights in women to create debts and alliances so that he can build a group of followers. Although most men aspire to the top (Gibbs 1963), usually only those related to powerful families can succeed. A big man may acquire wives and become a wife lender in several ways. As we have seen, people anxious to cement ties of reciprocity with him bring him wives. People may also promise a big man their infant daughter or even an unborn child, saying that if it is a girl it will be his wife, and if it is a boy, his ward. This kind of marriage gives the parents maximum control over the choice of their daughter's partner, and yields gifts and political protection from her betrothed husband for many years before the legal marriage even takes place. The betrothed husband

9. Whether these fictionalizations are successful is another matter. D'Azevedo (1962a: 514–15) implies that Gola fictionalizations are not successful, because Poro elders who belong to aristocratic lineages memorize the true descent of everyone of importance, and will check any young upstarts who try to usurp more power than the aristocrats feel they should have. I would guess, however, that successful fictionalization is a function of the status of particular people: those acquiring wealth and influence are smoothly absorbed into the dominant lineages, whereas those whose status remains low are always reminded that they are outsiders.

also helps support the girl in the Sande bush school, and buys her fine clothes—a mark of high status—to bring her out of the bush. (See also Little 1951 on Mende child betrothal, and Fortes 1962, Harris 1962, and La Fontaine 1962 on the importance of choosing affines carefully.)

Though infant betrothal is a convenient practice for parents, most girls do not relish the prospect of marrying the old men who have paid a good part of their rearing expenses. It is not easy to escape this commitment, for the man will demand reimbursement for his "property" (the girl) if she wishes to marry someone else. Even if she eludes him, he may yet profit from his investment: the man who takes her must repay him with clientship. In fact, most cases of infant betrothal end in this way. The old man who has invested in the girl seldom marries her, but authorizes the choice of her spouse and is reimbursed in the form of labor and clientship from her young husband. Informants say that infant betrothal was more common in the past than today. However, I heard of several recent cases in which infant betrothal was used to cement alliances with local men who derived their wealth and power from the "civilized" world.

Big men also use kin marriages—real or fictive—to acquire rights in women. According to the patrilineal ideology, the Kpelle cannot marry within their own lineages, nor should they marry close relatives to their mothers' lineages. Several exceptions, however, allow big men and parents to gain the maximum profit from their control of women and young men. Parents often try to use—or invent—ties of kinship in order to link themselves with a big man through the marriage of their daughter. They ask him to become the patron and protector of the family (kúmɛi káa nuu, 'look-over-us person'). As "head of the family" he will be obligated to offer them political protection, favors in court, and economic support.

A common kin tie parents try to use is cross-cousin marriage, which for the Kpelle means marriage between the descendants of siblings of the opposite sex. As we can see in Figure 1, the Kpelle have two kinds of marriage that are based on the cross-cousin

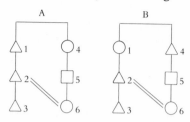

FIGURE I. *Two kinds of Kpelle cross-cousin marriages.*
△ = male; ○ = female; □ = male or female.

model. (See Bledsoe & Murphy, forthcoming, for more on Kpelle cross-cousin marriage.) Unlike most patrilineal societies, in which cross-cousin marriage would involve Man #2 and Woman #5, the Kpelle say that Man #2 and Woman #6 are usually the matched pair, as shown in both Diagram A and Diagram B: the cross-cousin's (#5) daughter (#6) is the potential spouse, instead of the actual cross-cousin. Although the origin of this rule is unclear, the rule gives the economic benefits of a young woman to an older man and preserves a gerontocratic power structure. Moreover, as we will see, powerful men have a much better chance of acquiring rights in cross-cousin wives than less important men.

If a big man decides not to marry the girl he has been promised, he can bestow her on a young man who may also be eligible as a cross-cousin to marry her. For example, he can give her to his son, Man #3 in both diagrams. (This is justified by the rule that theoretically permits all males in the agnatic line to marry women eligible for any of them, with the exceptions of their own mothers, daughters, etc.) By bestowing a wife on his son, Man #2 can strengthen his claim on the son's loyalty and labor. Similarly, if Man #1 in Diagram A is still alive, it is possible that he can claim the same girl (#6) as a potential spouse and give her to his son (#2) to tighten the knots of filial obligation. He can also give her to men who are not cross-cousins in order to create political ties of obligation with outsiders. Though both kinds of cross-cousin marriage are fairly common, my most interesting data concern the marriage shown in Diagram A. To understand this marriage we must first understand the -kêra/-mâleŋ relationship among the

Kpelle.[10] Ego's (#1 or any of his lineal descendants) sister's son or daughter (#5) is a -mâleŋ, as is any of the -mâleŋ's male or female children, grandchildren, great grandchildren, and so on, as long as they are the offspring of a man in the male line from the original sister's son or daughter. Reciprocally, ego's (#5) mother's brother (#1) is a -kêra, as is any of the -kêra's children, grandchildren, etc.

Kpelle informants would not agree with Radcliffe-Brown's portrayal of the mother's brother in African societies as demonstrative and indulgent (1950: 36). The -mâleŋ must obey his -kêra and give him anything he wants: labor, children, and in the old days even his life. In situations of extreme danger in the past, such as war, the -kêra could ritually sacrifice his -mâleŋ. Since sacrifices are outlawed now, the -mâleŋ may ritually sacrifice chickens for his -kêra or perform other services. When a local man, for example, was rushing to cut the trees on his farm before the rains came, he ordered his -mâleŋ to help.

Whereas a male -mâleŋ is used directly for labor and political purposes, a female -mâleŋ is used to acquire a son-in-law. The daughter of a male or female -mâleŋ is called a -mâleŋ-nèni ('-mâleŋ wife') by her -kêra. She inherits the -mâleŋ's obligation of complete obedience to the -kêra, as do her siblings and children (also -mâleŋs). If the -kêra desires, he may ask her parent to give her to him as a wife. The parent is obligated to do so, and at least in theory the daughter is obligated to accept. (I would expect a husband and wife to clash occasionally over the obligation to give a daughter to the wife's mother's brother, but I documented no actual cases of this.)

The -mâleŋ-nèni is often referred to as a túmu koi-kôleŋ ('snail in the cassava snake's abdomen,' a loose translation), or alternately túmu koi-kpêye ('opossum in the cassava snake's abdomen'). Like many descriptions of Kpelle sexual relations, these phrases employ food metaphors. Túmu, the cassava snake, is considered inedible. It refers to the sister's son or daughter who is ineligible for sexual relations with the -kêra. But snails or oppossums found undigested in

10. -Kêra and -mâleŋ are dependent nouns that are incomplete in Kpelle without an attached pronoun.

the cassava snake's abdomen (koi) may be eaten and are in fact great delicacies. The snails or oppossums in the túmu's abdomen, of course, refer to the progeny of the sister's son or daughter. These progeny may have sexual relations with the -kêra, and in theory are considered ideal spouses because of their obligations of obedience as -mâleŋs. But in fact, as two older men grumbled, they make terrible wives because they share relatives with their husbands and can flaunt their husbands' orders with impunity, knowing that common relatives will intervene to prevent severe beatings. Older men use beliefs such as this to rationalize giving túmu koi-kôleŋs to younger men, who may or may not be related, in exchange for the younger men's indebtedness.

In the old days, informants say, if the -mâleŋ's child was a boy, he was not called a túmu koi-kôleŋ but a kâloŋ ('chief'), an ironic term considering that he had to serve his -kêra like a slave. Now, of course, it is difficult to enforce this obedience, but the moral obligation remains. Theoretically túmu koi-kôleŋs are still available to everyone who has an eligible cross-cousin's daughter, but in fact an eligible girl is usually offered by her parents to a powerful man from whom they seek patronage. By accepting this girl, the man not only accepts in-law obligations to her parents but also acknowledges their claim to blood ties with him.

When a man with little power or prestige requests a girl cross-cousin wife from his family, his relatives find ways to put him off, even though he is within his rights to have her. Zina, a poor young farmer from Zulotaa, came to Haindii one day to seek a wife among his relatives because he had been unsuccessful so far in his town. Hoping to avoid brideservice by claiming his -mâleŋ-nèni as a wife, Zina asked Moses, his father's sister's son (-mâleŋ), to give him Sally, Moses's sister's daughter, who was still a small girl. He had first gone to the girl's mother, but she put him off, telling him to ask Moses, who theoretically had authority within the family over her and the child. But Moses did not want Zina to have Sally either: he wanted a wealthier, more prestigious husband for her. So he told Zina to ask "the older people." The main older person in question was Henry, the -kêra of both Zina and Moses's mother

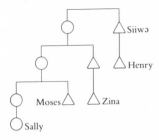

FIGURE 2. *Kin diagram of Haindii–Zulotaa family.*
△ = *male;* ○ = *female.*

(see Figure 2). Moses knew that Henry would refuse the request, because Henry was also technically eligible to marry Sally and wanted her for himself. Rather than test the goodwill of his -kêra, a very powerful man, Zina retreated to Zulotaa to renew his search there. Though the girl eventually escaped Henry's grasp (see Chapter 5), the most important point to note here is that her relatives would not give her to a poor young man. Hoping for generous loans and favors from Henry, who had a good job at Bong Mine and was building a following of several wives and clients, Sally's family diplomatically refused Zina.

Parents' Strategies

As we have seen, marriage is crucial to men's economic well-being and their political careers. Parents also have much at stake in their offsprings' marriages: rice farming requires long hours of tiring work, and parents fear the loss of their children's labor in their old age. Therefore marriage agreements are the outcome of negotiations between the girl's parents on the one hand, and the man or his family on the other, as both parties try to control the residence and labor of the young couple (see also Beidelman 1971).

Though parents want their children to marry, they caution them—their daughters in particular—not to marry strangers from different areas or tribes. A stranger can leave, taking his wife and any property the couple has accumulated, and he can also escape brideservice obligations. Because he has no local kin, no one can force him to return to his responsibilities. West African folktales such as the following, related to me one night by an older woman in Haindii, warn girls about the unreliability of handsome strangers:

Once there was a haughty young woman, a chief's daughter, who rejected the amorous advances of men with any sort of blemish or deformity. One day a bugu man [a hideous monster with large eyes, wrinkled skin, and gnarled limbs] heard about this girl and decided he wanted her. Setting out to her village from his home in the mountains, he passed a shiny black snake. "Lend me your skin," he said, and donned the snake's smooth, shiny skin, giving the snake his ugly wrinkled skin. Soon he came to the St. Paul River, where an animal with small dark eyes was swimming. "Lend me your eyes," he commanded, and exchanged his ugly large eyes for those of the animal. Meeting more animals along the way, he took their more comely hair, arms, legs, and feet, giving them in return his ugly features.

As soon as the reconstituted monster arrived in town, the haughty young woman quickly sized him up and noticed he had no blemishes or deformities. Without even waiting for the man to "approach" her, she killed a white chicken as a marriage sacrifice and informed her father she wanted to marry the unblemished stranger. After she left, the man came to her house and said, "ŋa íwêlii" ('I want you,' or 'I love you'). "ŋa faa," ('I agree'), she said immediately. So she prepared his rice, bath, and bed. That evening when they went to bed, he told her, "My home is far from here, so day after tomorrow I'm going to leave." "I'm going too," said the woman. "You should stay," he reasoned, but she insisted. The next day she announced to her relatives that she was going with him, but they said, "We don't agree. The man says he wants you, but you shouldn't leave." "Stay here," warned the man, "the place is far." But still she insisted, "I must go."

Everyone argued with her until they were tired, but the next day she packed and set out with the man. When they had walked for several hours, they met a snake with ugly wrinkled skin. Said the man, "Skin, skin, come down," and he gave the snake back its lovely smooth skin, taking back his own ugly skin. "Puii!" went the woman in distress. When they came to the St. Paul River they met an animal with large ugly eyes. Commanded the man, "Give me back my eyes," and put his own eyes back in. The woman whirled around in terror and tried to escape and go back to her people, whose wisdom she was beginning to appreciate. "Go in front," ordered the man, blocking her escape. "we are on our way now." So they continued on to the monster's home, stopping now and then for the monster to reclaim the rest of his hideous body parts from the other animals.

The story ends happily with the woman's twin brothers rescuing her from the monster and bringing her home to her kin. The moral, of course, is that young women do not know how to choose husbands: they are too easily swayed by handsome strangers, who inevitably betray them. Their elders, however, know that strangers may be evil spirits in disguise, and they should help young women choose husbands.

Stories like this, which direct a clear warning at fickle young girls, are closely related to parents' fears of losing their investments in their daughters. Parents prefer their daughters to marry men of known family, and they prefer them to have legal marriages, which afford anxious parents more security than unmarried "loving."

Parents also consider the benefits they could receive from various kinds of sons-in-law. They have three main choices: brideservice, bridewealth, and political and economic patronage. Most young men have little wealth or power, and must work to acquire wives. Older men may pay bridewealth, but because of their age and status will not be committed to brideservice. And rich patrons can bestow occasional favors but may not pay bridewealth, and certainly will not do brideservice. The rest of this section will explain more fully what determines the kinds of conjugal options parents want for their children.

Young parents, who can support themselves for many more years (or parents of any age who have a younger daughter whose future spouse can be drafted for brideservice), sometimes accept bridewealth from their daughters' husbands. Forty dollars, a huge sum for most men in traditional society, is the commonly mentioned price, though bridewealth may also consist of goats, kola nuts, cloth, and the like. A man who pays bridewealth for a wife technically frees himself from brideservice, though he may be called on for occasional gifts. It is important to note, however, that few young Kpelle men can afford to pay a full bridewealth when they are betrothed. Most men make payments to their in-laws for the duration of the marriage, counting every gift to them as another installment. Men may even try to count contributions for funeral expenses of deceased in-laws as bridewealth payments. Nevertheless, bridewealth payments are rarely completed to the satisfaction of the wife's parents. The man remains in a state of long-term obligation to his in-laws, who feel they can ask him for financial help at any time.[11]

Young men whose parents can afford bridewealth, or whose relatives paid bridewealth for them, are little better off at first. They are still indebted to their relatives, and must pay them back with labor and loyalty.[12] Therefore young men try to define bridewealth funds as their patrimony, or as their rightful share of corporate resources. Although I have no direct evidence, I suspect that fathers and other agnatic kinsmen try to define bridewealth as loans to be repaid if the young men display too much independence. In spite of the obligations they incur by having their relatives pay bridewealth, young men who can avoid brideservice and uxorilocal residence are eventually in a better position than men who must live uxorilocally, for they have more opportunities to establish political roots in their agnatic villages.

Other parents may decide that they need political patronage more than bridewealth. Such parents may be newcomers to the area, trying to establish a foothold by giving their daughter to the local chief, who may also bestow favors as the presiding judge in court cases. When parents give their daughters to big men for patronage, bridewealth is seldom appropriate, and brideservice is unthinkable.

Bridewealth may give parents a sudden windfall of wealth, and patronage may prove advantageous in times of trouble, but neither provides parents with long-term, committed labor. So important is farm labor, an informant asserted, that poor parents or those of advanced age often refuse bridewealth in favor of a son-in-law who will do brideservice. Parents who want labor from a son-in-law may give their daughter to an impecunious young man for only a token payment, but they require him to perform a lengthy brideservice and share whatever he earns in the outside world with them.

11. Bridewealth arrangements add to the difficulty in determining people's marital status, since sons-in-law can pay bridewealth in different ways and can pay in installments.

12. Kuper (1950: 96) has reported that a married Swazi man is never entirely free from his father's control, and must turn over all earnings to him as long as the son lives in his compound. The father may, if he wishes, give back a portion.

Though he eventually escapes these burdens as he grows older and his in-laws die, his labor and support last as long as the in-laws can stretch them out.

The case of Mɔlei is typical of young men's brideservice obligations. Mɔlei was about twenty-four years old and lived in Bamu, a small town in the bush near Digei. Despite his lack of education, Mɔlei clearly had an analytical mind. When I asked him how young men in traditional areas obtain wives, he responded with a metaphor: a young man has to "hold the cutlass head tight" (work hard). His own case was typical. He had sent his father's sister to the parents of the girl he wanted, asking them to "turn her over" to him as a wife. The parents responded favorably, sending word back that Mɔlei should come with his relatives to talk. When the delegation arrived, the girl's parents let it be known that they wanted brideservice. Mɔlei, however, wanted to make his own farm. So he suggested a compromise: whenever the in-laws needed some rice to tide them over the "hungry season," he would provide it from the farm he and his wife would make.

When the girl's parents agreed, Mɔlei thought he had gotten off easily. For a couple of years things went as he had planned. Although his farm was fairly close to that of his in-laws, he worked only on his farm and gave them surplus rice when they ran short. About two years later, however, they suddenly announced that they were too old and sick to make their own farm, and they moved in with Mɔlei and his wife. They helped him with his farm and got all their rice from him. Once a man marries, Mɔlei told me resignedly, he is obliged to help his wife's parents as long as they live—a refrain echoed by other young men.

Some prospective parents may let a son-in-law escape brideservice. Mɔlei's brother, for example, married a girl whose parents were young and had several unmarried daughters. These parents allowed Mɔlei's brother to take one daughter, with the same stipulation that he help them whenever needed. Since they were young and healthy, they probably would not need Mɔlei's brother's help—at least not for a good many years. But even then they would be more likely to call on one of their other sons-in-law, preferring to ask

TABLE 3. *Residence of fathers of married Digei men and women*

Relative	In same house	In same town	Out of town	Total
Husband's father	1 (12.5%)	6 (75%)	1 (12.5%)	8 (100%)
Wife's father	2 (25%)	4 (50%)	2 (25%)	8 (100%)
TOTAL	3	10	3	16

TABLE 4. *Residence of mothers of married Digei men and women*

Relative	In same house	In same town	Out of town	Total
Husband's mother	2 (20%)	8 (80%)	0	10 (100%)
Wife's mother	18 (64.3%)	8 (28.6%)	2 (7.1%)	28 (100%)
TOTAL	20	16	2	38

help from a man who was not well established and hence was more vulnerable to their demands.

The pattern emerging from cases such as Mɔlei's is one of daughters remaining with their parents and marrying husbands who are willing to perform brideservice (see also Harris 1962). Both Mɔlei and his brother owed primary duties to their wives' parents, whereas their sister and her husband supported Mɔlei's parents. Tables 3 and 4 lend statistical support to this statement. They show the residence of fathers and mothers of Digei couples who live in the same house. With the help of informants, I obtained information on 72 couples, but I have not included cases in which the spouses did not know where their parents lived, or whether their parents were alive or dead.[13] The figures presented here also exclude parents of married couples living in separate houses, and they exclude men living apart from their wives—a category that applies to wealthy men in particular.

Although Table 3 reveals no clear difference between the resi-

13. One Digei husband knew that his father was alive, but I did not find out where his father lived; four husbands and seven wives did not know whether their fathers were alive or dead, and six husbands and seven wives did not know whether their mothers were alive or dead. The fathers of 59 husbands and 57 wives were dead, whereas the mothers of 56 husbands and 37 wives were dead.

dence of married men's and women's fathers, more fathers seem to be living in the same town with their married children than in the same house or out of town. However, Table 4 does show strong differences between the residence of men's and women's mothers. Most mothers of married men live in Digei, but few live in the same house. Most mothers of married women, on the other hand, live in the same house with their daughters. In many of these cases, of course, such as Mɔlei's, brideservice merges with taking care of an aged mother-in-law. But in general the figures show that men house their mothers-in-law more often than their own mothers.

The preferred residence for a man and his family is virilocal, so that the man can be near his natal group for inheritance or possible succession to power. However, among lower-status families, which in most towns constitute much of the population, young men and their kin can rarely afford bridewealth, or even a large down payment on bridewealth. Many young men must therefore perform brideservice and support their wives' families or reside near them—perhaps permanently. Hence d'Azevedo's (1962a) observations of Gola residence and Gough's (1971) conclusions about the Nuer may be particularly apt for the Kpelle: wealthy men are usually the only ones who can afford to follow the preferred virilocal rules of the society.

The woman's parents have the most leverage in marriage negotiations, but the man's parents are just as anxious to control the young couple's labor and wealth after marriage, and in general they choose one of two strategies. The father may lend his son money or goods for his wife's bridewealth in order to fix his claim on the young man's labor. Alternatively, parents who cannot afford bridewealth may try to influence their son's choice of a wife, making sure that the new daughter-in-law lives nearby so that when they need support their son will be available to them, rather than working for his in-laws in a distant village.

Women's Strategies

As I noted previously, Kpelle legal rules allow men to achieve power and independence, but they restrict women. A woman in traditional society has few means of escaping legal subordination, since all her services legally belong to a man. Even though she might divorce her husband to improve her immediate situation, she cannot sabotage the system: her relatives reclaim their authority over her and try to find another husband for her as soon as possible. Both men and women in traditional areas often say that a woman without a man's legal control lacks self-respect, because she is prey to the advances of any man who wants her. (As we will see in the next chapter, however, being single has its virtues in areas near wage-labor centers, because there men have money to give their lovers.)

Because men control legal rights in women, women as a class cannot assume political roles. Individual women, however, may become secular political leaders by manipulating the male political system. A woman desiring a formal political role must escape male control and at the same time acquire dependent male clients. Rather than fight the system, an ambitious woman paradoxically uses men's rights in her to reach her objectives. Using a front man—a powerful husband or lover who delegates power and authority to her—she obtains male clients the same way men do, by controlling rights in other women and securing male labor and allegiance.[14] Eventually she will have enough autonomy to maintain control over her clients when her husband or lover dies. A woman in this position will have accumulated so many clients that no other men will try to enforce rights over her. (See Hoffer 1974 for an excellent case study of a Mende woman chief and her rise to power in Sierra Leone.) As we saw in the last chapter, certain women may also play important roles in the Sande secret society. However, much of the Sande leaders' power also derives from their relationship to powerful male relatives, and from their careful deployment of Sande initiates to men seeking wives. Though there are notable exceptions, it is rare for a woman in a traditional area to emerge as a political

14. The literature on African female husbands and chiefs bolsters this point, revealing that women may achieve or solidify high status by acquiring legal rights in other women (Herskovits 1937, Krige & Krige 1943, Uchendu 1965, O'Brien 1972, Hoffer 1974, and Krige 1974).

leader, independent of male control. The great majority of women lack formal, socially sanctioned authority over adults. Because men control political authority, most women must negotiate within family and domestic units, where economic security is their immediate concern.

Women in traditional society need two things for economic security: male farm labor to clear, burn, and fence a rice farm; and cash to pay the annual house tax as well as to buy clothes and household furnishings, pay medical expenses, and so on. For all people in remote areas, economic security is bound up in ties of obligation to others. For this reason a young woman usually prefers to marry legally in order to ensure her husband's support, and she initiates divorce only when her husband fails to work hard on the farm or support her family adequately. But even a woman who prefers legal marriage is reluctant to have "money behind" her, that is, bridewealth paid for her, in spite of the status this confers: she fears having to refund the money if she wants to divorce later. If she has a lover who is unable to refund the bridewealth, she must try to retrieve it from her relatives, who are rarely eager—or able—to comply. Therefore, a clever woman may try to construe economic transactions between her affinal and consanguineal relatives as 'loans' (kpa), rather than bridewealth payments (Collier 1971).

Acquiring cash is a particular problem for women in traditional areas because wage jobs are virtually nonexistent, and cash cropping is difficult. One way to acquire cash is through borrowing. Men have little trouble borrowing money from big men because big men use male debts as political tools. But borrowing is difficult for a woman. My explanation for this is based on the previous analysis of debt and men's rights in women. First, a big man's loan to a woman would be a political dead end, since people who control no rights in themselves or in others cannot reallocate their political loyalty. Most women are therefore useless as political allies or clients. Second, a man who lent money to a woman might be sued by those who legally owned rights in her—because women in traditional areas have few means of earning cash for repaying debts, the woman would immediately be suspected of repaying her debt with sexual favors. In giving herself to her creditor, a woman would, in effect, be giving away the property of the man who did own rights in her.

Though the society gives them little formal economic or political authority, women try to maneuver informally, using their domestic roles to make others comply with their wishes and to create a favorable environment for themselves. Several means are at their disposal. First, because women are valued as subsistence producers in rural areas, a woman can refuse to go on the farm unless her complaints are heard. Women can also refuse to perform household chores such as housecleaning, child care, fetching water and firewood, heating bath water, and washing clothes. When wives refuse to work, husbands have only two choices: to beat them, thereby risking court fines, or to accede to their desires. Performing the chores themselves is not a viable choice for Kpelle men, because women's chores take a considerable amount of time and are regarded as denigrating for a man. (See also Fortes 1949 and Green 1947). Bachelors try to find wives, lovers, or female relatives to take care of these tasks. However, for women who have to serve bachelor hangers-on as well as their husbands, patience quickly wears thin. A widower, for example, moved in with his sister and husband. Tired of taking care of two men who frequently demanded different meals at different times, the woman went out and found a lover for her brother to get him off her hands.

Women may also use their domestic roles to gain more control over their marital status: I suspect that widows seeking to avoid leviratic marriage refuse to cook for their husbands' brothers. In addition, women in polygynous households may manipulate food preparation and allocation to create more favorable domestic situations for themselves. Junior wives not wanted by senior wives, for example, invariably feel that they and their children are being shortchanged—and this is often the case. A senior wife keeps the key to the rice kitchen, preventing anyone from taking rice without her consent. Furthermore, she usually divides the rice into portions, even when a junior wife has cooked the meal, and may serve more rice to herself or her children than to others. A senior wife can also assign an unwanted junior wife undesirable tasks and otherwise make her life miserable. Such tactics invariably end in one wife divorcing the husband or moving to another house.

In one household, Lɔɔ-nɛŋ, a junior wife, was not getting along with her husband (whom she claimed was impotent) or with Kɔto, the senior wife who had not wanted her initially. Both wives shared cooking chores, each cooking one week at a time, but Kɔto always divided the cooked rice for the household members. After a particularly bad dispute, Kɔto locked the granary and refused to give Lɔɔ-nɛŋ any rice. Though Lɔɔ-nɛŋ continued to live in the head wife's house, she began to eat with a friend in another house. Eventually she divorced her husband and returned to her parents.

Women may also use their domestic roles to maintain custody of their children after a divorce, despite the patrilineal rules of the society. Because women control the granary and the cooking pot, people say that after their parents divorce children are better off with their own mother than with their father and a stepmother who might slight them in favor of her own children. (Of course, a man may use the excuse that a stepmother will neglect another woman's children to avoid supporting his children while they are too young to be of help. He expects that eventually the children will come back to him as their rightful owner, but few children do.)

By allocating food to people outside the family, as well as to kin, a woman can increase the number of people owing her favors. An analysis of Kpelle consumption units reveals that nonkin members of a consumption unit usually have ties to the woman in charge of the cooking pot.[15] For example, young students from the interior who come to Haindii to attend school are lodged and fed by local women. In return, they help with chores on the farm or in the house. Many students, in fact, must work so hard for their landladies that they miss weeks—or even years—of school.

In exchange for a woman's cooking services, bachelors may be asked to help with house and farm chores. Married women and

15. I define a consumption unit as a group of people eating from the same cooking pot; those who work on the same farm together and produce the same rice will usually eat rice from the same pot.

bachelor lovers sometimes strike up an arrangement in which a woman secretly cooks for her lover or brings him rice out of the family cooking pot. One young woman told me, "The wife will cook some rice her husband bought for the family and take some to her boyfriend. . . . Especially in Haindii, if you really want to watch it, you go to the river in the afternoon. You will find young men there, eating rice." A woman cannot ask her lover to help with chores, for her husband would soon discover the affair. Instead, the lover brings her clothes and money, which she construes as gifts from relatives.

As this discussion has shown, women try to use conjugal ties, domestic groups, and domestic production to their own advantage, maneuvering informally because men usually have authority over domestic resources. Women also use their children to advance them-selves politically and economically. Having neither formal author-ity over their children nor legal rights in them, women gain compli-ance from their children by emphasizing the ties of moral obligation and recalling the "suffering" they have undergone for them. Men and women alike told me they revered their mothers above every-one else and felt morally obliged to support them in their old age. Commitments such as these can be converted to political and eco-nomic capital by women seeking independence and security.

Divorced or widowed mothers can cash in on the labor of sons-in-law by moving in with their married daughters, who are glad to have them around for company, help with child care, and support in arguments with their husbands. Mothers may also try to arrange marriages for their daughters with powerful chiefs, just as men do. One divorced woman told me that she had taken both of her daugh-ters to powerful political figures: one to an educated chief who be-came an official in the national government, and one to the man who later took his place. In this case the mother had acted in her brother's name in bringing her daughters to the officials, since le-gally she did not control them. (The fathers of the girls had not re-imbursed the woman or her family for their expenses in raising them, so she knew she was safe in distributing them without their fathers' permission.) Though he had little part in the matter, her brother approved the arrangements because he would then become allied with the powerful officials through marriage. The girls were soon redistributed to young male clients, but their mother was assured of at least token patronage from two powerful men for the rest of her life.

Mothers of young men, on the other hand, may be instrumental in choosing wives for their sons, in order to keep the young couples close by and ensure daughters-in-law who will help with house and farm chores. (See also Hay 1976 on Luo women's investments in daughters-in-law.) Fearing the loss of her son to distant in-laws, a woman may ask a girl in her town to marry her son (ńee a ńenii wèli, 'my mother marries or "loves to" my wife'). I heard of several such cases in Digei, most of which produced amiable marriages.

A Digei woman named Bɛlɛ, for example, had six sons and no daughters. She was understandably anxious to acquire a congenial daughter-in-law to help her with her chores, and acted quickly when her oldest son reached marriageable age. Taking no chances on a girl in a distant town whose parents might want the new couple to live with them, Bɛlɛ asked a girl in a house only yards away to marry her son. This marriage—a relationship more between the women than the husband and wife—was instigated with the son's knowledge. But there are other instances, according to informants, in which a mother decides on her own to "marry" a girl for her son and brings her home to a very surprised bridegroom.

Older women without children to support them as well as those needing to draw on wider ties use what may appear at first to be a rather unlikely tactic: playing on people's fears of witchcraft. The Kpelle believe that witches eat the children of kin as well as nonkin if not given enough food. Most informants agreed that old women were more likely than old men to be witches. An old man told me that when a girl is small, she calls a piece of corn or cassava her baby and puts it on her back, just as grown women do with real babies (see Photograph 9). When the girl gets hungry, she roasts the "baby" and eats it. According to the old man, if her children fail to give her enough meat when she grows old, she remembers how she used to eat corn and cassava babies and begins to eat real babies,

9. *A small girl (right) carries a "cassava baby."*

spiriting them away to share with her cronies. One young man told me that people attribute the death of almost every baby to witches: "Parents often tell their children, 'Don't talk bad to old people, because harm might come to you. So take time [be careful]. Whenever they ask for something and you don't have it, well, tell them, 'I don't have it.' But if you do have it, give it to them.' " Naturally, old women can often get whatever they want from people who are anxious to protect their children. In administering my domestic organization questionnaire, I asked 79 women in Haindii and Digei if they ever gave food to old people not related to them; all said yes. Thus, even though one's own children are the best security, old Kpelle women may draw on wider ties by threatening witchcraft if they haven't enough to eat. Old Kpelle women do not starve.

In general, women in traditional areas escape restrictive ties to men and elders only when they are older and can rely on their grown children. As we will now see, however, women in more modern areas have outside opportunities to support themselves, so they can head domestic groups without legal restrictions much sooner than women in traditional areas. They also have more of a chance to earn cash. But like women in traditional areas, those in modern areas such as Haindii and Dobli Island still try to maintain strong bonds with their children and other people in their household, creating ties of debt and obligation with dependents whose labor and earnings they seek.

CHAPTER 5

The Transition to a Cash Economy

Two major economic and political changes have started to break down the Kpelle wealth-in-people system, on which traditional Kpelle marriage is based. First, opportunities to earn cash are giving people a new way to pay for goods and services, enabling them to sever economic ties of obligation to kin groups, chiefs, and religious leaders. Traditional social ties become more fragile since people have less to lose economically by breaking them. Increasingly, the Kpelle indebt themselves to kinsmen or local leaders only if they cannot achieve their goals using outside sources or a less binding means of exchange such as cash. (See Gluckman 1941 and Mair 1953 for insightful treatments of the effects of cash on traditional kin relationships.)

Opportunities for earning cash through wage labor, marketing, and cash cropping are changing social ties in the modern part of Fuama Chiefdom, as in other modern areas throughout Africa. A young man, for example, can now evade dependency and still obtain a woman. He need not rely on his father for bridewealth payments or take on the burden of performing brideservice for in-laws. By giving your in-laws a lot of money, one young man told me, you don't have to work for them and you can keep them at bay. Although a young man can achieve considerable independence from traditional obligations to parents and in-laws, he still needs a wife in order to obtain rights in children as well as domestic services such as cooking and cleaning. Moreover, many young men who work for wages marry to obtain subsistence food, because their wages are insufficient to meet their needs in a cash economy. (This problem exists in Liberia as a whole, as well as in other parts of Africa. See Fraenkel 1964, Meillassoux 1972, and Handwerker 1973.)

Men have direct access to cash through wage jobs. Women, on the other hand, have fewer opportunities to work for wages. Because they rarely attend school, many tribal women are ineligible for wage jobs in urban or concession areas, where they usually need a minimal knowledge of English. Moreover, many "civilized" people who control wage jobs see women as less desirable workers than men. The 1962 census of Liberia reported that only 3.6 percent of all women aged ten and over were classified as paid employees, in contrast to 32.8 percent of all men. (The 1974 census has categories which are less specific.) The lack of wage jobs spells hardship for many urban women, a trend observed in modernized areas throughout the world.

The second economic change affecting social relations in Kpelle areas is an increase in legal land purchases. Those with the most resources, usually people in Monrovia, buy land in remote areas for growing cash crops and for extracting minerals. Wealthy tribal people with power rooted in the traditional system also buy land to use for cash profits. In this way, they retain or even increase their power over their rural wives and clients, who must comply with their demands if they want land to farm.

Most women are at a disadvantage in relation to these wealthy land buyers, because their marketing profits are small and must be spent for subsistence goods instead of land purchases. (See also Handwerker 1973 on marketing among urban Liberian women, and Huntington 1975 on African market women in general.) In fact, women in Bong Mine told me that they had been forced into marketing because there is little subsistence farmland available. Bong Mine women who did not have market businesses seemed to be idle not because they wanted to be, but rather because they lacked the capital to begin such a business, and most expressed the hope they could do so soon.

For the most part, however, Fuama Chiefdom has escaped the ill effects of land grabbing and cash cropping. Although land near the roads is being sold rapidly, there is still enough farmland for slash-and-burn agriculture. Only in the southeastern part of the chiefdom near Bong Mine is farmland inadequate for subsistence needs. My study thus catches an economy in transition. In Digei, far away from motor roads, cash is scarce and land is plentiful. Haindii and Dobli Island, on the other hand, are in a more modern area where both cash and land are plentiful. The local people have enough farmland for their subsistence needs, and they are beginning to enjoy the economic benefits of new roads, nearby wage labor, and more numerous and larger local markets. The wealth-in-people system is beginning to break down, allowing women and young men—formerly the subordinates in the system—to escape the control of men and older people.

Young men can now subsist and achieve status without indebting themselves so heavily to older men and political leaders; they no longer need to wait for old age and the death of their creditors. However, even though they seek independence, many young men in Haindii and Dobli Island are not sloughing off the wealth-in-people system. Instead, they regard the new opportunities as a way to rise rapidly in both systems, and successful young men reach a level in the wealth-in-people system that they formerly would have attained only in their later years. Unlike young men in Digei, who can barely afford one wife, those in Haindii and Dobli Island who are earning cash wages often marry polygynously and readily take on clients of their own.

Similarly, Haindii and Dobli Island women have greater access to these new economic opportunities than Digei women. Though few women can secure wage jobs, they can pay for house taxes, male farm labor, and other essentials by selling agricultural produce in markets and by receiving cash gifts from lovers who work for wages nearby. Since marriage still hands the fruits of female production and reproduction to men and elders for their own purposes, many women with independent access to wealth prefer to be single[1] (see also Steady 1976). However, like young men, women continue to collect dependents when they can and try to keep their children committed to support them. Such actions show that women as well as young men are still operating in a wealth-in-people framework, trying to escape the control of superiors by acquiring legal rights in themselves, and at the same time trying to reestablish themselves in the system at a high level, controlling more people than was previously possible for them. In the rest of this chapter I will examine the effects of economic and social change on Kpelle marriage, being careful to note how a person's age relates to his or her ability to acquire wealth outside the traditional sector.

MARRIAGE AND DIVORCE RATES IN THE MODERN AND TRADITIONAL AREAS

Kpelle marriage benefits men more than women, and a variety of evidence indicates that women avoid marriage when other options for support are available to them. During my fieldwork I gathered data on differences in marriage and divorce rates between the mod-

---

1. The decline of traditional cooperative work groups provides an example analogous to marriage. The number of people working in a cooperative rice-farming group (kuu) seems to vary roughly with the distance from roads and wage labor centers: the farther away from a road or business area, the more people work in kuus together. For example, Gbaŋ-su, a small, remote village in the northern part of Liberia, was about four hours away from the nearest road, and far from major wage-labor areas. Here I saw kuus of 30 to 40 women planting rice. In Digei, the same distance from a road but closer to major labor centers, smaller groups of six to ten women were common. And in Haindii, located on a road and very close to Bong Mine, women often planted rice by themselves with occasional help from relatives or friends, but seldom in large kuus. (I did see a large kuu of about fifty women near Bong Mine, but these women were paid in cash, earning a dollar a day.)

I speculate that kuus are breaking down in modern areas for the same reason marriage is: more opportunities to acquire cash and support outside traditional social units mean less dependence—or reliance—on the labor of other people. Those with ready access to cash do not want to commit themselves to working in a group for a whole clearing, planting, or harvesting season. In fact, it seemed that people in Haindii often joined cooperative work groups because they were in a "jam." For example, a man had received some cash from his stepchildren for the purpose of paying men to cut and burn the trees on his farm. Because he "ate" the money, however, he had to join a kuu to prepare the farm before the rains came.

ern and traditional areas, and on the differential effects of wealth
on men's and women's marital status. (See the Appendix for an explanation of the marital categories.) Many of the statistics differentiate people according to age. Because most people have no accurate birth records, I did not attempt to estimate ages or calculate
them from historical events. Instead, I asked my informants to classify people on the basis of age categories important to the Kpelle.
Though this procedure masks data, especially in the categories that
cover a number of years, it does allow observations of the general
age groups I was interested in. Children and young people up to
about sixteen or seventeen were excluded from the present analysis
of marriage because only one girl on Dobli Island within this age
range was married.

A young woman, about sixteen to twenty-five years of age, is
called a nɛnî kpela, one experienced in "man business" and possessing fully developed secondary sexual characteristics. A young
man (naaŋa) is experienced in "woman business." Men and women
of this age are considered marriageable. What I call middle-aged
women (nɛnî kpanaŋ) are about twenty-six to fifty years old. Most
have borne at least two children, and many have children with
spouses as well as parents too old to work on the farm. A man of
this age is called a surɔ̂ŋ kpanaŋ. Old women (nɛnî pɔlɔ) are at least
fifty. Though they find it hard to maintain a farm, most receive the
help of their children. A man of this age is called sie-pɔ̂lɔ. (Nɛnî
pɔlɔ and sie-pɔ̂lɔ are also general terms of respect.) In the oldest
category, very old women (nɛnî pɔlɔ gɔ̂fé gɔ̀fé[2]) are unable to take
care of themselves and rely on others for most of their needs. Men
of this age are called sie-pɔ̂lɔ gɔ̀fé gɔ̀fé.

To help distinguish which women are married in Digei, Dobli Island, and Haindii, Table 5 shows the percentages of married
women who belong to different age groups. (See Tables A1 through
A3 in the Appendix for the marital statuses of women in the three

2. The term gɔ̀fè gɔ̀fé is derived from the shuffling sound old people make as they
walk with canes. Yɛ̀fé yɛ̀fé, which refers to the sounds made by even feebler old
people as they crawl, is a possible final category for old people. But since only one
woman in the total census was a nɛnî pɔlɔ yɛ̀féyɛ̀fé, she was counted as a
nɛnî pɔlɔ gɔ̀fé gɔ̀fé. (She died soon after the initial census was taken.)

TABLE 5. *Percentages of married women in Digei, Dobli Island, and Haindii, by age category*

| Town | Age category | | | |
	Young	Middle-aged	Old	Very old
Digei	55.3%	84.3%	42.9%	0%
Dobli Island	19.0%	46.2%	15.4%	0%
Haindii	24.1%	43.5%	27.3%	0%

SOURCE: Numbers combined from Tables A1–A3 in the Appendix.

towns.) The percentages show a consistent pattern for women in all three towns. In each town, fewer young women than middle-aged women are married. They have few children at this age and can rely on their parents or relatives to help provide for them. More middle-aged women are married than women in any of the other three groups. Because they need to support their children and their parents are old, they see marriage as the most reliable source of male labor and cash. Old women may have trouble finding husbands because they are beyond the childbearing age and can offer only domestic services to men. Though their conjugal options diminish with age, however, many old women say that they prefer to be single if they have support from their children. None of the very old women were married. The fact that women usually marry men of the same age or older may account for this finding, in addition to their preference for being single if they have younger relatives to support them.

The percentages of married men (Table 6) show similar patterns. (See Tables A4 to A6 in the Appendix for statistics on men's marital statuses in the three towns.) Though the number of old and very old men is extremely small, the fact that men often marry wives younger than themselves may explain why there are more married men than women in these age categories. This was true for the only very old married man in Dobli Island, who had been married to the same woman for many years. Some men, however, acquire wives as their economic and political status increases, even though they are very old. The only very old man in Digei, for example, was married

TABLE 6. *Percentages of married men in Digei, Dobli Island, and Haindii, by age category*

Town	Age category			
	Young	Middle-aged	Old	Very old
Digei	53.3%	91.8%	81.8%	100%
Dobli Island	13.0%	49.1%	50.0%	50.0%
Haindii	20.6%	61.1%	36.4%	0%

SOURCE: Numbers combined from Tables A4–A6 in the Appendix.

TABLE 7. *Marital statuses of women in traditional versus modern areas of Fuama Chiefdom*

Area	Marital status		Total
	Married	Other	
Traditional (Digei)	94 (65.7%)	49 (34.3%)	143 (100%)
Modern (Haindii and Dobli Is.)	106 (36.9%)	181 (63.1%)	287 (100%)
TOTAL	200 (46.5%)	230 (53.5%)	430 (100%)
$\lambda_{xy} = .23, \lambda_{yx} = .26^a$			

SOURCE: Numbers combined from Table A7 in the Appendix (excluding unknowns).

NOTE: The whole population of Digei, Dobli Island, and Haindii is included in these statistics. Because no sample was involved, I could not fairly assume that the people in the three towns represented a random sample of all West Africans, Liberians, or Kpelle, since many of the residents of the three towns share a common history and are closely related. Therefore, the Lambda, a measure of association between dependent and independent variables, was used as the nonparametric statistic.

[a]The predictability of marital status on the basis of areas of origin, as measured by λ_{xy}, is .23. The predictability of area of origin on the basis of marital status, as measured by λ_{yx}, is .26.

to a young woman he had obtained through his position as an important town elder and cash crop producer.

Although the modern and traditional areas of Fuama Chiefdom have similarities in the age distribution of married women and men, the total percentages of married people reveal striking differences between the two areas. Table A7 in the Appendix shows the total number of women of marriageable age in various conjugal arrangements in Digei, Dobli Island, and Haindii. Table 7 simplifies these figures, showing only the percentages of married women and of women in all other categories in the traditional and modern areas. These tables show that in Digei 66 percent of the 143 women of marriageable age are legally "turned over" to a man in marriage, whereas the remaining 34 percent are divorced, widowed, separated, "loving to" a man, not yet married, or of unknown marital

TABLE 8. *Marital statuses of men in traditional versus modern areas of Fuama Chiefdom*

Area	Marital status		Total
	Married	Other	
Traditional (Digei)	74 (85.1%)	13 (14.9%)	87 (100%)
Modern (Haindii and Dobli Is.)	78 (45.3%)	94 (54.7%)	172 (100%)
TOTAL	152 (58.7%)	107 (41.3%)	259 (100%)
$\lambda_{xy} = .15, \lambda_{yx} = 0$			

SOURCE: Numbers combined from Table A8 in the Appendix (excluding unknowns).

NOTE: The λ_{yx} statistic shows no predictability of area of origin on the basis of marital status, but this does not invalidate generalizations from the table. Lambda only detects association for combinations in which knowledge of the independent variable helps to predict the value of the dependent variable. In this instance, knowledge of marital status does not improve the chances of guessing the area of origin, even though the percentages show high association.

TABLE 9. *Male/female ratios in Digei, Dobli Island, and Haindii*

Town	Age category				Total
	Young	Middle-aged	Old	Very old	
Digei					
Males	15	61	11	1	88
Females	47	71	21	5	144
M/F	.32	.86	.52	.20	.61
Dobli Island					
Males	23	57	4	3	87
Females	42	78	13	4	137
M/F	.55	.73	.31	.75	.64
Haindii					
Males	34	60	13	0	107
Females	58	92	22	2	174
M/F	.59	.65	.59	0	.62

NOTE: Figures include all current residents of marriageable age.

status. In marked contrast, only 37 percent of the 287 women of marriageable age in Haindii and Dobli Island are married.

Table 8 shows similar differences for men in the modern and traditional areas. (See also Table A8 in the Appendix.) Though the differences in numbers of married people in the two areas appear great, we must control for the possibility of differences in male/female ratios among people of marriageable age. Table 9 shows that the male/female ratios for the three towns vary to some degree among age categories. (Digei's small number of young men, for ex-

TABLE 10. *Number of marriages extant, ending in divorce, and ending in death for Digei, Dobli Island, and Haindii*

Town	Extant marriages	Marriages ended by divorce	Marriages ended by death	Total	Total *less* widowed
Digei	85	43	14	142	128
Dobli Island	44	71	10	125	115
Haindii	54	87	9	150	141

NOTE: Unknowns and older women are excluded from the enumeration.

ample, is probably due to the absence of older school boys and young men who have migrated for wage labor.) But the male/female ratios for all marriageable people are nearly the same in all towns, a finding that suggests that marriage and marital instability vary independently of sex ratios in these towns.

Divorce rates are another indicator of the differences between the modern and traditional areas of Fuama Chiefdom. With more economic opportunities for women in modern areas, divorce rates should be higher in Haindii and Dobli Island than in Digei. Since the divorce histories of old women were dim in informants' minds, I used the histories of young and middle-aged women.[3] The four cases of permanent separation were counted as divorces, because the distinction was minimal to informants. I excluded marriages whose endings were uncertain and women who never married, thereby restricting the analysis to 110 women in Digei, 111 in Dobli Island, and 133 in Haindii. As we can see in Table 10, only in Digei is there a greater number of extant marriages than marriages ended by divorce. In Digei, 66.4% of marriages with both partners still living are extant, whereas in both Haindii and Dobli Island only 38.2% of marriages are extant.

Table 11 shows that for Digei women, 75.4 percent of all terminated marriages (Ratio B) ended in divorce, and 33.6 percent of all known marriages, excluding those ending in death (Ratio C) ended

3. Using only women is a methodological weakness, but it was so difficult even to keep people's names, whereabouts, and relationships straight that it would have been impossible to count all the marriages ever contracted by matching women to specific ex-husbands.

TABLE 11. *Divorce ratios for Digei, Dobli Island, and Haindii*

Town	Marriages ended by divorce (1)	All marriages ended (2)	Ratio B (1) ÷ (2)	All marriages with both partners still living (3)	Ratio C (1) ÷ (3)
Digei	43	57	75.4%	128	33.6%
Dobli Island	71	81	87.7%	115	61.7%
Haindii	87	96	90.6%	141	61.7%

NOTE: The divorce ratios are those of Barnes (1967). Not included is his Ratio A. Unknowns and older women are excluded from the enumeration.

in divorce.[4] The statistics for Dobli Island and Haindii contrast strongly with those for Digei. For Dobli Island women, 61.7 percent of all known marriages ended in divorce; of all terminated marriages, excluding those ending in death, 87.7 percent ended in divorce. Similarly, 90.6 percent of all Haindii women's terminated marriages ended in divorce, whereas 61.7 percent of all known marriages, excluding those ending in death, ended in divorce. (One possible interpretation of these results is that the larger number of young people in the modern area might be the cause of the increased divorce rates because people in this age group divorce more often. However, a glance at the appendix, Tables A2, A3, A5 and A6, reveals that most of the young people in Haindii and Dobli Island have never married.) Though my divorce statistics on men are inadequate for the purpose of examining differences in men's divorce rates between the two areas, the cases I have seem to correspond with the statistical results for women.

WHO WANTS TO MARRY? WEALTH AND MARITAL STATUS OF MEN AND WOMEN

So far we have seen that in Digei there is a high percentage of married people and a low divorce rate among women; and in Dobli

4. The divorce ratio formulas used are those of Barnes (1967: 61). Ratio B is "the number of marriages ended in divorce expressed as a percentage of all marriages in the sample that have been completed by death or divorce." Ratio C is "the number of marriages ended in divorce expressed as a percentage of all marriages except those that have ended by death."

Island and Haindii, a low percentage of married people and a high divorce rate among women. However, these statistics do not tell us who is most anxious to marry or divorce, men or women. Statistics on wealth, though they cannot be regarded as conclusive, help to answer this question. I contend that most men in both areas are anxious to marry legally in order to acquire greater control over women's productive and reproductive services. Robert, a man in Haindii, was perhaps an extreme example of a man bent on keeping his wife. When he found that his wife was having an affair, he was so anxious to keep her from running off with her lover that he permitted the two to share a room in his house, hoping his wife would eventually give up her lover of her own accord. Women, on the other hand, are less eager than before to subjugate themselves in marriage. In order to obtain male farm labor and small amounts of cash for taxes and other necessities, women who have few means of support outside of marriage—a category that includes most women in Digei—will want to marry legally. Women who have greater access to wealth outside marriage, as many women in modern areas do, will prefer the single life.[5] Several measures of wealth will be used to examine these assertions.[6]

Owning a House

Owning a house is an indicator of wealth and independence for both men and women. Behind almost every Kpelle adult I found a house story: people with houses were proud to relate at great length how they acquired them, whereas people without houses often harbored deep resentments at whoever or whatever they saw as re-

5. This conclusion is implicit in the results of the studies that find women usually initiating divorce actions (for example, Fortes 1935, Forde 1941, and E. N. Goody 1973). This conclusion is also implicit in the work of Colson, who found that divorced or widowed Tonga women are eager to set up their own households, perhaps living with male relatives who do not intervene too deeply in their affairs: "Old women chuckle happily at their independence. [On the other hand] old men who are single desperately try to find themselves wives through whom they can once more establish a household unit catering to their wishes and giving them prestige" (Colson 1958: 105).

6. Access to wealth should not be regarded as a single causal explanation. The argument presented here merely seeks to demonstrate strong associations between wealth and marital preferences.

sponsible for that condition. According to my thesis, men who own houses are more likely to be married than those without houses because they can provide shelter to women who cannot afford it. Women, on the other hand, are less likely to be married if they own houses, since they have shelter independently of husbands who would restrict their freedom.[7]

Owning a house (pέrε-nàmu, being a 'house owner') contributes to independence in several ways. First, houses offer an escape from the domination of in-laws. A female house owner does not have to compete for food and resources with co-resident in-laws, nor does she have to work for a mother-in-law she dislikes. Similarly, a man tries to avoid living with his wife's parents, who will undoubtedly attempt to extract money and labor from him. A young man in Haindii recounted to me two other advantages of owning a house. For one thing, he said, it is hard to beat your wife in front of her parents, even if she deserves it; for another, having your own house keeps your own parents at a restful distance. In fact, he declared, living with your own parents may be even worse than living with your wife's. If you live with her parents and they spend money on her, they may claim that you have to reimburse them in work or cash. But you can rejoin, "Wasn't that your daughter you spent the money on? You didn't spend it on me." On the other hand, said the young man, if you are living with your own parents and they spend money on your wife, you have no excuse when they remind you of your obligations to them. This will hurt your feelings and make you determined to have your own house and provide your wife with everything yourself.

A person who owns a house not only acquires independence from family elders, but also gains power over a spouse or concubine. When I asked one informant why it is important to own a house, she quoted a Kpelle proverb that stresses the liability of being a tenant: "You can't have your finger in a man's mouth and knock him

7. House ownership cannot be completely separated from occupation and household size and composition, the variables tested later. House ownership and occupation should be regarded as manifestations of wealth rather than accurate measures of wealth.

on the head." That is, if someone living in your house mistreats you, you can evict him. A man has a great deal of control over his wife if he owns the house she lives in, and she must be diligent in caring for his needs if she wants to stay. She must be sexually faithful to him, restrict her visits to relatives, show deference to in-laws, and try to get along with any co-wives who live in the house.

A female house owner, on the other hand, can resist her husband's attempts to dominate her and use her labor for his own purposes. "When a women has a house," a female informant asserted, "she thinks she is the only woman, the most powerful woman on earth!" She can take on outside lovers with less fear of economic reprisal by her husband, and be less diligent in taking care of her husband and freer in her comings and goings. A woman in Haindii, for example, said that her mother had a lover who had come to live with the family. Whenever he ordered people around too much, he was swiftly reminded that he was just a visitor. Even the children in the household sometimes threatened to evict him or successfully urged their mother to deny him access to the rice kitchen.

A female house owner can extend her control over other household members besides husbands and lovers. She can take on bachelors and students, for example, asking them for rent or labor in exchange for a place to eat and sleep. Bana, a female house owner in Haindii, took schoolchildren as boarders. I used to pass her zinc-roofed house almost every day on my way into town, and it was rare not to see Bana and her old mother Galoŋ stirring a boiling vat of water and palm oil out in the yard or cracking palm nuts on the porch. David and Alfred, two teenaged schoolboys, were usually hauling loads of palm nuts to be processed, pounding palm nut pulp in a large tub, or helping to crack the kernels. It was several months before I began to put two and two together, and eventually I asked Galoŋ (and later a relative of hers) how she and her daughter had acquired their house and how they made a living without the help of an adult man. I learned that Bana's ex-husband Tokpa had built the house with his earnings from Bong Mine. After it was built, however, Bana's relatives began to visit for longer and longer periods of time, until Galoŋ, Bana's two sisters, and assorted small nieces and nephews were all living in the house with Bana and Tokpa. Tokpa began to complain that everyone was eating the food he provided from his meager earnings, and that no one was helping with household or medical expenses or with the house tax. Tokpa's fights with Bana and her family grew more bitter. Finally the couple decided to divorce and agreed to divide the "properties." Tokpa took the "cane juice" still (worth $350), and Bana took the house (along with the radio, the dishes, and the bed), since she was maintaining the children. To support themselves, Bana and her relatives decided to take in schoolboys to help process and sell palm oil. With the profits they would pay men to cut and burn a rice farm for them. When David and Alfred appeared from a town farther up-country to go to school in Haindii, Galoŋ and Bana took them in and put them to work. The year before I came, Galoŋ said, the family was doing so well that they did not need to grow their own rice, but could buy rice and pay their household expenses with the profits from the oil they sold in the Haindii market. Bana had a current lover but wanted to "see his ways" before she agreed to marry him. Since the family was doing well without a man, she did not need to rush things.

In addition to helping small family units gain economic independence, owning a house offers people a base from which to seek political power in the larger community. If a man can play host to visiting dignitaries in a modern house with a zinc roof, a cement floor, and "civilized" beds (soft imported mattresses on wooden or metal frames, as opposed to the traditional straw mats or the more recently introduced burlap sacks filled with dried palm leaves), he can impress them with his wealth and put them in his debt. A woman can also use her house to build political power. A woman in another chiefdom whom I learned about through two sources persuaded her lover to build her a house and then took in local girls as wards and boarders. By lending the girls out to important men in exchange for gifts and political recognition, she ultimately amassed enough wealth and power to become a paramount chief.

Kpelle men and women are alike in their desire to be house owners, but differ in their ability to acquire houses. Building a house is generally regarded as men's work.[8] Women with cash may commission houses, but those without cash must try to acquire houses indirectly, through husbands and lovers. For example, a woman who is divorcing her husband may be awarded a house if it was built while the couple was married and if she can prove she was not at fault in the breach. A woman rarely gets everything the couple has accumulated even if the husband is found at fault, but she often gets the house because she is regarded as the best guardian of the children, who must be fed and sheltered.

Women, of course, play up their caretaker roles, especially when houses and other "properties" are at stake. They also insist that their husbands are responsible for making co-wives happy with their housing arrangements. Kpelle informants agree that if two co-wives "make palaver" constantly, the husband must either divorce one wife or build her a separate house. Yɔŋgɔ, a Haindii woman about 25 years old, took advantage of this practice, acquiring not only a house but also a divorce. Yɔŋgɔ lived with her husband, her aged mother, and three co-wives, as well as assorted children belonging to each of the wives. It was not a congenial household: the women quarreled constantly over chores, food, and children. Finally Yɔŋgɔ decided she had had enough, but she realized if she tried to divorce her husband right away she would be given few or none of the group's "properties." She particularly wanted her own house. Since her husband would not build her a house if he knew she was bent on divorce, and since she had no more claim to a house than his other wives if she were to remain married, she asked her husband to build a separate house for her old, sick mother,

---

8. Although houses and lots are not legally registered in the towns I studied, the initial house owner is usually the one who organized the work to build the house and paid for materials. The cheapest way to build a house is to use materials from the nearby forest; the owner need only buy one day's food and drink for people who help daub the house with mud. Building a more modern house can be quite expensive, however, depending on the owner's time, money, and desires. Options include zinc roofing; sheets of particle board in place of raffia ceiling mats; cement for floors and wall coatings instead of mud; screens for windows; planks for roof frames, doors, and windows; hooks and locks for doors and windows; and commercial paint for the roof and walls. All these luxuries could total $1,000 in 1974, a huge sum of money for most Kpelle.

whose drinking and belligerence annoyed everyone in the household. Her husband and his other wives readily agreed to this solution to their problem. As soon as the house was built, however, Yɔŋgɔ divorced her husband and moved into the new zinc-roofed house with her mother. When her angry husband demanded compensation for the house, Yɔŋgɔ obtained the money from her current boyfriend, who was working for Bong Mine.

Older women may acquire houses after their husbands die by playing on filial obligation. The Kpelle say that brothers and sons inherit goods from a man when he dies, but in fact women in Haindii and Dobli Island usually take over most of their husbands' property. (I have little comparative data from Digei.) In a survey of house owners on Dobli Island, for example, I found that only one man inherited houses from a dead relative, in this case his brother; all the rest were inherited by women. This can be attributed in part to the emigration of men for wage labor, but several young men told me that their widowed mothers had begged to be allowed to remain in their houses. When Kpelle men die, the disposition of their houses and other valuables is often couched in terms of their children's inheritance. But I heard of no cases of women giving houses to their children when they grew up. No sons or daughters would stoop to claim their inheritance by evicting their mothers, though a widowed mother is sometimes obliged to share a house with her son and his wives and children.

Old women may ask their grown children to build houses for them and pay their house taxes. Or a local chief may assign an unmarried old woman a house no one else is using and exempt her from the house tax on the grounds that she is incapable of acquiring cash—especially if she has no living children, or children who seldom visit. The fact that old women are often released from this need for money to build a house and pay taxes accounts in part for their independence from ties to spouses. Those few divorced or widowed old women who have the option of remarrying are not constrained to remarry for economic reasons, and old women who want to divorce their husbands may do so without fear of abject poverty.

TABLE 12. *Number of houses owned, by sex, in traditional versus modern areas of Fuama Chiefdom*

| | Number of houses owned by: | | |
Area	Men	Women	Total
Traditional (Digei)	74 (87.1%)	11 (12.9%)	85 (100%)
Modern (Haindii and Dobli Is.)	134 (71.6%)	53 (28.3%)	187 (100%)
TOTAL	208 (76.5%)	64 (23.5%)	272 (100%)
$\lambda_{xy} = 0, \lambda_{yx} = 0^a$			

SOURCE: Numbers combined from Table A9 in the Appendix.
   [a]On λ values, see the notes to Tables 7 and 8.

Table 12 confirms that fewer women than men own houses, and that the percentage of women house owners is markedly higher in the modern area than in the traditional area. (See the breakdown for individual towns in Table A9 in the Appendix.) I attribute this higher percentage to the greater opportunities for women in Haindii and Dobli Island to hold wage jobs, grow cash crops, sell produce in markets, and acquire rich lovers—in short, to their greater direct access to cash to pay for labor and materials.

As we have seen, a woman who owns a house can take care of her family without relying on a husband, whereas a man who owns a house can offer shelter to one or more women who have no better alternative. We would accordingly expect the majority of male house owners to be married and the majority of female owners to be unmarried. Tables 13 and 14 dramatically bear out this expectation (see also Tables A10–A15 in the Appendix).

An important difference between the modern and traditional areas emerges when we note the ages of female house owners. Some old female house owners were unlikely to be married, regardless of house ownership, because they were beyond childbearing age and had children to support them. Some of these women were given old thatch-roofed houses that no one else wanted, and were eliminated from the house tax rolls. Similar numbers of old women in all three towns owned houses (six houses in Haindii were owned by old women, four in Dobli Island, and four in Digei). But there were more young and middle-aged female house owners in Haindii (22,

TABLE 13. *Marital statuses of male house owners versus non-house owners in Digei, Dobli Island, and Haindii*

| House owner status | Marital status | | Total |
	Married	Other	
House owner	167 (83.9%)	32 (16.1%)	199 (100%)
Non-house owner	15 (16.5%)	76 (83.5%)	91 (100%)
TOTAL	182 (62.8%)	108 (37.2%)	290 (100%)

$\lambda_{xy} = .56, \lambda_{yx} = .48^a$

SOURCE: Numbers combined from Tables A10–A12 in the Appendix.

NOTE: In Tables 13 and 14, people are the units of analysis rather than houses. People who own more than one house are counted only once. People of uncertain marital status are excluded, as are houses whose owners are unknown. Absent house owners are included, however, because many were gone only temporarily.

[a]On λ values, see the notes to Tables 7 and 8.

TABLE 14. *Marital statuses of female house owners versus non-house owners in Digei, Dobli Island, and Haindii*

| House owner status | Marital status | | Total |
	Married	Other	
House owner	4 (6.6%)	57 (93.4%)	61 (100%)
Non-house owner	196 (52.7%)	174 (47.3%)	370 (100%)
TOTAL	200 (46.4%)	231 (53.6%)	431 (100%)

$\lambda_{xy} = .11, \lambda_{yx} = 0^a$

SOURCE: Numbers combined from Tables A13–A15 in the Appendix.

NOTE: See note to Table 13.

[a]On λ values, see the notes to Tables 7 and 8.

or 84.6 percent) and Dobli Island (21, or 77.7 percent) than in Digei (7, or 63.6 percent). These differences, plus the fact that few female house owners were married, tend to support the generalization that young and middle-aged women in the modern areas can support themselves without husbands by paying house taxes with money from outside sources.

Household Size and Composition

Also related to wealth are patterns in the size and composition of households.[9] Household size provides information on the number of people available for domestic labor, whereas household compo-

9. Data on the size of the house and the number of rooms per house were not collected.

TABLE 15. *Average household size in Digei, Dobli Island, and Haindii*

Town	Number of oc- cupied houses	Total number of people present	Average house- hold size
Digei	80	428	5.35
Dobli Island	83	364	4.39
Haindii	92	508	5.52
TOTAL	255	1,300	5.10

sition helps in analyzing authority relations in the house. As we will see, most households headed by single women are larger than those headed by single men, thus giving single women a greater potential source of domestic labor. Moreover, there are more households headed by women in the modern area.

To distinguish a household from a kinship or domestic function unit, I have defined it here as a group of people sleeping under the same roof. Table 15 demonstrates that the average household size in the three towns is about the same, despite the differences in the towns' proximity to roads and jobs. This finding should make us skeptical about assertions that domestic groups are breaking down in modern areas. However, the relationships of the residents to each other and the composition of the households have changed in the modern area. Tables 16 and 17 will prove this point.

To analyze the composition of households in the three villages, I used a typology based on that of Carter (1970), who studied the Loma, a tribal group north of the Kpelle area. My household typology is as follows:

(1) *simple monogamous,* a married (or cohabiting) pair with or without children of one or both partners
(2) *complex monogamous,* a married (or cohabiting) pair with or without children, plus other kin or nonrelated persons
(3) *simple polygynous,* a husband and two or more wives (or co-habiting women) with or without children of the wives and/or husband
(4) *complex polygynous,* a husband and two or more wives (or

cohabiting women) with or without children of the wives and/or husband, plus other kin or nonrelated persons

(5) *simple male,* a male with or without his children

(6) *complex male,* a male with or without his children, plus other kin or nonrelated persons

(7) *simple female,* a female with or without her children

(8) *complex female,* a female with or without her children, plus other kin or nonrelated persons

In cases of ambiguity I used the house owner (pέrε-nâmu) or household head (pέrε ŋuŋ-tuê nuu) as the unit of analysis because he or she has the most authority in the house and can legally expel anyone if there is disagreement. For example, in a household consisting of a middle-aged male house owner and his wife, plus his aged father, the aged father would not be considered the household head. Rather, this would be a complex monogamous household. I have excluded from the analysis eight cases in which it was hard to determine who was the household head. These cases included temporary female household heads whose husbands were away, female house owners living with men who might also be considered household heads by the Kpelle because of male dominance ideologies, and a young boy who legally inherited his father's house, even though his mother was still alive.

Table 16 shows the distribution of household composition types, and Table 17 presents a simplified version of these types. Besides the obvious fact that Dobli Island and Haindii have fewer conjugal unit households (types 1–4) than Digei, we can see several interesting patterns in these tables. First, there are more complex female households (type 8) than simple female households (type 7) in all three towns. Conversely, there are fewer complex male households (type 6) than simple male households (type 5). Furthermore, Table 16 shows that female households (type 7 and 8) are more numerous in all three towns than male households (types 5 and 6). As these observations indicate, female units are more likely to collect residents (not including their own children) than male units. One explanation might be that female units are more successful in attract-

TABLE 16. *Household types in Digei, Dobli Island, and Haindii*

Household type	Digei	Dobli Island	Haindii	Total
1. Simple monogamous	24 (30.0%)	27 (33.8%)	13 (15.1%)	64 (26.0%)
2. Complex monogamous	26 (32.5%)	15 (18.8%)	26 (30.2%)	67 (27.2%)
3. Simple polygynous	6 (7.5%)	4 (5.0%)	5 (5.8%)	15 (6.1%)
4. Complex polygynous	4 (5.0%)	5 (6.3%)	6 (7.0%)	15 (6.1%)
5. Simple male	5 (6.3%)	6 (7.5%)	7 (8.1%)	18 (7.3%)
6. Complex male	2 (2.5%)	0	2 (2.3%)	4 (1.6%)
7. Simple female	6 (7.5%)	11 (13.8%)	7 (8.1%)	24 (9.8%)
8. Complex female	7 (8.8%)	12 (15.0%)	20 (23.3%)	39 (15.9%)
TOTAL	80 (100%)	80 (100%)	86 (100%)	246 (100%)

TABLE 17. *Three basic household types in Digei, Dobli Island, and Haindii*

Household type	Digei	Dobli Island	Haindii	Total
Conjugal unit (types 1–4)	60 (75.0%)	51 (63.8%)	50 (58.1%)	161 (65.4%)
Male (types 5–6)	7 (8.8%)	6 (7.5%)	9 (10.5%)	22 (8.9%)
Female (types 7–8)	13 (16.3%)	23 (28.8%)	27 (31.4%)	63 (25.6%)
TOTAL	80 (100%)	80 (100%)	86 (100%)	246 (100%)

NOTE: Numbers combined from Table 16.

ing male residents because women are willing to perform domestic services, such as cooking, which men perform only with the greatest reluctance. Moreover, female units may be more successful in attracting female residents—women seeking shelter during marital disputes, after divorces, and so on—because it is easier for female residents to escape subordination to female household heads than to male household heads.

I also found that female households were much larger than male households, especially in the modern area where residents in unmarried female households outnumbered those in male households by almost three to one. Though women may have to work hard cooking for these residents, they also acquire labor for house and farm work. Galoŋ and Bana, described earlier in the chapter, used student labor in their palm oil business. Another case in point was Miata, a middle-aged woman living on Dobli Island. Until a few

TABLE 18. *Married and unmarried household heads in simple and complex female households in traditional versus modern areas of Fuama Chiefdom*

Area	Unmarried	Married	Total
Traditional (Digei)	8 (61.5%)	5 (38.5%)	13 (100%)
Modern (Haindii and Dobli Is.)	41 (82.0%)	9 (18.0%)	50 (100%)
TOTAL	49 (77.8%)	14 (22.2%)	63 (100%)
$\lambda_{xy} = 0, \lambda_{yx} = 0^a$			

SOURCE: Numbers combined from Table A16 in the Appendix.
  ^{a}On λ values, see the notes to Tables 7 and 8.

years before I met her, she had been living with a well-to-do doctor whenever he came from Monrovia to visit his family. Miata had gotten some cash from him and from her father to build a big zinc-roofed house and to buy a sugar cane still. Putting relatives and local students to work, she made and sold "cane juice" and charged other sugar cane growers to brew their alcohol in her still; she was able to buy a rice farm with the profits. As she grew wealthy and earned a reputation for generosity (lending money to students and hospital patients and to those who were having trouble paying their taxes), even more people were attracted to her household. When I knew her, she had in her house, her own two sons, a new lover who worked for Bong Mine, a junior wife (technically a junior concubine) of her own choosing, her four younger brothers and sisters, and occasional student boarders, all of whom brought money into the household through their labor or kin ties. Miata was not included in my household composition calculations because she had a resident lover who might have been considered the household head. But it was clear to me and to everyone who told me about her that she had built up the household and the "cane juice" business by herself, and would therefore tolerate no challenges to her authority.

Some might argue that the larger percentage of female household heads in the modern area is not the result of women's economic independence, but might merely reflect a greater number of wealthy men who can build separate houses for their economically dependent wives. Table 18 discredits this argument. It shows that the percentage of married female heads of single and complex households is greater in Digei than in the modern towns. (Table A16 in the Appendix breaks this down for Dobli Island and Haindii.) As Yɔŋgɔ's case showed, of course, female household heads in the modern area may acquire independence by asking their husbands to build houses for them, and then divorcing their husbands. But this supports rather than detracts from my argument that women in the modern area use male resources to gain independence.

Occupation

In trying to determine in what ways people's occupations are associated with wealth, it is again necessary to take marital status into account. Wealth per se is hard to measure in a subsistence economy because it is bound up in the social networks of wives and clients that men command. Therefore, I collected data on occupations that would give people wealth and status beyond ordinary rice farming or subsistence. I do not mean to imply that people could support themselves solely from these occupations, or that these occupations are reliable indicators of wealth. I merely take them as indicators of extra income. Since people have different occupations in the traditional and modern areas of the chiefdom, and since different options are available to men and women, I will discuss occupations in more detail in the following two sections on men's and women's wealth and marital status.

Men's Wealth and Marital Status

Since men get more benefits from marriage in the Kpelle wealth-in-people system than women (legal rights in children, adultery fees, domestic services, and so on), I am assuming that most men try very hard to hold on to women. Men with lucrative occupations should be able to do so more easily than others, because they can provide women—and their relatives—with houses and with cash for buying Western goods and other desirable commodities. Hence, it is more likely that men with additional sources of wealth beyond subsistence ("wealthy men," as I will call them) will be married than men without such sources of wealth. Table 19 examines the

TABLE 19. *Marital status of wealthy versus nonwealthy men in Digei*

Economic status	Marital status		Total
	Married	Other	
Wealthy	20 (90.9%)	2 (9.1%)	22 (100%)
Nonwealthy	53 (82.8%)	11 (17.2%)	64 (100%)
TOTAL	73 (84.9%)	13 (15.1%)	86 (100%)
$\lambda_{xy} = 0, \lambda_{yx} = 0^a$			

SOURCE: Numbers combined from Table 21 and Tables A17–A18 in the Appendix.
^{a} On λ values, see the notes to Tables 7 and 8.

marital status of wealthy and nonwealthy men in Digei. (Table 21 and Tables A17–A18 in the Appendix examine this for different age categories.) Digei men have access to wealth in any of several ways: (1) cash crop production—sugar cane, citrus fruits, and rubber (records for coffee, cocoa, and other minor crops were incomplete); (2) ownership of a shop; (3) wage jobs; (4) political office in the local government; (5) religious office in local secret societies; and (6) traditional roles as diviners and curers. Rice production cannot be used here as an indicator of wealth, because data on the amount of rice produced and sold were not available. Men whose economic or marital statuses were unknown are excluded from the table.

The percentages in Table 19 show only weak relations between marital status and wealth among Digei men. I reason that in Digei a man's access to cash through lucrative occupations is not as important as in Haindii. Men here are wanted mainly for their labor in clearing and burning farms; parents and women stress the importance of holding on to a man who works hard. A Digei woman I know, for example, feared that her son-in-law, a diligent worker on the farm, would soon divorce her daughter because of the girl's laziness. Therefore, she began to wash her son-in-law's clothes and cook for him—chores normally done by a wife—and persuaded him to stay.

In contrast, Table 20 shows that in Haindii wealthy men are usually married, and nonwealthy men are usually unmarried. (See Table 22 and Tables A19–A20 in the Appendix, which break the

TABLE 20. *Marital status of wealthy versus nonwealthy men in Haindii*

Economic status	Marital status		Total
	Married	Other	
Wealthy	33 (78.6%)	9 (21.4%)	42 (100%)
Nonwealthy	11 (21.6%)	40 (78.4%)	51 (100%)
TOTAL	44 (47.3%)	49 (52.7%)	93 (100%)
$\lambda_{xy} = .55, \lambda_{yx} = .52^a$			

SOURCE: Numbers combined from Table 22 and Tables A19–A20 in the Appendix.
  [a]On λ values, see the notes to Tables 7 and 8.

figures down by age group.) Here access to cash for men seems clearly associated with being married. In the same vein, it is interesting that all of the fifteen polygynists in Haindii (a figure not in the tables) had access to outside wealth, through government offices, teaching in the local school, running a shop or trading, and wage employment at Bong Mine or Firestone Rubber Plantation. In contrast, four out of the twelve polygynists in Digei had no outside access to wealth, but had achieved power and acquired women through the traditional system.[10]

It is also instructive to compare the two towns with respect to the ages of wealthy and nonwealthy men. Tables 21 and 22 show the marital statuses of young men in Digei and Haindii. (See Tables A17–A20 in the Appendix for data on economic and marital statuses of middle-aged and old men in Digei and Haindii.) Digei, first of all, has no wealthy young men, and there is roughly an equal number of married young men and young men in all other categories. In Haindii, on the other hand, associations between age, marital status, and wealth are striking. Only seven young men in Haindii are married, and only eight are wealthy. Hence, it is significant that five of the young married men are wealthy. (Two of the three unmarried wealthy young men were my husband's research assis-

10. As Mair (1953: 136) points out in distinguishing West African marriage from that of Central and Southern Africa, polygyny is still economically advantageous in areas where subsistence cultivation has not given way to wage labor. Although wage labor is assuming greater importance for the Kpelle, subsistence cultivation still supports most people in non-urban areas.

TABLE 21. *Marital status of wealthy versus nonwealthy young men in Digei*

Economic status	Marital status		Total
	Married	Other	
Wealthy	0	0	0
Nonwealthy	8 (53.3%)	7 (46.7%)	15 (100%)
TOTAL	8 (53.3%)	7 (46.7%)	15 (100%)
$\lambda_{xy} = 0, \lambda_{yx} = .53^a$			

NOTE: Unknowns are excluded.
[a]On λ values, see the notes to Tables 7 and 8.

TABLE 22. *Marital status of wealthy versus nonwealthy young men in Haindii*

Economic status	Marital status		Total
	Married	Other	
Wealthy	5 (62.5%)	3 (37.5%)	8 (100%)
Nonwealthy	2 (8.3%)	22 (91.7%)	24 (100%)
TOTAL	7 (21.9%)	25 (78.1%)	32 (100%)
$\lambda_{xy} = .29, \lambda_{yx} = .38^a$			

NOTE: Unknowns are excluded.
[a] On λ values, see the notes to Tables 7 and 8.

tants, who had just begun their jobs, and the third was for all practical purposes married, having lived with his woman's family for at least six years and produced two children.)

Furthermore, in contrast to Digei, where no young men had more than one wife, one young Haindii man had two wives and two young men on Dobli Island had two wives (data on polygyny are not included in the tables). After the initial census was taken the young polygynist in Haindii acquired a third "trial" wife, though this marriage appeared doomed because of co-wife disputes. Another wealthy young man moved to Haindii after the census was taken. This man had been fired from Bong Mine, but had acquired a wife during his employment. With his savings, he opened a cane juice shop in Haindii and bought a battery-powered record player. He soon did a healthy business, especially on market day when people had money to spend. It was not long before a second wife appeared, and the young man seemed bent on a third.

In interpreting Tables 21 and 22 and the related tables in the Appendix (A17–A20), we should keep in mind the caution that wealth may be a result as well as a cause of marriage. However, as my figures for middle-aged and old men in Digei show, access to wealth outside the traditional system affords few more advantages in acquiring wives than traditional labor. Moreover, although older Digei men may acquire more than one wife through the traditional system or through outside cash opportunities, young Digei men must settle for one wife, for whom they must usually perform bride-service.

In Haindii, on the other hand, access to outside wealth is strongly associated with marriage for men of all ages. Furthermore, some young men are now acquiring wealth on their own, marrying more women than they could have in the traditional system, and marrying earlier than nonwealthy young men in Haindii. It is important to note, however, that although wealthy young men appear to be circumventing powerful older people in a way unavoidable to them before, many young men are still investing their income from the modern world back into the traditional wealth-in-people system, marrying legally and polygynously when they can. (Handwerker's 1973 study of urban Bassa in Liberia supports this observation, showing that men from rural areas begin marrying polygynously when they can afford to.)

Young men who begin to acquire wealth also inevitably collect clients, in much the same way that traditional men do. Harry, an assistant of my husband's, is an excellent example. Bill (my husband) had taught Harry in the Peace Corps and knew he was a good student and a reliable worker. When Bill went back to Liberia to do anthropological research, Harry came to see him. Harry had been living in Zulotaa and making a rice farm there with his brother. He was dressed in tattered clothes, and was quite dejected because he owed a Zulotaa chief eleven dollars for a fine he could not pay. Therefore, he had to quit school and work for the chief. Like most debts, this one was extending indefinitely. Playing the Liberian patron role, Bill "redeemed" Harry; he gave him the eleven dollars to pay the debt and taught him how to transcribe Kpelle tapes.

With the money he began to earn from Bill, Harry bought new kwi ('modern') clothes. Because he was now an attractive son-in-law prospect, parents were quite willing to let him "love to" their daughters, so we began to see him with new girlfriends. He also began to acquire clients in a way that few other young men do. He paid his brother to make a rice farm and build a house for him in Zulotaa, thus in effect placing his older brother in a subordinate client relationship. On market days his new patron role blossomed. Relatives and acquaintances from neighboring towns would find him at the market and ask him for money to pay court fines, taxes, and so on. Many of these were older people, who were themselves the patrons and creditors of younger men. Harry was a generous creditor and also began to pay for goods and services he formerly could not afford, instead of saving his money for future school fees, as we were perhaps naively urging him to do. Harry was not trying to escape the traditional wealth-in-people system; rather, he was re-investing in it.

Though most wealthy men of all ages seek clients and wives, an important qualification for men's desires to hold on to women must be added. Wealthy men may be more likely to marry than non-wealthy men, but they also tend to divorce more often, because they are frequently married to several wives at a time and because they know they can easily find other women. Although my divorce figures for males are too incomplete to distinguish which men divorce most often, Cohen has found that high-status Kanuri men (Nigeria) marry as well as divorce frequently: those men "who are best able to provide for their wives divorce more than the lower status men and have fewer stable unions of long duration. . . . [Furthermore,] higher status men are stricter and more dominant with their wives and therefore have a lower threshold of divorce than their poorer low status neighbors who are more dependent upon wives and must therefore think twice before divorcing them" (1971: 139).

Cohen did not separate urban from rural men in his cross-tabulations. Nor are high-status Kanuri women strictly comparable to Kpelle women, because Kanuri women are often Muslims and hence live in seclusion. Nevertheless, this finding, which corresponds with my knowledge of Kpelle men, differentiates a subclass of rich men who know that they can easily acquire other wives if they dispose of an undesirable woman. Such Kpelle men also give up their wives to other men to build a base of political support. Hence, although rich men are nearly always married at any given time, frequently to several women, most of them have had many divorces.

A court case I heard about in Haindii involved a powerful man named John who made it a practice to become engaged to young women and let them go if they caused him trouble. Even though he did not marry most of these women legally, his case reveals a great deal about the marital strategies of powerful men. One day I happened to see a group of people standing outside the clan chief's door, listening to a woman palaver. Unlike most houses, the chief's house had a walled-in porch, with several chairs and a small table. This room was frequently used for secret political affairs and for legal cases that important people did not want aired in the public courthouse. Deciding not to intrude, I later asked a witness about the case. I learned that the palaver involved John, a patrilateral cousin of Dumu's and the son of a deceased powerful official in the chiefdom. John had been educated at the Lutheran mission near Haindii and he owned a cane juice shop that his wife ran. These attributes, my informant declared, made him so conceited that at times he even failed to show proper respect for Dumu.

John had been married for many years to Suaa, a woman about forty years old who had borne him five children after she divorced her first husband. He had no other wives at this time, but had had a series of girlfriends, some of whom had come to live with him and Suaa. The recent palaver involved one such girlfriend, Gbilika, a woman of about nineteen, who had been living with her parents in a village farther up in the bush. Two years before, John had asked Gbilika to marry him. However, he wanted her to stay with her parents for a while so that the two of them could get a chance to "see each other's ways." He would come up to sleep with her and would bring gifts of money and clothes to her family from time to time. Soon, he promised, they would exchange the token to marry legally. Because John was a wealthy and powerful man, Gbilika and her parents agreed. My informant was careful to note that no one "stood for" John in the arrangement, since he declared that he was a big man and needed no one to stand for him.

After a while, however, it became apparent that John did not intend to marry Gbilika or even support her and her parents. When he visited he rarely brought them money, and as time passed his visits became less frequent. Gbilika's parents began to urge her either to make John exchange the token so that he would be legally obligated to help out more, or to get rid of him and find someone else. Gbilika decided to bring the matter to a chief in Haindii. Because the chief was related to John, he held the case in the privacy of the clan chief's house. After Gbilika explained her side of the story, the chief turned to John and asked him if he wanted to marry the girl. Before answering, John called the chief over to "hang head" (talk privately). Then he went to fetch his wife, Suaa, insisting that she should make the decision, since she would have the most contact with a second wife. When the two returned to the court, Suaa declared that she did not want this girl as her second wife. John turned to the chief and said regretfully, "I wanted to marry Gbilika, but Suaa doesn't want her. So out of respect for my head wife, I can't marry her." Hearing this, Gbilika said she would drop the matter and go back to her people. She probably still wanted to marry John, my informant said, but it would have been shameful and embarrassing to say that she still wanted him after she had been rejected.

Knowing that my informant was close to John's family, I prompted him to explain more of the "inside business" and to give me his interpretation of these facts. My informant revealed that John did not want the financial burdens of another wife plus her relatives, who would constantly demand money and favors. He was very much attached to Suaa, however, because she made a lot of money in the shop. John had originally given her some capital to set up the shop, but she was such a good businesswoman that she soon returned his investment and began making large profits. Not only did she support herself and the children in the house, as a wife should, but she was able to give him money when he needed it.

When it came to other women, however, John was a "rascal man," my informant said. He wanted only children from them, for prestige and for support in his old age. He might "love to" a woman for a while, but as soon as she had a baby he would leave her and provide little child support, figuring that the child would help him in his old age just because he was its father. Gbilika, however, had apparently become impatient and threatened to leave before she had any children. Rather than marry her, John decided to get rid of her, knowing that more docile women were available. So when he "hung head" with the chief, he must have confided that he would tell his wife Suaa to refuse Gbilika when asked if she wanted the girl. According to my informant's interpretation, John was invoking the cultural ideal that a head wife should approve a second wife in order to justify his own desires. And the chief, John's relative, was willing to help him carry out his fiction.

Several days later I interviewed Gbilika, whose interpretation of the case coincided with that of my informant. Husband business, she complained, was hard: "John hasn't given me anything to 'satisfy' [compensate] me, except the rice farm he helped me and my father make." When I asked if Suaa's "hand was in the matter" in scheming to get rid of her, Gbilika assured me no, not at all. In fact, Suaa had been very good to her, telling her all about John and his ways. In court that day, when Suaa said that she did not want Gbilika, everyone knew what was going on. People acted as if they believed John, but they knew from his past and from the kind way in which Suaa had really treated Gbilika that John was trying to trick people. Because he was such a powerful man, I could easily see why people allowed him to make his definition of reality prevail.

The Kpelle examples plus Cohen's statistical evidence (1971) may suggest an alternative interpretation to the one I have presented. We might hypothesize that there are higher divorce rates in

Haindii and Dobli Island not because Kpelle women choose to escape marriage in areas where cash is available, but because men who earn cash may decide that legal obligations to a wife are burdensome as well as expensive. Such men may divorce their wives, placate them by allowing them to keep their houses and children (as evidenced by the dearth of single male households), and move in with female house owners who are willing to provide domestic and sexual services in exchange for male labor, an increasingly valuable commodity as more and more men move to wage labor areas.

I believe that rich men do indeed cast off fractious wives, and that young men in modern areas are in general less eager to marry, unless they can manage to avoid burdensome debts. However, the interpretation that many men with cash are forgoing legal marriage would be hard to support for several reasons. First, living with a female house owner, as we have seen, is precarious for a man. He is subject to her whims, and may be evicted if he makes palaver with other members of the household. Second, he has no legal check on her affairs with outside men. Though this in itself would not prevent a man from obtaining a woman's domestic and sexual services, unmarried men express jealousy when their partners "love to" other men, and they worry about losing whatever claim they have on the woman's children. (I heard about several court cases in which unmarried men tried to sue their women's lovers in order to reclaim their women and "pregnancies," but were unsuccessful because they were not legally married.) Finally, and most persuasively, Haindii men cohabiting with women are rarely wealthy, by the criteria used in this chapter, whereas wealthy men are almost always married. (See Tables 20 and 22 in the text, and Tables A19–A20 in the Appendix.)

It appears that although rich men may contribute to the higher divorce rate in Haindii and Dobli Island by marrying and divorcing more often, they are almost always married to one or more women, and usually remarry quickly after a divorce. Nonwealthy men, on the other hand, lack the means to keep their wives satisfied, so they must live with relatives or with female house owners who have little patience with domineering guests. These men are the casualties of the new system, unable to acquire the wealth that women know is now available from other sources, and hence unable to hold on to wives. The figures on women's wealth and marital status in the next section add further support to this argument.

Women's Wealth and Marital Status

The conclusion that men of average or low wealth and status are not rejecting women has a logical converse: women are rejecting men. A woman with sources of wealth beyond subsistence farming would desire independence because a husband might try to restrict her freedom and use her income for his own purposes. Hence, we would expect that wealthy women, found mainly in Haindii,[11] could support themselves and would not be married. However, it is difficult to distinguish women with independent access to wealth from women who are dependent on men for cash incomes. For example, several wealthy women in Haindii were dependent on their husbands, who gave them capital and a room to open a shop, or helped them plant and harvest each crop; at least two women had husbands who used political connections to find local wage jobs for them. Some women had wealthy male relatives in the area who gave them money periodically, and others had wealthy lovers who had been married in Christian ceremonies to "civilized" women in Monrovia. (Because they were members of the church, these men could not legally marry more than one wife.) Such women could not be classified as independently wealthy. To a certain extent these ambiguities apply as well to the figures on female house ownership examined above, but in general

11. That women in Haindii have more access to cash than Digei women is supported by three questions on my domestic organization questionnaire, administered to 44 Haindii women and 35 Digei women. Question #74 asked the women if they had paid anyone cash during the preceding year to prepare farms for them. Twelve women (27.3 percent) in Haindii said that they had, in contrast to two women (5.7 percent) in Digei. Question #87 asked women if they had market businesses. Nine women (20.5 percent) in Haindii said they ran shops, whereas only one woman (2.8 percent) in Digei said she did. And Question #92 asked women if they had participated in a susu (a savings association in which people give a fixed amount of money weekly to each member in succession, until everyone has collected) during the preceding year. Twelve women (27.3 percent) in Haindii and no women in Digei said they had participated in such an association.

TABLE 23. *Marital status of wealthy versus nonwealthy women in Haindii*

Economic status	Marital status		Total
	Married	Other	
Wealthy	6 (28.6%)	15 (71.4%)	21 (100%)
Nonwealthy	54 (43.9%)	69 (56.1%)	123 (100%)
TOTAL	60 (41.7%)	84 (58.3%)	144 (100%)
$\lambda_{xy} = 0, \lambda_{yx} = 0^a$			

^{a}On λ values, see the notes to Tables 7 and 8.

I consider house ownership a more reliable indicator of wealth than access to cash and occupation.

Table 23 shows that women in Haindii with independent access to the same kinds of wealth that men may have (see the criteria listed for men, p. 141) are less likely to be married than those without such access. (Since my data for women's access to wealth in Digei are even less reliable than those for Haindii, I do not examine them here. I do know of several cases of unmarried "medicine" women and one unmarried female shopkeeper in Digei, though.) Wealthy women tend to be single or to be married to men with good incomes themselves. Of the twenty-one wealthy women in Haindii, fifteen were not legally married, whereas four were married to wealthy men.[12] Only one wealthy woman was married to a nonwealthy man. Her case, however, shows what is likely to happen when a woman's wealth exceeds that of her husband. This woman, a tireless worker on the rice farm, had managed to support her family for years with only minimal help from her husband, a drunk and a 'for-nothing' man (núu kpéni), as the locals called him. As her children grew up, she put them to work farming sugar cane and was able to use her initial earnings to expand the farm and pay outsiders to work. She could now easily afford to buy clothes and

12. Similar findings have appeared in two urban studies. Handwerker (1972–74) reports that poor market women in Monrovia are either unmarried or married to men without good incomes. Women running shops, on the other hand, are either unmarried or married to men with good incomes. And Harrell-Bond (1976) notes that urban women in Sierra Leone prefer to marry men of higher social and economic status.

pay taxes and school fees. Because her husband began to take advantage of her new wealth, demanding money from her for his drinking, her friends were urging her to divorce him. When I left she was about to do so.

On the basis of my data for Haindii, the following generalization may be advanced: wealthy men want to marry women of any class because women provide productive and reproductive services (see also J. Goody 1971), but wealthy women, if they marry at all, only want to marry men whose wealth and status equals or surpasses their own (see also Little 1951).

WOMEN'S SOURCES OF WEALTH IN HAINDII AND DOBLI ISLAND

The previous sections have shown that women with independent access to wealth prefer the single life, unless they can marry men who will bestow great wealth or status on them. I have argued that Haindii and Dobli Island, which are close to roads, markets, and wage jobs, present more opportunities than Digei for women to acquire wealth and become independent of marital ties.[13] It remains to examine more closely the ways in which women actually acquire wealth in the modern setting.

Though education and wage jobs are unavailable to most women, even in the modern area, women here can raise cash crops or make palm oil to sell in Haindii's weekly market, and invest their earnings in small shops or "table markets" on their front porches. As noted above, it is difficult to distinguish independently wealthy women from those who gain wealth through connections to men. These ambiguities, however, point to a major source of female wealth: sex and children, which women use to gain some control over men. Ironically, as we will see, once women acquire wealth through husbands or lovers, they often try to cut their ties to these

13. Similar patterns have been noted among Kgatla women of Southern Africa (Schapera 1940) and among Tonga women of Central Africa (Colson 1958). See also Wilson 1977, a study that parallels mine in documenting how economic and social change has affected people of different sexes and generations among the Nyakyusa-Ngonde of Malawi and Tanzania.

men. Age categories (young, middle-aged, and old) are particularly helpful in examining women's marital strategies in modern areas.

Young Women

Young women, first of all, welcome the new opportunities to prolong the single life before marriage. Realizing that marriage will bring them obligations and restrictions they can now postpone, most girls in Haindii and Dobli Island follow two main pursuits before marriage, which can often be profitably combined: school and men. Though many girls in Haindii and Dobli Island go to the nearby public schools, few are graduated even from the sixth grade. Their parents usually take them out of school, insisting that girls with too much education become hard to handle and leave for greener pastures in the city—often an accurate perception. Many of the girls who do remain in school must help support themselves to justify their education to their parents, but few part-time jobs are open to them in comparison with boys. Cash cropping takes many hours of work, as does marketing, and may necessitate missing many days of school.

Girls find it difficult to earn cash by doing housework for people outside their families because people in Haindii and Dobli Island still associate housework with sexual services. A Peace Corps volunteer I knew was paying the young wife of an important, educated man to cook his meals and wash his clothes. Unaware of the inseparability of housework and sexual services in the people's minds, he was astonished by the husband's repeated outbursts of jealousy. Swearing that he had no sexual interest in the man's wife did no good. Finally, after one night when the hysterical, screaming husband nearly beat his door in, he dismissed the woman and arranged to have one of his unmarried female students cook and wash for him. The new housekeeper had a lover, but because she was unmarried, the Peace Corps volunteer had no more trouble. When the girl later had a child by her lover, however, he discovered much to his surprise that many people had been assuming he was enjoying her sexual favors, and that they had attributed the fatherhood of the child to him.

Since few sources of support are available, many impecunious girls with ambitions to educate themselves take on lovers who pay their school fees and living expenses in exchange for sexual privileges. This practice is especially common in private mission-operated schools closer to Monrovia, which officially frown on students' sexual activities. One girl told me that her lover was posing as an uncle who paid her expenses and picked her up from school each weekend so that she could "visit the family." In all such cases the Liberian principal knew the truth of the matter, but for occasional gifts of money he helped the girls and their lovers perpetuate the myth. Indeed, he must have profited greatly from the rules prohibiting sexual affairs among students.

Parents in Haindii and Dobli Island still try very hard to choose partners for their daughters, in hopes of ensuring support from dutiful spouses. Like mothers in Digei, those in Haindii and Dobli Island may try to find wives for their sons, but because sons are less dependent on economic ties to their parents, they are less likely to give in to appeals based on moral obligation. I did find that in the modern area parents were often successful in convincing their daughters to marry particular men—but these marriages usually lasted only a few months or even weeks. After the first time, daughters generally made their own decisions, regardless of their parents' desires. (See also Mair 1953, Colson 1958, and Oppong 1974.) The túmu koi-kôleŋ relationship (cross-cousin marriage) and infant betrothal, both involving the distribution of young daughters, are similarly less binding in the modern system. The case of Sally and Henry, previously discussed in Chapter 4, will illustrate.

Siiwɔ, a man living in Zulotaa, was given his sister's daughter's daughter (his cross-cousin) as a wife when she was an infant. Infant mortality is high, however, and this child soon died. Since Siiwɔ was still entitled to a wife from his sister's grandchildren through a kind of prenatal sororate, he was promised the next girl born of the same woman. Misfortune struck again, and this girl drowned when she was small. Cross-cousin status was finally conferred on Sally (her "civilized" name), the last infant girl born of the same woman. By this time, however, Siiwɔ had grown very old, so he gave his son

Henry conjugal rights in the infant. Henry, who lived in Haindii, was a young man when he acquired rights in Sally, but he was a desirable husband because he had a good job at Bong Mine.

For a while all went according to plan. Though Sally was sent to Monrovia to be educated and to do housework for a distant relative, she wrote to Henry, played with him and asked him for money when he came to visit, and told him that she would soon come back to Haindii to be his wife. As she grew older, however, her attitude changed. Henry had acquired three other wives as she was growing up, and now had several children—all living in one house, where Sally was to live also. She realized what going back to Haindii would now entail: few of the modern conveniences she was used to, constant squabbles with wives who were less "civilized" than she but senior in authority, and a lack of employment opportunities in anything other than laborious farmwork or petty trading.

When Sally announced her decision to stay in Monrovia and marry a man there, her family was furious. Her mother was particularly angry that she was disobeying her kin and destroying their good relations with Henry, who had been a magnanimous creditor because of his claim on Sally. Whenever Sally visited her family, her mother and other relatives beseeched her to come back and live with Henry, instead of living with a distant stranger over whom they had no control, and who was in effect stealing Henry's "property." All this was to no avail: Sally remained firmly opposed and even declared that she was pregnant by her lover. Henry, of course, was incensed. He had lost not only a wife but also his years of monetary investment—food, clothes, and gifts for Sally as well as gifts and uncollected loans to members of her immediate family. This money was unlikely to be recovered because the family lived in the bush and had few opportunities to acquire cash. If Sally had not gone to Monrovia and gotten all those "civilized" ideas, Henry fumed, she would have had no opportunity to support herself without obeying her kin and marrying him.[14]

14. Several Kpelle men I knew vowed that they would never marry a city woman, or even a woman who had grown up in a town such as Haindii or Dobli Island. They preferred "country girls," whom they believed were happy with the simple pleasures

Though institutions such as infant betrothal and cross-cousin marriage are becoming less binding, most parents still put pressure on their daughters to marry. As this last example has shown, many parents now prefer wealthy husbands for their daughters rather than diligent rice farmers, hoping that a wealthy son-in-law will give them money to buy commercial goods occasionally and help them hire farm labor. Not all parents, however, still want their daughters to marry. Late in my fieldwork I heard about a case in Haindii that illustrates this change in parents' attitudes. Although I did not witness the hearing, I questioned several people about it to get corroboration. The case involved Kutu, an unmarried girl about eighteen years old, who was brought to a "house matter" (less formal than a "court matter") by her parents. The parents complained to the officiating elder that Kutu was "loving around," and declared that they wanted her to confess her boyfriends' names. According to most witnesses, Kutu eventually revealed the names of twelve boys from Haindii, Dobli Island, and Bong Mine. (Some said as many as nineteen; the lowest estimate was eleven.) The elder decreed that all the lovers would have to pay the court costs, even though they were not present, because they had collectively lost the case.

Kutu's parents left the "house matter" still complaining about the crumbling morals of the younger generation. But everyone I talked to, including some people close to the family, said that in fact Kutu's parents were secretly encouraging her to "love around." The year before, my informants declared, the same thing had happened. Ten young men's names were confessed, and all were ordered to come up with five dollars apiece to compensate Kutu's parents for "damages" to their daughter. The same thing had happened the previous year, after Kutu had come out of the Sande bush school. (Lest anyone think that men have no recourse in trickery, someone

---

of a farm and children. Realizing, however, that even "country girls" might change their life-styles in a "civilized" area, they preferred to leave their wives up-country if they got wage jobs in order to protect them from the corruptions of fine clothes, money, and independence.

later reported that one of the boys refused to be sued by Kutu's parents, claiming that when she propositioned him she told him she was married in order to alleviate his fears of a lawsuit. Therefore, he would consent to be sued only by a husband.)

Middle-aged Women

In contrast to middle-aged women in Digei, those in Haindii and Dobli Island often opt out of marriage. Moreover, if an economically independent woman decides to remarry after a divorce or the death of her husband, she will have time to choose a good husband. During my fieldwork my husband and I unwittingly created a test case for my later realization that women's marital options expand when they begin to earn cash independently of men. We hired Tɛɛ-ma, a divorced woman about twenty-eight years old, as our cook and housekeeper. One morning, a few months after Tɛɛ-ma had been hired, she came running in with a frightened look on her face. Yakpalo, her younger sister's husband and a former student of my husband's from his Peace Corps days, was coming over to tell us to fire her. "Don't listen to him," she begged.

Soon Yakpalo arrived. After the preliminary greetings and inquiries after our health, he got to the business at hand. "I want you to pay Tɛɛ-ma and let her go," he said to Bill. "She is causing 'confusion' [disputes] in the home between me and my wife Zɔmɔ and her family." (Yakpalo and Zɔmɔ lived with Zɔmɔ's family.) Bill, he reminded us, had first tried to hire Zɔmɔ because she was his former student and housekeeper. But because she now had two small children to care for, her family had suggested Tɛɛ-ma, who could have no more children. By including himself as part of the family that had gotten Tɛɛ-ma the job, Yakpalo tried to convince Bill that he had a right to take her job away.

"Because of Tɛɛ-ma's 'confusion,'" Yakpalo complained, "I must move out of the house. She says she has a job with you people and is earning her own money, so she doesn't need the money I earn from Bong Mine. She is 'spoiling my luck,' so now I want to 'spoil' hers by taking her job away. She has been complaining about my way of life, while she herself has had lovers." Bill agreed gravely that the matter sounded serious. Having no intention of firing Tɛɛ-ma, he told Yakpalo in true Liberian fashion, "Wait until tomorrow, and we'll take the palaver to the quarter chief," who also happened to be Tɛɛ-ma's father.

When Tɛɛ-ma came over to wash dishes for us the next morning, I asked her to come in and talk. With my assistant interpreting, Tɛɛ-ma told her side of the story. "When I was married to Bɔi-ma," she began, "Yakpalo first approached me for 'love.' I refused him, insisting he was my younger sister's husband, and to 'love to' him would cause palavers between me and my sister." Tɛɛ-ma was referring to the ambiguity about seniority that would result if an older sister became a junior wife or concubine in her younger sister's household. Yakpalo came to her again after the birth of Zɔmɔ's first child because Zɔmɔ was observing the taboo on sexual relations while the child was nursing. However, Zɔmɔ suspected that Yakpalo was turning his attentions—and giving his wages—to lovers outside the family, so she finally asked Tɛɛ-ma to "love to" Yakpalo and keep him busy until she finished nursing the baby.

In the meantime, all was not well between Tɛɛ-ma and her husband Bɔi-ma, who often drank and beat her. She had taken him to court before, but had never managed to stop him from beating her. Now, however, she had an excuse to divorce: in the clan chief's court she "confessed Yakpalo's name" as a lover. The chief returned Tɛɛ-ma to her family, and Bɔi-ma eventually settled for a small fine from Yakpalo.

Because she was now unmarried, Tɛɛ-ma did not feel that she had to reserve her attentions to Yakpalo. While married to Bɔi-ma, she had been "loving to" another man whose name she did not want to confess, and she saw little reason to terminate the affair now that she was "loving to" Yakpalo. When Yakpalo began to object that she was not only acting immorally but was also bringing "disease" into the family, she agreed to give up other lovers. But then Yakpalo himself began to take on other lovers. He tried at first to deny it, but the family had been gathering evidence. One day, for example, a girl brought him some "country bread" (uncooked powder made of rice and sugar), a highly suspicious act, since the exchange of food between men and women often means that they are having sexual relations. Things came to a head one market day, a few days before Yakpalo came to ask us to fire Tɛɛ-ma. Another girl came by the house and asked for Yakpalo. When he came back from the market and was told about her, he went down the road after her. At that, Tɛɛ-ma became angry and declared she had her own money from her housekeeping job with us; she didn't need him anymore. Fuming, Zɔmɔ declared that she didn't want him either. But Tɛɛ-ma acting in her role as an older sister, advised Zɔmɔ not to give up Yakpalo because she had more at stake in holding on to him. Eventually it was decided that George, their older brother, would be summoned to settle the matter between Zɔmɔ and Yakpalo. But in the meantime, Yakpalo had to move out of the house.

Looking across the road to where the family lived, I could see Yakpalo moving out. Zɔmɔ, her children, and her family were watching him go. In the yard were all his belongings: clothes, buckets, an axe, a cutlass, a bed, and even the radio Bill had given Zɔmɔ long ago in exchange for her cooking services. (The radio was eventually recovered.) Sad but calm, Zɔmɔ remarked that Yakpalo was taking all the "properties" he gave her, even Alice, a fourteen-year-old distant relative he had brought down from the bush to help Zɔmɔ with her chores.

Deciding the time was ripe to get the decision we wanted, Bill and I walked over to talk to the quarter chief, Vani, who was sitting on the porch watching his son-in-law move out. When Bill told the chief that we were ready to discuss firing Tɛɛ-ma, Yakpalo retreated into the house, saying he was not ready to discuss it. Vani shook his head hurriedly, saying to Bill, "I thought you and I gave her the job," implying that Yakpalo had no right to take her job—and income for the household—away. Several weeks later Yakpalo was trying to get Zɔmɔ back. Realizing that life would be difficult for him in her family's house, he used his earnings to buy building materials and eventually built a house for Zɔmɔ and the children. Even then he had not exactly torn Zɔmɔ away from her family: the new house was scarcely 50 yards from theirs.

It is unlikely that an incident like this would have taken place in

Digei. In Haindii, however, women have more opportunities to earn cash independently of a spouse's control. Tɛɛ-ma did not need Yakpalo's money or labor, for she could use her earnings from working with us to pay men to work on her rice farm that year. She eventually married a man of her own choice, and began to take English lessons at a nearby literacy center in order to gain a skill she would need in the "civilized" world.

Like women in traditional areas, women in modern areas often use their sexuality to apparent advantage. Adultery has long been a complaint in Kpelle courts, and certainly has not diminished since men began to earn wages, since men can now give their lovers more munificent gifts of clothes and money to buy food.[15] However, these gifts intended for luxury and subsistence may be converted into capital investments: several women told me that they had used the money their lovers had given them for clothes to expand their market businesses instead. Women compete for rich lovers, and usually drop men who cannot afford gifts in favor of those who can.[16] Of course, women married to low-status men often find it harder to advance than single women. Afraid of arousing their husband's suspicions, they are reluctant to accept gifts from their

15. This situation may be reversed in the case of women with rich elderly husbands, if there are many other wives in the household. These women may not receive gifts from their lovers; because they are economically secure, they may delight in supporting fine young lovers secretly with the money their husbands give them for food and clothes.

16. Some of the answers to my domestic organization questionnaire substantiate the fact that women receive economic help from their lovers. Question #64, for example, asked women how they acquired meat. Eight women (18.2 percent of the sample) in Haindii said that their lovers sometimes supplied them with meat, in contrast to three women in Digei (8.6 percent) who said that their lovers sometimes gave them rice. Finally, eight women (18.2 percent) in Haindii and two (5.7 percent) in Digei said that their lovers gave them clothes. Again, however, these data must be read with caution. Though the interviewer was careful to distinguish between 'lover' (wɛli) and 'husband' (surɔ̃ŋ) when questioning these women, the two words are often used interchangeably. Furthermore, the data presented here do not specify how much money women acquired from their lovers. Such data would be unreliable to say the least, because of informants' memory lapses or attempts to hide touchy information. Nevertheless, lovers seem to play a more provident role for women in Haindii. (Actually I believe the percentages are quite low, especially for Haindii women, who may be more likely to have lovers; because their husbands were often present during the interviews, women were reluctant to admit having lovers.)

lovers. For this reason, an informant told me, many women in places like Haindii do not want husbands.

Because women in Haindii and Dobli Island try to acquire money from lovers, a woman may distribute sexual favors to more than one man at a time, telling each that he is the only man she wants. This strategy, however, is risky: if the competitors discover each other, all of them may drop her. To manage such situations women have a whole repertoire of tricks to hide husbands from lovers, lovers from husbands, and even lovers from other lovers. Their complex techniques of deception could fill a small volume. Women with lovers in different towns, for example, may use different names to prevent men who might happen to compare notes from discovering they are "loving to" the same woman. Alternatively, single women may tell their lovers they are married, because the lovers would not become jealous of men they believed were legal husbands. One such instance was related to me by a divorced woman in Haindii, who made it a policy to tell each of her lovers she was married. She fooled two men, each of whom thought that the other was the husband who could sue him for adultery. One of the woman's lovers gave her money to buy some food. When the meal was ready, the two sat down to eat. But before they could begin, she heard another lover coming. She quickly told the first, "My husband and his relatives are coming. Quick! You go hide!" When he had hidden, the new lover came in, saw the food, and commended her on preparing it just in time for his arrival. The two sat down together and began to eat. Halfway through the meal, the woman suddenly announced that she heard her husband coming. When the second lover had scurried out, she summoned the first lover, who then finished the meal with her, rejoicing that the "husband" had not seen him.

A more involved story was uncovered by my assistant during a court hearing and through subsequent questioning of the parties involved, as well as their friends and neighbors. This case illustrates a scheme carried out jointly by a married couple, first to use the wife as bait and to falsify her marital status, and then to manipulate the husband's identity for material gain. A woman named Maa was married to a man who lived and worked in Bong Mine and came to see her in Haindii occasionally. She lived in the house he built her and grew rice to send to him. Maa not only appeared single, but cultivated the image and told strangers that she was unattached in order to make herself seem more available for sexual liaisons. Near the end of my stay in Haindii, a man from up-country who was a very important medicine man in Poro society began "loving to" her. On her encouragement, he moved in and helped her begin a rice farm. One day Maa's husband came home from Bong Mine, announced that he was married to her, and threatened to take the intruder to court. However, he seemed afraid of the medicine man's power, and appeared to relent. With Maa and her brother as witnesses, the husband gave the lover a dollar token and, according to later testimonies, presumably told him he could live with his wife. The husband then went back to Bong Mine.

Several weeks later he reappeared, summoned the lover to court, and sued him for $150 plus court expenses for "loving to" his wife after he had been ordered out. (The fact that Maa and her lover had just harvested the rice may have been an important factor in the husband's timing.) The medicine man protested that the husband had given him a marriage token and had thus legally transferred Maa to him. Because of his high status, he said, Maa's husband gave the token to him rather than the other way around, as was usually the custom. He asked Maa and her brother to back him up. To his dismay, however, both swore that the token had only symbolized the friendship between the two men: the husband had in fact ordered the lover to move out.

Probably no outsider will ever know what actually happened during the crucial exchange of the token, so anxious were both sides to have their own definitions of the situation prevail. But because of the witnesses' oaths, the court chief found the lover guilty and fined him a total of $53, including a basic adultery fine, court fees, the husband's transportation expenses, reimbursement for the husband's lost day of work, and so on. The lover moved out in humiliation, the husband went back to Bong Mine with his adultery fine, and Maa, gloating publicly over being able to keep the rice harvest and part of the fine, went back home—to set the trap again, people said.

Uneducated women like Maa may settle for labor and occasional gifts of cash from their lovers. But even women with education and skills find it hard to obtain good jobs, promotions, and political office in the larger society without help from lovers. By having affairs with powerful men, women can establish a kind of patron-client relationship—a pattern as common in Liberia as in Hollywood or Washington. I mentioned earlier, for example, the woman who lent her young female boarders to visiting dignitaries. The same woman also used her lover, a high government official, to help her win an elected government position.

Florence, an attractive woman about twenty-eight years old, was another case of a woman using sexual services to advance in the "civilized" world. Florence told me that she had been trained in Monrovia as a "civilized" midwife and had been working at the Bong Mine hospital for seven years. However, her salary of $50 per month was inadequate because she had to rent a room in the expensive Bong Mine area and had neither a farm nor the time to produce subsistence food. Therefore, Florence began to work as a prostitute on the side. With her earnings she bought a three-bedroom house and began to reclaim her investment by renting two of the rooms to friends.

One day about two years before I talked with her, Florence was visiting a customer, who happened to show her a newspaper ad from a school in Chicago offering correspondence courses in dental assistant's training. Excited by the prospect of a better-paying job, she sent the school $300 for tuition and soon received her textbooks and lessons. A year and a half later she received her diploma and passed the test to become a student nurse at a hospital in Monrovia. When I talked to her in 1974, Florence had begun to work as a student nurse and was making $175 per month. At the end of a two-month trial period, they would either let her go or hire her permanently, raising her salary to $300 per month. "They will keep me," she said confidently, "because I'm 'loving to' the director. He gave me forty dollars last month to go find a good house to live in.

He's a rascal man, though, and I know I'm not the only girlfriend he has [besides his wife]. Men are tricky. That's why I'm trying to make my money independently."

Even though middle-aged women in modern areas are trying to escape restrictive conjugal bonds, they still try to maintain control over their children. In traditional areas, as we have seen, middle-aged women maneuver informally to find spouses for their children and to claim brideservice from their daughters' husbands. In more modern areas, however, women can act more directly to obtain filial support. Divorced women who have housed, fed, and educated their children can try to claim support on their own behalf. They forcefully remind their relatives that they raised their children with little help from the children's fathers, whose legal claim to financial benefits from these marriages concomitantly decreases.[17]

Moreover, middle-aged women view their children as assets even before they are old enough to marry. In Digei children's labor is used almost exclusively in the subsistence sphere. In Haindii and Dobli Island, however, older children make great quantities of palm oil, which their mothers sell in the market, and they may help with cash cropping. Some women use the labor of other people's children as well as their own. For example, women who head households feel free to call on student boarders for help with cash cropping or making palm oil, as we saw earlier in the case of Bana and Galoŋ. So fluid is the system of wardship and child care in Liberia, and indeed throughout West Africa, that even barren women can acquire children's labor. One such case involved a Haindii woman about forty years old who lived near the market area. Noai had a small shop in her house, and sold cane juice, palm oil, and assorted small items. One day I interviewed her to find out how she managed to get along so well without a husband.

"I was the first child of my parents." Noai began. "There were four others besides me. Two of the youngest died, leaving three of

17. In fact, Murray 1976 argues that contemporary Lesotho bridewealth transactions are less the result of men bargaining over the productive and reproductive capacities of women, than of women bargaining over the wage labor potentials of men.

us. When you come up in life, the first blessing you should have is a child. I never had a child of my own. That is the pitiful thing [malôŋ mɛni, 'sorrowful business'] that has happened to me. Since God has not sent me that blessing, he is sending it to my sisters. Whenever sisters have children, they belong to all of them. So since God is sending children to my sisters, he is sending them to me too.

"When my first husband found I was barren, he threatened to divorce me. So I approached my younger sister and brought her to my husband. She had a child, so he kept her but divorced me. Since then my relatives have helped me to get along. Now and then I find a boyfriend, but they aren't permanent husbands, so I can't rely on them. Now, though, my mother is blind and my father is sick, so they can't help me. I am so pitiful! The only thing that has helped me is the children my sisters sent because they took pity on me. One boy is in high school, away from home most of the time, but the other three live here and go to school here. These boys helped me to open my shop, and they made a sugar cane farm and sold palm oil for me."

Despite Noai's self-pity and her story of woe, her neighbors described a very different woman. Said one informant, "The people who have known Noai from a young age say she is terrible to the men she has lived with. Noai got money from a husband or a lover to build the house she lives in. So when a man comes into her home to live, it is hard for her to respect him. Everything that goes on there, she will have to know about. Anything she doesn't like, she will let the man know. When men came into her home, she used to beat them. And you know the nephews who are living with her? Sometimes she orders all of them to jump on her boyfriends and beat them." Noai had little need for a permanent husband, even though she was by no means rich, for she could pay men to clear and burn her rice farm with the money she made from her shop and her nephews' labor.[18]

18. Protestations of sorrow and self-pity such as Noai's were not uncommon among the women I talked to. In some instances, of course, unmarried women did have a hard time earning a living. But in most cases there seemed to be little relation between the degree to which a woman complained about her lot and the indepen-

As Chapter 4 has demonstrated, the most important female function in men's eyes is bearing children. Even though Kpelle marriage rules give men legal rights in female reproduction, women can use their children as part of a strategy to change their marital situations or to obtain support from men. In this patrilineal society, the man is considered the "owner of the pregnancy" (koo-nàmu, 'belly owner'). A woman who divorces is legally obligated to give up her child to its father when it is old enough. Legal rules also state that if a man other than the husband is the "owner of the pregnancy," he must pay the husband a fine and take care of the woman from the time she is pregnant until she has finished nursing the child. At that point the woman should return to her husband, leaving the child with its father. In most cases, however, actuality is quite different from legal ideals, for women in Haindii seldom give up their children to biological fathers. And they frequently use the opportunity of living with the "owner of the pregnancy" to divorce their husbands, by convincing their lovers to repay their husbands for bridewealth and other expenses.

Children are useful to their mothers in yet another way. Since extramarital affairs are common, the biological fatherhood of a child is often in doubt. A woman can try to obtain support from a man by claiming that he is her child's father—even if she herself is not certain. (See Bledsoe, forthcoming, for an examination of changes in Kpelle fatherhood patterns.) Because men have more access to money in the modern area, a woman here can use this strategy to best advantage. She can press a wealthy man for money to support the child and send it to school, "eating" a great deal of the money herself in the process. And she will eventually benefit from the child's education when he gets a good job and begins to support his poor old mother, who reminds him how much she suffered and sacrificed to raise him herself. A woman who succeeds at this maneuver maintains her own independence from marriage,

---

dent assessment of her neighbors. In fact, said the person who told me about Noai, evoking pity is a common tactic that women use to get money and favors from rich people like me.

and at the same time keeps her children bound to her in moral and economic ties of obligation.

Miata, the Dobli Island woman with the large household and cane juice business, succeeded at this ploy. For several years she had been "loving to" a doctor. When he left the country for specialized training, however, Miata took on another lover. When the doctor came back ten years later, Miata introduced him to Aaron, the son she had borne while he was away, and told him that Aaron was his child. The doctor began to give Miata money to support Aaron, even though he had brought back a foreign wife. While he was married to this foreign wife everything was fine, since she treated Aaron like her own son and even brought him to Monrovia to go to school and live with her and the doctor. Unfortunately for Aaron, the doctor divorced this wife and married an educated Kpelle woman who was a teacher in a Monrovia high school. This new wife disliked Aaron intensely. Worse still, she was wise to the "country women's ways." "This boy is not for you [not your child]," she declared. "All those country people are just fooling you." So despite Miata's protests that Aaron was "for the doctor," he was sent back home. However, since she was now making money from a cane juice business the doctor had helped her set up, Miata was able to pay for her son's schooling.

As this story shows, true biological fatherhood is often irrelevant. Even while the doctor was married to the foreign woman, he himself may have doubted that Aaron was really his son. But he liked having a boy around to do household work, as shown by the fact that he took another boy in as soon as Aaron left. His decision to turn Aaron out was undoubtedly based more on his new Kpelle wife's resentment of Aaron's privileged position as a son in the household than on his doubts about his own paternity.

Musu, a woman in Haindii, also tried to manipulate the social identity of her child's father for her own ends. But in contrast to Miata, who fixed her son's relationship to only one man, Musu decided to switch the identity of her daughter's father after the child was several months old. Musu had married Samuel, a local schoolteacher and political protégé of a powerful chief. She had begun "loving to" him while she was a student in the fourth grade (she was about fifteen at the time: most Kpelle students are sent to school much later than American students). After Musu had a son by Samuel, she and Samuel decided to marry, and went with Musu's relatives to Dobli Island in order to have Dumu conduct the "turning over." After a time, however, quarrels broke out in the household. Disliking Samuel's senior wife, Musu refused to work on their common farm. And since Musu felt that Samuel was not giving her enough money, she tried to arouse his jealousy by flirting with other men. Samuel flew into terrible rages when he saw this, threatening to kill those he suspected of "loving to" Musu. Exasperated, he finally took her back to Dumu, and according to his story, turned her over to her people—that is, divorced her.

Soon Musu began "loving to" a man named Richard and moved in with him. Samuel, seeing someone else interested in Musu, grew jealous and began "loving to" her secretly again. To cloud matters even more, Musu became pregnant and bore a daughter, whom she claimed was "for" Richard. When Richard tired of her, however, Musu had to move out and began telling people that her daughter was really by Samuel. She also began to say that Samuel and Dumu hadn't really turned her over to her people after all—Dumu had merely urged the couple to get along better. But Samuel knew that Musu now had little leverage against him, he apparently did not want to raise a child whose fatherhood was in doubt. (I inferred from similar cases that Richard might reassert his claim when the child was grown, and try to take her without reimbursing Samuel for his expenses.) Therefore Samuel decided to maintain the original definition of the situation: Musu's daughter was not by him. Furthermore, though Samuel was willing to "love to" Musu, he was unwilling to claim publicly that they were still married.

Subsequent quarrels I witnessed showed that Musu was still trying to make her own definition of the relationship prevail and Samuel was still resisting. Reading in my house one afternoon, I was startled by shouts and shrieks from Musu's house down the road. Joining several other curiosity seekers, I ran to her house and peered around the corner into the back yard. Sobbing hysterically,

Musu was chasing Samuel, trying to hit him and claw at him. As she snatched up a piece of firewood and swung at him, she spotted me in the crowd, and wailed loudly in English that Samuel was 'loving to" a "for-nothing" girl in town and was giving her money, while neglecting Musu, his real wife, as well as his own children. Samuel finally escaped to his head wife's house, suffering only minor scrapes, a torn shirt, and humiliation.

On another occasion, I was buying some canned mackerel at the Lebanese store in town, when Musu stormed up the road with her infant daughter on her back, crying loudly and shouting at Samuel, who was hurrying ahead of her. "You just want the 'name' [status] of having children and don't want to spend money to buy clothes for them," she cried to him in English, again for the benefit of me and the Lebanese man. Musu seemed to know that by embarrassing Samuel in public, screaming and alluding to "his" children, especially in front of "civilized" people, she could get exactly what she wanted from him. By this time, a lot of people had stopped to listen to the palaver. Turning to me, Samuel tried to explain that Joseph, the Lebanese merchant, had "credited" Musu ten dollars for clothes and food for her children. She had paid him five dollars a few days before this incident, after waiting several months for the bureaucratic process to deliver her salary from cooking at the local school (fifteen dollars). But she had repaid other debts and had spent the rest of the money on frilly nightgowns and jewelry, which Samuel considered wasteful. "I got her the job at the school," he told me indignantly. "She should use that money to pay for her children's things. But now she wants me to pay the debt. I gave her three dollars to pay part of it, but now she wants the other two as well." Finally, edging away from the crowd that had gathered, he succumbed to Musu's tirade, paid Joseph the remaining money, and hurried off, complaining loudly about Musu's lack of responsibility toward "her" children.

Old Women

Old women in the modern area, like those in Digei, do not usually want to remarry after a divorce or a husband's death. As one informant put it, old women are beyond the age when they should be told what to do by husbands or relatives. Since an older woman does not want a husband's legal control over her, she must rely on other means of subsistence. As we have seen, she may benefit from her children's subsistence labor and from their marriages, and resort to witchcraft threats if all else fails.

Financial help from children working for wages in urban areas is another important source of support for old women who now have an alternative to following the strict Kpelle patrilineal rules that widows should become the wives of their dead husbands' brothers or older relatives. In the modern area such marriages rarely take place anymore; even in more traditional areas the practice is waning. One man told me that after his father's death his mother had urged him to compensate the dead man's family so that she could remain single. She also asked for money to pay her house tax, so that she could be independent of other relatives' control. However, because more young people now leave the rural areas in search of wage jobs and tend to stay away for long periods of time, they are less likely to provide the kinds of support or compliance their mothers would like. Consequently, fewer mothers are able to arrange their children's marriages for their own benefit. In Haindii, for example, the single case I recorded of a mother "marrying" a woman for her son failed because the son had taken on "civilized" ways while working for wages, and felt that he wanted a more "civilized" wife than the traditional girl his mother had picked out.

Rachel, a woman about twenty-two years old, told me that her mother-in-law, Kɔpu, had tried to "marry" another girl several years ago for her eldest son, Peter. The girl Kɔpu chose was fairly traditional by most measures. Although she lived in Haindii, she had no education. Her parents were poor rice farmers who had little income. Kɔpu liked the girl, who was a hard worker, and decided to approach her parents and ask them to give her to Peter as a wife. After some negotiations, in which the parents agreed to let the girl live with Kɔpu in exchange for occasional gifts of money from Peter, the deal was closed. Everyone was satisfied—until Kɔpu told Peter about his new wife. Peter had several years of education and a well-paid job in Monrovia. Citing his newly acquired "civilized" ways, he refused the girl his mother had chosen in favor of Ruth, a more educated and "civilized" girl he had met in Monrovia. From Kɔpu's point of view, however, Ruth was next to useless as a daughter-in-law because she did not speak Kpelle (having been raised in an English-speaking household in Monrovia), refused to do farmwork, and disliked cooking on a crude fire. Because tension inevitably rose between Ruth and other members of Peter's family, she and Peter rarely visited Haindii.

Old women with no children or those whose children and grandchildren do not help them are pitied by others, and often describe their situation in tragic terms. In a sense, they are justified. Moral ties of obligation seem to dissolve quickly when economic dependency is gone, in part because older relatives' requests for money are major threats to people's small businesses as well as to their social mobility. (Gluckman 1941 and Oppong 1974 make similar observations.) Many urban people consequently visit their mothers and other rural relatives as little as possible.

In the eyes of old people, marriage is directly related to filial obligation because it brings them added support from a son-in-law or daughter-in-law and his or her family. Since they have much to lose as their children's and grandchildren's marriages break up, old women voice loud complaints about the breakdown of marriage and morality among younger people (see also Barnes 1951 and Green 1947). An old woman in Haindii, for example, sued her granddaughter in the clan chief's court in order to force her to reveal her lover's identity. The old woman complained that the girl was living away from home with her lover, who was partaking of the girl's sexual favors without a commitment to marry her and help support her poor old grandmother.

Two recent changes in marriage patterns and economic conditions highlight the trends I have discussed. First, more and more tribal people, especially those in urban areas, have decided to get married in church, a change hailed by missionaries and local elites as a sign of development (da mari kɛ, 'they marry' in a "civilized" way, an expression based on the English word "marry") The early black American settlers in Liberia brought with them the rule that forbids polygamy to people married in a Christian ceremony. Although church marriage has become a sign of status for tribal people, this trend has not changed basic social relations. Sexual affairs seem to be as common among people who have married in church as among those who have not, and polygyny has continued in a somewhat different form: many men who marry in church have "country wives" to whom they are not legally married, a pattern common to elites elsewhere in West Africa. Children from these unions may be recognized or denied as the occasion demands.

Second, during 1974, the year I was in Liberia, prices for commercial goods and local foods climbed sharply as a result of worldwide inflation. Women who relied on cash commodities and had to hire male farm labor were finding it hard to make ends meet. This trend may begin to reverse women's marital strategies in areas such as Haindi and Dobli Island. One woman, who had been relying on gifts from her lovers, said that her standard of living was dropping as prices rose and her lovers ran short of money. Nowadays, she complained, a woman needed a husband—as well as her lovers—to keep her going.

CHAPTER 6

Conclusion

I went to Liberia to investigate Kpelle women and their positions in society, particularly with respect to marital institutions. Naively, I assumed that all women would regard marriage as a burden, and that they would form bonds of solidarity with other women in family groups, secret societies, trading partnerships, and the like. As my fieldwork progressed, however, I began to see differences in women's marriage goals in traditional and modern settings. I also noticed significant differences in the options open to old women and young women, and I realized that other women used the young as well as other women for their own purposes. Family membership also emerged as an important determinant of women's strategies. I deduced, for example, that institutions such as the Sande society functioned less for female solidarity than for older aristocratic men's and women's political ambitions. Finally I realized that an accurate picture of Kpelle marriage could not brush men aside, both as members of the society (which they almost always dominated) and as marriage partners. This last chapter, in setting the findings of my fieldwork in a larger theoretical framework, reflects my concern with the effects of social stratification and economic development on African conjugal patterns, and on African women as well as men.

THE JURAL FRAMEWORK OF MARRIAGE AND
MARITAL INSTABILITY

In order to explain marriage patterns in Fuama Chiefdom, I have discussed the legal concept of rights in people in the context of people's social strategies. The combined approach sees rights in people as resources to be used by individuals seeking political and economic status. Since Chapter 3 has already traced the concept of legal rights in people in the anthropological literature, this section examines the jural model of social organization from which this concept is derived. Because a thorough treatment of the jural model is beyond the scope of this book, my analysis will focus on the way in which the model has been used to explain marriage and marital instability in African societies.[1]

The jural model of social organization has been employed by theorists such as Radcliffe-Brown, Evans-Pritchard, Fortes, and Gluckman. Here "jural" refers to

certain aspects or elements of right and duty, privilege and responsibility, laid down in the rules that govern social relations. . . . It is, therefore, distinctive of these features of right and duty, privilege and responsibility, that . . . they have the backing of the whole society. That is to say, they derive their sanction from the political framework of society. They thus have "public" legitimacy in contrast to the "private" legitimacy of rights and capacities based solely on moral norms or metaphysical beliefs. (Fortes 1969: 89)

The jural model assumes that people behave the way they do because legal rules tell them how to behave and punish those who deviate. Radcliffe-Brown (1950) and Evans-Pritchard (1940, 1945), for example, postulate that traditional African societies are organized on the principle of perpetuating the descent group by recruit-

---

1. This study does not attempt to cover the literature on marital instability. See Cohen (1971) for a systematic review. Studies of particular importance, other than those discussed in the text, are those of Lévi-Strauss (1969) and Leach (1957), who stress the role of women and marriage in creating links between groups. These authors argue that the stability of legal marriage varies with the groups' desire to maintain political alliances. Also relevant is Cohen (1971), who develops a psycho-cultural explanation for marital instability among the Kanuri of Nigeria.

ing or reproducing new members and by forming alliances with outside groups. The acquisition of legal rights in people—especially in women—is invoked as the chief mechanism that binds people to groups and thus perpetuates descent groups. Marriage is the institution that best fulfills these functions. A group that acquires legal rights in a woman thereby acquires productive and often reproductive rights in her, as well as in-law relationships with her natal kin. Her own kin group, on the other hand, usually acquires brideservice or bridewealth, which can be used to finance marriages for its male members.

Since the jural model of marriage assumes that behavior follows rules—that people stay with those who control legal rights in them—the fact that many marriages do not last forces proponents of the model to explain why some rules are broken so frequently. Some theorists hypothesize a relationship between the rate of divorce in a society and the extent to which descent groups possess rights in women. When a man's lineage acquires most of the reproductive (genetricial) rights and domestic and sexual (uxorial) rights in a woman, divorce will be infrequent because both lineages maintain a large investment in the marriage—a pattern found primarily in patrilineal societies. When a woman's lineage retains many rights in her, as in most matrilineal societies and some patrilineal societies such as the Somali (Lewis 1962), bridewealth is low and conjugal ties have little effect on the interests of the lineage, making divorce easy and therefore frequent (Gluckman 1950, 1972; Fallers 1957; Ackerman 1963; Mitchell 1961). Retaining the basic jural scheme, Gibbs (1960, 1963) argues that the Kpelle of Panta Chiefdom have a high divorce rate because they lack clearly defined corporate kin groups to enforce sanctions on conjugal partners, and because ambiguous marital norms permit frequent deviation from patrilineal rules. It must be noted that some of the strongest advocates of the jural approach have been interested in how people pursue strategies within the range of culturally accepted norms and laws (for example, Fortes 1962) and how people try to manipulate norms to their advantage (Gluckman 1955). But deviations from marital norms are usually treated as exceptions, and most theorists who discuss marriage and marital instability believe that jural rules generally determine behavior.

One important example of the way in which jural theorists attempt to explain the disruption of social groups and marital institutions is found in studies of urbanization and industrialization in Africa. Comparing groups in their traditional and more modern settings, these studies argue that the importance of individual success in the urban environment has broken down the ideology and controls of corporate descent groups, releasing people from kin group pressure that had formerly constrained their behavior. According to these theorists, disruptive changes in social organization have resulted. Wilson (1941) and Mitchell (1961), for example, showed that where the policies of colonial governments discouraged women from moving to the city, the value of individual women as domestic laborers increased and there was greater competition among men for women to perform these chores.

Some researchers (for example, Ardener et al. 1960, Ardener 1962) argue that women in wage labor areas are freed from traditional kin group constraints on their behavior. Such women can easily find men with cash to pay for sexual services, thus producing a high divorce rate. Demographic imbalances are claimed to be a major causal factor as well: disproportionate sex ratios increase the value of women's sexual services in wage labor areas, where men predominate. (These studies, however, provide no comparative data to test the hypothesis that divorce rates increase as men begin to outnumber women.) This explanation may indeed account for divorce rates in some urban or wage labor areas, but it does not explain the case of Fuama Chiefdom, in which divorce rates differ but the ratio of adult males to females is nearly the same for both the traditional and the modern areas.

Many studies based on the jural model correctly recognize the importance of legal rights in conjugal relations, but they usually assume that marriage is the normal condition for all adults. Thus they tend to focus on the role of legal rules in first marriages, which are notoriously unstable, and do not take into account strategies women use as they acquire more economic resources. The fact is that most Kpelle women do regard marriage as normal and desirable. However, when they become old enough to rely on grown children or wealthy enough to forgo marriage, they espouse the norm for everyone but themselves.

More problematic are the logical assumptions the jural model makes about behavior and human nature, in particular the assumption that if rules break down, chaos and social disintegration may result. For example, some studies of urbanization claim that the breakdown of legal marriage and the migration of unmarried women to urban centers are harmful to society. (See Comaroff & Roberts 1977 for a critique of this argument.) Studies such as Ardener et al. (1960) and Ardener (1962) present a picture of irresponsible mothers and wives abandoning their crucial moral obligations to home and family, contracting disease, and depleting the labor force by lowering the birth rate—all in favor of a life of carefree temporary liaisons. Certainly some women seek temporary liaisons, but these relationships are more usefully regarded as a rational means to an end. Young women's flights to the city represent social disintegration primarily from the point of view of men and older people in rural areas, who thereby lose their most important means of gaining security and advancement.

AN ALTERNATIVE VIEW OF WOMEN, MARRIAGE, AND FAMILIES

In contrast to the jural model, which assumes that people behave the way they do because rules punish deviance, a processual model focuses on the interactions and exchanges among people, and views rules as a language by which people justify their behavior. Proponents of this approach do not deny that rules can act as sanctions; rather, they argue that rules do not determine behavior in such a mechanistic way as the jural model would suggest. (See also Roberts 1977 and Comaroff & Roberts, forthcoming, for critiques of the jural model as it has been applied to African marriage.) In the processual model, social chaos does not result from people's actions because it is assumed that people make rational choices, depending on what is possible in given social and cultural situations. Legal anthropologists have made strong cases for both models (see, for example, Collier 1973; Moore 1978; Comaroff & Roberts, forthcoming). However, some recent studies are now exploring an in-between course, focusing on the interplay between norms and self-interested behavior (Gulliver 1964, 1969; Hamnett 1977). For example, Comaroff and Roberts (forthcoming) show that although rules may influence social action, they also provide a general cultural gauge by which people may evaluate their own and others' behavior in order to gain strategic advantage.

A clear demonstration of the interplay between Kpelle norms and self-interested choice can be found in the case of John, the wealthy man who reneged on his promise to marry Gbilika (Chapter 5). In devising a strategy, John used the Kpelle rule that a senior wife must approve the choice of subsequent wives, and he fabricated his court testimony and that of his wife around this rule. But even more important in the context of this study is the fact that the processual model better explains the actions of lower-status people who invoke rules that conflict with those espoused by dominant members of the society. For example, a woman seeking a divorce may manipulate rules in order to escape social control: she may claim that her husband fails to support her adequately or that he beats her, both of which are culturally accepted grounds for women to obtain a divorce without serious loss of property in the settlement. In many cases, of course, a woman may have suffered such mistreatment. But such charges are often false, or they may be true because the woman provoked her husband to mistreat her so that she could divorce him. Similarly, women may invoke rules in order to justify their demands, as we saw in the case of Musu (Chapter 5), who tried to exact money from the man she claimed was her husband on the grounds that he should support the children she had borne.

Like the jural theorists, I have used the concept of legal rights in people in analyzing Kpelle marriage. Unlike them, however, I have treated legal rules as resources as well as sanctions. This position supports the works of Barth (1959, 1966), Bailey (1969), and Whitten and Whitten (1972), who discuss social organization in terms of social strategies.[2] (See Asad 1972 for an analysis of the limitations of this view of social rules.) Viewing rules as resources as well as constraints allows us to recognize that divorce is not necessarily tragic for conjugal partners (see Cohen 1971 and E. N. Goody 1973), but can be a means by which people may attain certain goals (see Fortes 1962 and La Fontaine 1962). Instead of labeling divorce as a consequence of the breakdown of social sanctions, we can understand why divorce is a rational alternative for women who seek more autonomy, and why there are so many "exceptions" to formal marriage rules that favor men and older people. In this framework, moreover, the issue of marital instability in different societies becomes subordinated to larger issues of economic and political stratification. We must ask why, and by whom, marriage is contracted: who benefits from marriage?

Women as Seekers of Power

The findings presented in this book raise a number of important issues. First, I have viewed women as well as men as social actors with needs and goals of their own. Like men, women use marriage and divorce as tools for their own purposes. Because women act in their own interests when possible, they frequently disrupt male strategies of advancement: for example, by divorcing men who seek to accumulate wives and clients. Approaches that underestimate the significance of women's goals and strategies "have limited utility, because they treat women as actors seeking to minimize unpleasantness instead of as actors trying to maximize goals; and once the unpleasantness has been minimized, there is no further basis for prediction" (Collier 1974: 90).

Although studies employing the jural model frequently take note of the few women who succeed in the public arena (women chiefs, female husbands, ritual leaders, wealthy market women, and so

2. Scholars have used similar approaches in studies of marriage among the Kaguru of Tanzania (Beidelman 1971) and the Basotho of Lesotho (Murray 1976), and in studies of marriage in the United States as well (Blood & Wolfe 1960, Bernard 1964, and Stack 1974).

on), they generally stress the fact that men control rights in most women's labor, sexual services, and children. In spite of the fact that these studies correctly define the legal dimensions of African marriage, they often make the mistake of accepting the natives' view that because women had no legal rights in themselves, they lacked the means to increase their status and acquire power.

Moreover, jural approaches tended to overemphasize the differences between men's and women's sources of authority and power, reserving the public sphere for men and the private sphere for women. Many of the studies using the model do, of course, describe people's strategies outside the legal system (for example, the informal ways in which women exercise power and influence, especially in their homes). However, by treating women as legal minors these studies tend to obscure the importance of women's political and economic ambitions in the wider society. Since they assumed that desires are always consistent with rules, they conclude that most women are uninterested in—and incapable of—acquiring power and status. I argue instead that we must ask how women, like any other low-status group, acquire wealth and power[3] within the system of legal rights in people.

My view of women as social actors draws an important assumption from authors who view women as seekers of power rather than passive pawns of men. Collier, for example, remarks: "The model woman of my argument . . . is not the affectionate daughter, hardworking wife, or loving mother who gets into trouble while making the best of a difficult situation, but the cold, calculating female who

3. For my present purposes, I am defining power as "an actor's ability to induce or influence another actor to carry out his [or her] directives or any other norms he [or she] supports" (Etzioni 1961: 4). Authority, on the other hand, "is the right, not the ability, to exercise power over others" (Beattie 1959: 357). The distinguishing feature of authority is legitimacy. Beattie's (1959: 347) observation that "authority may exist without power, just as power may exist without authority" is important for the consideration of women and other "lower participants" in the social order. Most Kpelle women, like other African women, have little authority, but exert control over others through influence or persuasion. Influence, in Parsons's terms, is the ability to bring about "a decision on alter's part to act in a certain way because it is felt to be a 'good thing' *for him* [or her]" (1967: 367). Since politics broadly defined is the distribution of power and authority (Cohen & Middleton 1967: ix), women as well as men engage in political activity.

uses all available resources to control the world around her. My model woman seeks power: the capacity to determine her own and others' actions. . . ." (1974: 90)[4]

Although studies such as these recognize that women have political aspirations of their own, some commit the same error as earlier studies, the error of overemphasizing the differences between men and women. They frequently argue that women acquire power and prestige in special ways open to them only, such as becoming leaders of women's secret societies, or at least that women can acquire power independently of the male status system. Moreover, some studies mistakenly associate a high female status with the heavy productive roles women must bear (see Chapter 1).

A number of these works also overemphasize character differences in men and women. Unlike studies that underestimated women as social actors, however, these postulate that women have some innately superior qualities.

[Ibo] women do play an influential part, not only by native custom but because of their inherent vitality, independence of views, courage, self-confidence, desire for gain and worldly standing. More than the men, they seem to be able to co-operate, to stand by each other even in difficulties, and to follow a common aim. The men, except when they are among strangers in a distant place, do not seem to have any common link which goes beyond their immediate town and one cannot easily imagine any situation which would overcome their mutual suspicion and unite them in a common impulse or incline them to acknowledge the leadership of a "stranger," even though that stranger lived but a few miles away. Yet, among the women, there seems to be something—perhaps merely the bond of sex—that links them up over wide areas so that a woman's call to women would echo far beyond the boundaries of her own town . . . there does seem to be an intangible communion, normally latent and without visible organization, but so profoundly felt that the slightest stir sets the whole body trembling. (Leith-Ross 1939: 22)

Similarly, Paulme claims that "the influence exerted by women is due rather to their liveliness, their independent spirit, and their inexhaustive energy, than to rights recognized by custom, and the

4. See also Leith-Ross 1939, P. Ottenberg 1959, Lloyd 1965, Gough 1971, Paulme 1963, Rosaldo & Lamphere 1974, and Hafkin & Bay 1976.

manner in which they are brought up certainly accentuates these innate qualities" (Paulme 1963: 6). The problem with seeing women
as innately different from men or as superior, and with postulating
separate female power bases, is that such a view places women outside the world of social relations that men dominate. This book has
argued the opposite: that both men and women seek power and status. Moreover, there are important similarities in the resources
available to Kpelle men and women. Both use other people—the
young as well as women—to attain power, security, and status.

Women's Resources

In order to help identify and explore the resources available to
men and women, Rosaldo (1974) has proposed a distinction between public and domestic realms of authority that is similar to
Fortes's (1969) earlier distinction between public and private
realms. When we use this distinction to analyze the Kpelle, we find
that most Kpelle women are relegated to domestic groups, and that
few women hold legal rights in themselves or in others. Ordinarily,
women do not have the right to expect others to prepare their
meals, heat their bath water, or clean their clothes, nor do they have
legal rights in bridewealth or brideservice from their children's marriages. A man, on the other hand, acquires domestic support for his
ambitions in the public realm simply by birthright and by marriage.
A woman seeking political advancement thus begins with a double
handicap: advancement requires her to retain the benefits of her
labor and reproduction, but marriage and the legal system fix her to
the domestic realm and hand the benefits of her services to men.
Hence, women must work much harder than men to derive support
from the domestic sphere. Though the distinction between public
and domestic realms is useful in revealing the kinds of resources—
and handicaps—that African men and women have, we must keep
in mind the important connection between the two spheres, especially as it affects women. Men and women rarely gain public success without domestic resources: both need the labor of children
and of women attached to the household (Huntington 1975), and
women need support from husbands and lovers. (See also Sudar-

kasa [1976, n.d.] for a critique of the distinction as it applies to African societies.)

Because most women are confined to the domestic realm, those whom they can most effectively use as political tools are other members of their domestic group: husbands, children, and other women. However, since anthropologists often treat these ties as sacred—or do not treat them at all—it is necessary to distinguish the people women can use to further their ambitions, and to point out what particular methods are available to women by virtue of their positions in the social structure.

The idea that women use other women for their own interests is unacceptable to some feminist writers. However, this study assumes that women have no innate tendency to unite with other people, and do so only when they can benefit from the relationship (see also Lamphere 1974 and Leis 1974). Thus women, as social actors, do band together on occasion: co-wives square off against husbands, market women form trade unions (Lewis 1976), and so on. But given the structure of Kpelle society and the ways in which rewards are achieved, women will act independently when they can gain advancement by doing so. They may compete with other women for scarce rewards and they may profit from the work, marriages, and sexuality of other women (see also Lewis 1976 and Steady 1976). Huntington makes a similar point about systems in which women do the bulk of the agricultural work: "in female farming systems, men subjugate women and women subjugate other women and their own female children in a system of thoroughgoing and self-perpetuating exploitation" (1975: 1008).

Equally disquieting to some is the fact that women use not only other women, but also their closest relatives in pursuit of their own goals. For example, although husbands may be obstacles, they are also the chief sources of labor, cash, houses, and political advancement for ambitious women. In treating conjugal relations so dispassionately, however, I must reiterate the caution stated in the first chapter of this book: most Kpelle spouses who stay together for any length of time feel affection for each other. Furthermore, not all interactions between husbands and wives are based on self-interest.

But I believe that my emphasis on the goal-oriented side of Kpelle conjugal relations is not misplaced. In fact, Kpelle spouses see each other in many ways as outsiders.

Perhaps because of the corporate nature of lineage descent, people's primary allegiances are usually those to consanguineal kin. Consanguineal ties (which include filial ties) are regarded as more important and enduring than those with spouses (see also Little 1973 and Harrell-Bond 1976). Therefore, Kpelle spouses have few inhibitions about expressing conjugal ties in pragmatic terms. Especially after marriage, relations between men and women are frequently marked by distance and by a businesslike attitude focusing on rights and obligations. Recall, for example, how Kpelle women answered my question about whether it is better to be married or single (see Chapter 4). Though embarrassment may have been a factor in these replies, it is significant that none of the Kpelle women mentioned companionship or love, as a woman from the United States might. Furthermore, the Kpelle do not speak in terms of tragedy or emotional trauma when they refer to divorce and adultery.[5]

Since Kpelle sexual affairs also have pragmatic overtones, we must be equally careful to recognize our own cultural biases when analyzing these relationships. Though some observers have treated extramarital affairs dispassionately (for example, Oberg 1938, Schapera 1940, Forde 1941, Nadel 1942, Little 1951, Mair 1953, Colson 1958), others have viewed African women's affairs with disapproval—either condemning the activities of a very large number of African women, or arguing that in analyzing social mobility we should overlook the socially unapproved avenues of mobility that some women choose and concentrate instead on the more self-reliant and socially approved means of upward mobility (Brown 1975, Hafkin & Bay 1976). Moreover, condemnation is not restricted to Westerners. Brain (1976) reports that many elite Tanzanian men publicly deplore cohabitation and the activities of "good-time" girls, while privately enjoying the company of those

5. This, of course, brings into question Western assumptions about the universality and almost biological necessity of romantic love.

girls—a finding that corresponds with my own observations of Liberian elites. Brain believes that elite Tanzanians "in rejecting colonial rule have nevertheless retained attitudes about appropriate sex roles not very different from those found in bourgeois Victorian England (1976: 274)."

Though elites may have absorbed such attitudes from colonial rule, traditional Africans also condemn extramarital sex. But my observations point to a crucial difference between Western attitudes and traditonal Kpelle attitudes. Most Westerners stress the moral disrepute of women who carry on affairs, and view accepting money for sexual favors as a sign of humiliating subservience. But for most Africans, traditional as well as modern, accepting money for sex is not in itself debasing. Even women whom the local people recognize as full-time prostitutes (especially the successful ones) are often admired for their business skills, associations with important people, traveling opportunities, and independence—a point supported by studies dealing with Nigeria (Leith-Ross 1939), Tanzania (Leslie 1963), and Sierra Leone (Little 1973, Harrell-Bond 1976).

From the Kpelle point of view, the use and misuse of female sexual services are best seen in legal perspective. Whereas men are not bound by legal constraints on their sexual behavior, women's sexual services are legally owned by male relatives and husbands. Parents fear losing bridewealth or brideservice if their marriageable daughters have affairs. Similarly, if a man does not consent to his wife's affair, he sees the affair as an infringement on his rights and as damage to his property. Though women lack the legal backing that men have, women whose husbands are carrying on affairs are often equally upset—but not for emotional reasons, as Westerners might think. Rather, Kpelle wives complain about lovers and prostitutes mostly because they worry about family resources slipping through their husbands' frivolous hands. Moreover, Western attitudes not only place condemnation where it does not belong, but also obscure the importance of female sexuality as a resource in men's and women's ambitions of advancement. I have found, as have many other observers of traditional West African societies (for example, Meek 1931, Little 1948, Gibbs 1960, and Green 1947), that the practice of allowing a wife to take on a lover is one of the primary sources of labor and political support for wealthy men. And for women, conversely, lovers represent a primary source of outside support, as well as an avenue of escape from restrictive marriages. To ignore extramarital affairs is to ignore the crucial role they play in African political and economic life.

Although discomfort with treating relations between men and women dispassionately may be a Western cultural bias, when we consider the bonds between mother and child we find that Africans and Westerners have similar views. The Kpelle, for example, feel discomfort in probing these bonds, which most Kpelle consider the most sacred of all. Nevertheless, Huntington's (1975) observation that women use their own children as well as other women to acquire labor and support shows that it is necessary to analyze this relationship objectively. As I have argued, many Kpelle women seek to benefit from their children's subsistence and cash crop production as well as from the earnings of their educated children. Mothers also demand a share in the bridewealth or brideservice their children's marriages bring.

Fathers as well as mothers seek these benefits, of course, and a consideration of both parents in relation to their children reveals a largely overlooked pattern: the group that shoulders the heaviest burden of productive labor in African societies is not women, but rather the young. As my evidence has shown, both men and women look forward to an old age in which the young support them. In fact, the distinction between the old and the young may ultimately be more important in understanding people's goals and strategies in many African societies than the distinction between men and women, even though the latter is the one to which our attention is most often drawn by anthropologists and natives alike. Since women are able to gain control over the young using the traditional wealth-in-people system, it is easy to understand why many women, especially older ones, complain on the one hand about the breakdown of marriage and filial obligations, but on the other hand reveal by their own actions a desire for independence—a question raised at the beginning of this book.

Although men and women share similar goals, they have different methods of seeking advancement and their options are directly related to their legal status. Because men have recognized authority in kinship and other groups, they have legal backing for securing status and power. Men's use of the benefits derived from women and children is therefore unquestioned. But women, because they are defined as legal inferiors, must rely heavily on resources that are often viewed as nonlegal and therefore suspect: illicit use of their sexual services, informal negotiation, trickery, and appeals to moral obligation.

Bailey's (1969) typology is helpful in analyzing the kinds of moral resources women have. He distinguishes "moral" relations (those rooted in ideals or altruism, in which thoughts of reward are absent) from "contract" relations (those based on a specified reward for services rendered). Since relationships within domestic groups are defined in moral rather than contractual terms (Collier 1974), women with no outside resources can gain the most power by appealing to moral obligation, love, altruism, and guilt. Although women are reluctant to admit that they use their families in these ways, "there are advantages in translating even moral obligations into the language of resources. . . . A moral resource is nonetheless a resource, and therefore open to questions about relative cost" (Bailey 1969: 26). Older Kpelle women who tell tragic stories of their children's neglect can arouse public indignation in a way men cannot.

However, in Western societies as well as among the Kpelle, there are more pitfalls in the use of moral resources than in the use of contractual resources such as legal rights. In English the word that best describes informal maneuvering and the use of emotional appeals to gain compliance is "manipulation," a word with negative connotations. Hence, when women's political strategies in domestic groups are exposed, it is easy to label these strategies manipulation, thereby condemning them (Collier 1974: 91). Because people view attempts to manipulate family relationships as deplorable—an observation that applies to the Kpelle primarily in terms of mother-child relations—the slightest misuse of these ties can bring humiliation on a woman and quickly turn public sympathy for her into resentment. Moreover, in order to keep others in line, women must continually preach the need for moral sanctions and the value of altruism. This strategy ultimately places their own behavior under intensified public scrutiny. When women fulfill selfish ends by preaching selflessness, the revelation of their own failures to act altruistically will be doubly damning.

Since legal rights in people are reinforced by the weight of the judicial system, they represent a surer means of gaining power. Therefore, Kpelle women seeking independence, wealth, and status begin by obtaining legal rights in themselves, and then attempt to claim legal rights in their children. Eventually they may be able to establish contractual ties with powerful patrons, and in turn take on dependent clients in their roles as chiefs, secret society leaders, and household heads. Women can play the wealth-in-people game more easily when they control production and reproduction legally, just as men do, instead of counting on nonlegal moral sanctions.

I suggest that a reluctance to examine women's extramarital affairs and their political activities within their families and in relation to other women has led us in recent years to consider women as somehow special or above the messy world of self-interest, and as separate from men but equal to them in social status. Because most women must operate within the confines of domestic groups, this reluctance has prevented us from working toward an understanding of women's most common strategies. Rather than ignore or minimize the significance of female subordination and of women's use of sexual resources, families, and other women, I have dealt squarely with these issues. To do otherwise is to misconstrue the place of women in society and to underestimate their political ambitions. We must preserve a dispassionate attitude even when studying what to us constitute the most sacred bonds: the bonds between husband and wife, mother and child, and one woman and another. By taking such a position we can examine women's lives and their relations much as we would any other social phenomena.

During my fieldwork I observed significant differences in the lives of women in traditional and modern areas, and I would like to end by assessing Kpelle women's prospects for the future. Women in Haindii and Dobli Island seem motivated to change their way of life by the carrot instead of the stick. Although women who try to divorce know that they will lose their husbands' labor and perhaps their houses and crops, they hope to replace these losses with greater gains: economic independence or richer husbands. These women see change as a positive force primarily because they have access to land for subsistence farming, which enables them to support their families and engage in entrepreneurial activities. (Brain 1976 and Hay 1976 have noted similar patterns among East African women with land to farm.)

However, an ominous trend threatens to reverse women's initial gains very soon. In Haindii, Dobli Island, and Digei, land is freely available to women either because they are longtime residents or because they have relatives in the area. But as land passes into private ownership, and the fertility of subsistence farmland decreases owing to shortened fallows, women's security will be jeopardized, for women are almost invariably the first to lose rights in land when it grows scarce. Moreover, government programs designed to facilitate modernization too often neglect women; the programs concentrate on training men for skilled jobs in industry and on teaching men agricultural techniques that produce more food from smaller plots of land (Boserup 1970). Most urban women without education have few options other than petty trading, housekeeping for wealthy urbanites, and relying on husbands and lovers (see also Pellow 1977). Though urban trading is often treated as a sign of independence and wealth, only a few older women who are free from domestic duties actually undertake such ventures: "The geographical mobility and economic activity of women merchants, and the spectacular financial success of some, makes them obviously more fortunate than female farmers, but a little good fortune for a very few should not be confused with the authority and power which is the birthright of men in these societies" (Huntington 1975: 1009).

Similarly, the income that women derive from prostitution and lovers is seldom enough for steady upward mobility in areas where subsistence farmland is unavailable and men's wages are low. Prostitutes such as Florence (see Chapter 5) who can invest their incomes in real estate and professional training are most likely to advance. But most women lack the education or personal connections to do so. Moreover, most women who try to accumulate capital must share their earnings with relatives to ensure reciprocity when they themselves are in need. Though most studies have noted a decided drop in women's status as modernization proceeds, I have been careful to avoid the "romantic myth of the independent, self-sufficient African woman farmer and trader" (Huntington 1975: 1011) when discussing traditional Kpelle society. Indeed, as we have seen, both men and women rely on the labor of others.

However, many women in Fuama Chiefdom find themselves—at least temporarily—in a happy situation. They have used cash from marketing and from their lovers to free themselves from restrictive marital ties, and at the same time have kept a grip on traditional levers of control: children, clients, and access to subsistence farmland. The loss of adequate farmland and the scarcity of adequate wage jobs, both of which seem unavoidable, may soon force Fuama women to redefine themselves as dependent wives of men who earn money in the cash economy.

Reference Matter

APPENDIX

Supplementary Tables

MARITAL STATUSES OF WOMEN AND MEN
(TABLES A1–A8)

The following eight tables present full data on the marital statuses of women and men in Digei, Dobli Island, and Haindii. These data have been selected and combined for presentation in the text as Tables 5–8 in Chapter 5. Tables A1–A6 display a detailed breakdown of the marital statuses of women and men by age in the three towns; Tables A7 and A8 show women's and men's marital statuses for all ages combined in the three towns. In all eight tables the heading "Marital status" is subdivided into seven categories: "married," "loving," "divorced," "separated," "widowed," "never married," and "unknown." The term "married" refers to couples in which the woman has legally been "turned over" to the man by her kin. "Loving" refers to cohabiting unmarried couples or to people engaged in one serious affair. However, a man married to one woman and "loving to" another in the same household was classified as married. "Divorced" people are those who have divorced their legal spouse, and are not currently "loving to" anyone. "Separated" couples are married people living apart who are for all practical purposes divorced, except for the legal termination of the marriage by their kinspeople. A "widowed" person is one whose legally married spouse has died, and he or she is not currently married or "loving to" anyone. The term "never married" refers to those who have not married legally; although these people may have had "loving" affairs in the past, they are not currently "loving to" anyone.

Having just explained all these categories in a manner that is fairly clear to Westerners, I must caution the reader that actual conjugal arrangements are much messier than these neat categories would have us believe. The distinction between "loving" and "divorced," for example, is often a very arbitrary one, since sexual affairs are so common. This, I believe, accounts for the fact that there are no "divorced" men in Haindii and few in Dobli Island and Digei (see Tables A4 through A6, and Table A8). Similarly, the number of widowed old women in all three towns is great not only because they outlive their older husbands, but also because women in this age group have grown children to support them—therefore they are less likely to engage in sexual affairs for economic reasons than younger women are.

In the light of these problems, the categories are more reliably grouped as "married," "never married," "unknown," and "other." Only these are used for statistical purposes. Manipulating the data on any other level is to be discouraged. (The divorce ratios in Table 11, Chapter 5, however, use the histories of women's legal marriages, and are not concerned with present marital status. Therefore, they are fairly reliable.) Even the four simplified categories are not to be regarded as infallible, because relationships are often so ambiguous. For example, I did not try to trace all the legal rights in a woman to see if these rights were owned by a big man instead of the man she was living with. Legally, the big man might also be considered a husband if the woman was "turned over" to him. But the practice of loaning wives has changed, especially in Haindii. A big man may still arbitrate disputes between a man and the woman he has given him, and he makes certain that the husband who is living with the woman knows he is indebted to the big man. However, the husband generally has the right to collect adultery fees if the woman has been "turned over" to him, and he owns rights in the children she produces. Furthermore, couples frequently disagree on whether they are legally married. I have tried to put such cases in the "unknown" column, but some couples vacillated frequently, depending on how they were getting along at the time.

TABLE A1. *Marital statuses of women in Digei*

Age category	Marital status							
	Married	"Loving"	Divorced	Separated	Widowed	Never married	Unknown	Total
Young	26 (55.3%)	12 (25.5%)	1 (2.1%)	1 (2.1%)	0	7 (14.9%)	0	47 (100%)
Middle-aged	59 (84.3%)	3 (4.3%)	6 (8.6%)	0	2 (2.9%)	0	0	70 (100%)
Old	9 (42.9%)	0	1 (4.8%)	0	11 (52.4%)	0	0	21 (100%)
Very old	0	0	0	1 (20.0%)	4 (80.0%)	0	0	5 (100%)
TOTAL	94 (65.7%)	15 (10.5%)	8 (5.6%)	2 (1.4%)	17 (11.9%)	7 (4.9%)	0	143 (100%)

TABLE A2. *Marital statuses of women in Dobli Island*

Age category	Marital status							
	Married	"Loving"	Divorced	Separated	Widowed	Never married	Unknown	Total
Young	8 (19.0%)	10 (23.8%)	11 (26.2%)	1 (2.4%)	0	9 (21.4%)	3 (7.1%)	42 (100%)
Middle-aged	36 (46.2%)	18 (23.1%)	15 (19.2%)	0	3 (3.8%)	0	6 (7.7%)	78 (100%)
Old	2 (15.4%)	2 (15.4%)	2 (15.4%)	0	7 (53.8%)	0	0	13 (100%)
Very old	0	0	1 (25.0%)	0	3 (75.0%)	0	0	4 (100%)
TOTAL	46 (33.6%)	30 (21.9%)	29 (21.2%)	1 (0.7%)	13 (9.5%)	9 (6.6%)	9 (6.6%)	137 (100%)

TABLE A3. *Marital statuses of women in Haindii*

Age category				Marital status				
	Married	"Loving"	Divorced	Separated	Widowed	Never married	Unknown	Total
Young	14 (24.1%)	20 (34.5%)	4 (6.9%)	0	0	17 (29.3%)	3 (5.2%)	58 (100%)
Middle-aged	40 (43.5%)	24 (26.1%)	13 (14.1%)	0	6 (6.5%)	0	9 (9.8%)	92 (100%)
Old	6 (27.3%)	2 (9.1%)	5 (22.7%)	0	7 (31.8%)	0	2 (9.1%)	22 (100%)
Very old	0	0	0	0	1 (50.0%)	0	1 (50.0%)	2 (100%)
TOTAL	60 (34.5%)	46 (26.4%)	22 (12.6%)	0	14 (8.0%)	17 (9.8%)	15 (8.6%)	174 (100%)

TABLE A4. *Marital statuses of men in Digei*

Age category				Marital status				
	Married	"Loving"	Divorced	Separated	Widowed	Never married	Unknown	Total
Young	8 (53.3%)	4 (26.7%)	1 (6.7%)	0	0	2 (13.3%)	0	15 (100%)
Middle-aged	56 (91.8%)	2 (3.3%)	1 (1.6%)	0	0	1 (1.6%)	1 (1.6%)	61 (100%)
Old	9 (81.8%)	0	1 (9.1%)	0	0	1 (9.1%)	0	11 (100%)
Very old	1 (100%)	0	0	0	0	0	0	1 (100%)
TOTAL	74 (84.1%)	6 (6.8%)	3 (3.4%)	0	0	4 (4.5%)	1 (1.1%)	88

TABLE A5. *Marital statuses of men in Dobli Island*

Age category	Marital status							
	Married	"Loving"	Divorced	Separated	Widowed	Never married	Unknown	Total
Young	3 (13.0%)	1 (4.3%)	2 (8.7%)	0	0	17 (73.9%)	0	23 (100%)
Middle-aged	28 (49.1%)	19 (33.3%)	3 (5.3%)	0	0	0	7 (12.3%)	57 (100%)
Old	2 (50.0%)	1 (25.0%)	0	0	1 (25.0%)	0	0	4 (100%)
Very old	1 (50.0%)	0	0	0	1 (50.0%)	0	0	2 (100%)
TOTAL	34 (39.5%)	21 (24.4%)	5 (5.8%)	0	2 (2.3%)	17 (19.8%)	7 (8.1%)	86 (100%)

TABLE A6. *Marital statuses of men in Haindii*

Age category	Marital status							
	Married	"Loving"	Divorced	Separated	Widowed	Never married	Unknown	Total
Young	7 (20.6%)	4 (11.8%)	0	0	0	21 (61.8%)	2 (5.9%)	34 (100%)
Middle-aged	33 (61.1%)	17 (31.5%)	0	0	0	1 (1.9%)	3 (5.5%)	54 (100%)
Old	4 (36.4%)	3 (27.3%)	0	0	1 (9.1%)	2 (18.2%)	1 (9.1%)	11 (100%)
Very old	0	0	0	0	0	0	0	0
TOTAL	44 (44.4%)	24 (24.2%)	0	0	1 (1.0%)	24 (24.2%)	6 (6.1%)	99 (100%)

TABLE A7. *Marital statuses of women in Digei, Dobli Island, and Haindii*

Marital status	Digei	Dobli Island	Haindii	Total
Married	94	46	60	200
"Loving"	15	30	46	91
Divorced	9	29	22	60
Separated	1	1	0	2
Widowed	17	13	14	44
Never married	7	9	17	33
Unknown	0	9	15	24
TOTAL	143	137	174	454

TABLE A8. *Marital statuses of men in Digei, Dobli Island, and Haindii*

Marital status	Digei	Dobli Island	Haindii	Total
Married	74	34	44	152
"Loving"	6	21	24	51
Divorced	3	5	0	8
Separated	0	0	0	0
Widowed	0	2	1	3
Never married	4	17	24	45
Unknown	1	7	6	14
TOTAL	88	86	99	273

HOUSE OWNERSHIP, HOUSEHOLD HEADSHIP, AND MARITAL STATUS (TABLES A9–A16)

The following eight tables present full data on relationships among sex, marital status, residence, house ownership, and household headship. These data have been selected and combined for presentation in the text as Tables 12–18 in Chapter 5. Table A9 examines the number of houses owned by men and women in Digei, Dobli Island, and Haindii; Tables A10–A15 compare the marital statuses of male and female house owners versus non-house owners in the three towns; Table A16 compares the marital statuses of women who were heads of both simple and complex households in the three towns. On λ values, see the notes to Tables 7 and 8 in text (pp. 124, 125).

TABLE A9. *Number of houses owned, by sex, in Digei, Dobli Island, and Haindii*

Town	Number of houses owned by:		Total
	Men	Women	
Digei	74 (87.1%)	11 (12.9%)	85 (100%)
Dobli Island	60 (69.0%)	27 (31.0%)	87 (100%)
Haindii	74 (74.0%)	26 (26.0%)	100 (100%)
TOTAL	208 (76.5%)	64 (23.5%)	272 (100%)

TABLE A10. *Marital statuses of male house owners versus non-house owners in Digei*

House owner status	Marital status		Total
	Married	Other	
House owner	65 (94.2%)	4 (5.8%)	69 (100%)
Non-house owner	9 (50.0%)	9 (50.0%)	18 (100%)
TOTAL	74 (85.1%)	13 (14.9%)	87 (100%)
$\lambda_{xy} = 0, \lambda_{yx} = .28$			

NOTE: Unknowns are excluded.

TABLE A11. *Marital statuses of male house owners versus non-house owners in Dobli Island*

House owner status	Marital status		Total
	Married	Other	
House owner	33 (73.3%)	12 (26.7%)	45 (100%)
Non-house owner	1 (2.9%)	33 (97.1%)	34 (100%)
TOTAL	34 (43.0%)	45 (57.0%)	79 (100%)
$\lambda_{xy} = 0, \lambda_{yx} = .28$			

NOTE: Unknowns are excluded.

TABLE A12. *Marital statuses of male house owners versus non-house owners in Haindii*

House owner status	Marital status		Total
	Married	Other	
House owner	39 (70.9%)	16 (29.1%)	55 (100%)
Non-house owner	5 (12.8%)	34 (87.2%)	39 (100%)
TOTAL	44 (46.8%)	50 (53.2%)	94 (100%)
$\lambda_{xy} = .52, \lambda_{yx} = .46$			

NOTE: Unknowns are excluded.

TABLE A13. *Marital statuses of female house owners versus non-house owners in Digei*

House owner status	Marital status		Total
	Married	Other	
House owner	2 (18.2%)	9 (81.8%)	11 (100%)
Non-house owner	92 (69.7%)	40 (30.3%)	132 (100%)
TOTAL	94 (65.7%)	49 (34.3%)	143 (100%)
$\lambda_{xy} = .14, \lambda_{yx} = .28$			

NOTE: Unknowns are excluded.

TABLE A14. *Marital statuses of female house owners versus non-house owners in Dobli Island*

House owner status	Marital status		Total
	Married	Other	
House owner	0	24 (100%)	24 (100%)
Non-house owner	46 (43.8%)	59 (56.2%)	105 (100%)
TOTAL	46 (35.7%)	83 (64.3%)	129 (100%)
$\lambda_{xy} = 0, \lambda_{yx} = 0$			

NOTE: Unknowns are excluded.

TABLE A15. *Marital statuses of female house owners versus non-house owners in Haindii*

House owner status	Marital status		Total
	Married	Other	
House owner	2 (7.7%)	24 (92.3%)	26 (100%)
Non-house owner	58 (43.6%)	75 (56.4%)	133 (100%)
TOTAL	60 (37.7%)	99 (62.3%)	159 (100%)
$\lambda_{xy} = 0, \lambda_{yx} = 0$			

NOTE: Unknowns are excluded.

TABLE A16. *Number of married and unmarried household heads for simple and complex female households in Digei, Dobli Island, and Haindii*

Town	Unmarried	Married	Total
Digei	8 (61.5%)	5 (38.5%)	13 (100%)
Dobli Island	19 (82.6%)	4 (17.4%)	23 (100%)
Haindii	22 (81.5%)	5 (18.5%)	27 (100%)
TOTAL	49 (77.8%)	14 (22.2%)	63 (100%)

MARITAL STATUSES OF MEN BY ECONOMIC
CATEGORY AND AGE CATEGORY (TABLES A17–
A20)

The following four tables present data on the marital statuses of middle-aged and old wealthy and nonwealthy men in Digei and Haindii. Tables 21 and 22 in Chapter 5 present data on the marital statuses of young men in these two towns. I do not include a table for very old men in Digei, because there was only one such man, who was wealthy and married. In Haindii there were no very old men. On λ values, see the notes to Tables 7 and 8 in text (pp. 124, 125).

TABLE A 17. *Marital statuses of wealthy versus nonwealthy middle-aged men in Digei*

| Economic status | Marital status | | Total |
	Married	Other	
Wealthy	16 (88.9%)	2 (11.1%)	18 (100%)
Nonwealthy	40 (95.2%)	2 (4.8%)	42 (100%)
TOTAL	56 (93.3%)	4 (6.7%)	60 (100%)
$\lambda_{xy} = 0, \lambda_{yx} = .53$			

NOTE: Unknowns are excluded.

TABLE A 18. *Marital statuses of wealthy versus nonwealthy old men in Digei*

| Economic status | Marital status | | Total |
	Married	Other	
Wealthy	3 (100%)	0	3 (100%)
Nonwealthy	6 (75.0%)	2 (25.0%)	8 (100%)
TOTAL	9 (81.8%)	2 (18.2%)	11 (100%)
$\lambda_{xy} = 0, \lambda_{yx} = 0$			

NOTE: Unknowns are excluded.

TABLE A 19. *Marital statuses of wealthy versus nonwealthy middle-aged men in Haindii*

| Economic status | Marital status | | Total |
	Married	Other	
Wealthy	26 (83.9%)	5 (16.1%)	31 (100%)
Nonwealthy	7 (35.0%)	13 (65.0%)	20 (100%)
TOTAL	33 (64.7%)	18 (35.3%)	51 (100%)
$\lambda_{xy} = .33, \lambda_{yx} = .40$			

TABLE A 20. *Marital statuses of wealthy versus nonwealthy old men in Haindii*

| Economic status | Marital status | | Total |
	Married	Other	
Wealthy	3 (75.0%)	1 (25.0%)	4 (100%)
Nonwealthy	1 (16.7%)	5 (83.3%)	6 (100%)
TOTAL	4 (40.0%)	6 (60.0%)	10 (100%)
$\lambda_{xy} = .50, \lambda_{yx} = .50$			

NOTE: Unknowns are excluded.

REFERENCES CITED

Ackerman, C. 1963. "Affiliations: Structural Determinants of Differential Divorce Rates," *Amer. J. Sociol.*, 69: 13–20.

Adelman, I. 1961. *Theories of Economic Growth and Development.* Stanford, Calif.

Alldridge, T. J. 1910. *A Transformed Colony: Sierra Leone As It Was, and As It Is, Its Progress, Peoples, Native Customs and Undeveloped Wealth.* London.

Ardener, E. 1962. *Divorce and Fertility: An African Study.* London.

Ardener, E., S. Ardener, and W. A. Warmington. 1960. *Plantation and Village in the Cameroons: Some Economic and Social Studies.* London.

Asad, T. 1972. "Market Model, Class Structure and Consent: A Reconsideration of Swat Political Organisation," *Man*, n.s. 7: 74–94.

Bailey, F. G. 1969. *Stratagems and Spoils: A Social Anthropology of Politics.* New York.

Barnes, J. A. 1951. *Marriage in a Changing Society: A Study in Structural Change Among the Fort Jameson Ngoni.* Rhodes-Livingstone Institute Papers, no. 20.

———. 1967. "The Frequency of Divorce," in A. L. Epstein, ed., *The Craft of Social Anthropology.* London.

Barth, F. 1959. "Segmentary Opposition and the Theory of Games: A Study of Pathan Organization," *J. Roy. Anthrop. Inst.*, 89: 5–21.

———. 1966. *Models of Social Organization.* London. Royal Anthropological Institute Occasional Paper no. 23.

———. 1967. "On the Study of Social Change," *Amer. Anthrop.*, 69: 661–69.

Beattie, J. 1959. "Checks on the Abuse of Political Power in Some African States: A Preliminary Framework for Analysis," *Sociologus*, 9: 97–115. Reprinted in 1967 in R. Cohen and J. Middleton, eds., *Comparative Political Systems: Studies in the Politics of Pre-Industrial Societies.* Garden City, N.Y.

Beidelman, T. O. 1971. *The Kaguru: A Matrilineal People of East Africa.* New York.

Berger, I. 1976. "Rebels or Status Seekers? Women as Spirit Mediums in

East Africa," in N. J. Hafkin and E. G. Bay, eds., *Women in Africa: Studies in Social and Economic Change.* Stanford, Calif.

Bernard, J. 1964. "The Adjustment of Married Mates," in H. T. Christensen, ed., *Handbook of Marriage and the Family.* Chicago.

Bledsoe, C. H. 1976. "Women's Marital Strategies Among the Kpelle of Liberia," *J. Anthrop. Research,* 32: 372–89.

———. Forthcoming. "The Manipulation of Kpelle Social Fatherhood," *Ethnology.*

Bledsoe, C. H., and W. P. Murphy. Forthcoming. "The Kpelle Negotiation of Marriage and Matrilateral Ties," in S. Beckerman and L. S. Cordell, eds., *The Versatility of Kinship.* San Francisco.

Blood, R. O., and D. M. Wolfe. 1960. *Husbands and Wives: The Dynamics of Married Living.* Glencoe, Ill.

Boserup, E. 1965. *The Conditions of Agricultural Growth: The Economics of Agrarian Change Under Population Pressure.* Chicago.

———. 1970. *Woman's Role in Economic Development.* New York.

Brain, J. L. 1976. "Less than Second-Class: Women in Rural Settlement Schemes in Tanzania," in N. J. Hafkin and E. G. Bay, eds., *Women in Africa: Studies in Social and Economic Change.* Stanford, Calif.

Bretton, H. L. 1974. *Power and Politics in Africa.* Chicago.

Brown, B. B. 1975. "Review of Kenneth Little, *African Women in Towns,*" *African Studies Association Review of Books,* I.

Cancian, Frank. 1976. "Social Stratification," in B. J. Siegel, ed., *Annual Review of Anthropology.* Palo Alto, Calif.

Carter, J. E. 1970. "Household Organization and the Money Economy in a Loma Community, Liberia." Unpublished Ph.D. dissertation, University of Oregon.

Clower, R. W., G. Dalton, M. Harwitz, and A. A. Walters. 1966. *Growth Without Development: An Economic Survey of Liberia.* Evanston, Ill.

Cohen, R. 1971. *Dominance and Defiance: A Study of Marital Instability in an Islamic African Society.* Washington, D. C. American Anthropological Association Studies, no. 6.

Cohen, R., and J. Middleton. 1967. "Introduction," in R. Cohen and J. Middleton, eds., *Comparative Political Systems: Studies in the Politics of Pre-Industrial Societies.* Garden City, N.Y.

Cole, Michael, J. Gay, J. A. Glick, and D. W. Sharp. 1971. *The Cultural Context of Learning and Thinking.* New York.

Collier, J. F. 1971. "The Dynamics of Debt in Kpelle Politics." Unpublished manuscript.

———. 1973. *Law and Social Change in Zinacantan.* Stanford, Calif.

———. 1974. "Women in Politics," in M. Z. Rosaldo and L. Lamphere, eds., *Woman, Culture, and Society.* Stanford, Calif.

Colson, E. 1958. *Marriage and the Family Among the Plateau Tonga.* Manchester, England.

Comaroff, J. L., and S. Roberts. 1977. "Marriage and Extra-marital Sexuality: The Dialectics of Legal Change Among the Kgatla," *J. Afr. Law,* 21: 97–123.

———. Forthcoming. *Rules and Processes: The Cultural Logic of Dispute in an African Context.*

Crosby, K. H. 1937. "Polygamy in Mende Country." *Africa,* 10: 249–64.

Dalton, G. 1965. "History, Politics, and Economic Development in Liberia," *J. Econ. Hist.,* 25: 569–91.

d'Azevedo, W. L. 1959. "The Setting of Gola Society and Culture: Some Theoretical Implications of Variations in Time and Space," *Kroeber Anthrop. Soc. Pap.,* 21: 43–125.

———. 1962a. "Common Principles of Variant Kinship Structures Among the Gola of Western Liberia," *Amer. Anthrop.,* 64: 504–20.

———. 1962b. "Some Historical Problems in the Delineation of a Central West Atlantic Region," *An. N. Y. Acad. Sci.,* 96: 512–38.

———. 1971. "Tribe and Chiefdom on the Windward Coast," *Rural Afr.,* 15: 11–29.

Dorjahn, V. R., and A. S. Tholley. 1959. "A Provisional History of the Limba, with Special Reference to Tonko Limba Chiefdom," *Sierra Leone Stud.,* 12: 273–83.

Douglas, M. 1963. *The Lele of the Kasai.* London.

Etzioni, A. 1961. *A Comparative Analysis of Complex Organizations: On Power, Involvement, and Their Correlates.* New York.

Evans-Pritchard, E. E. 1940. *The Nuer: A Description of the Modes of Livelihood and Political Institutions of a Nilotic People.* Oxford.

———. 1945. *Some Aspects of Marriage and the Family Among the Nuer.* Rhodes-Livingstone Institute Papers, no. 11.

———. 1951. *Kinship and Marriage Among the Nuer.* Oxford.

Fallers, L. A. 1957. "Some Determinants of Marriage Stability in Busoga: A Reformulation of Gluckman's Hypothesis," *Africa,* 27: 106–23.

———. 1964. "Social Stratification and Economic Processes in Africa," in M. J. Herskovits and M. Harwitz, eds., *Economic Trans. in Africa.* Evanston, Ill.

———. 1973. "Introduction," in *Inequality: Social Stratification Reconsidered.* Chicago.

Forde, D. 1941. *Marriage and the Family Among the Yakö in South-Eastern Nigeria.* London: L.S.E. Monographs on Social Anthropology, no. 5.

Fortes, M. 1935. *Marriage Law Among the Tallensi.* Accra, Ghana.

———. 1949. *The Web of Kinship Among the Tallensi.* London.

———. 1950. "Kinship and Marriage Among the Ashanti," in A. R. Radcliffe-Brown and D. Forde, eds., *African Systems of Kinship and Marriage*. London.

———. 1962. "Introduction," in M. Fortes, ed., *Marriage in Tribal Societies*. Cambridge, England.

———. 1969. *Kinship and the Social Order: The Legacy of Lewis Henry Morgan*. Chicago.

Fraenkel, M. 1964. *Tribe and Class in Monrovia*. London.

Fulton, R. M. 1972. "The Political Structures and Functions of Poro in Kpelle Society," *Amer. Anthrop.*, 74: 1218–33.

Gay, J. 1973. *Red Dust on the Green Leaves: A Kpelle Twins' Childhood*. Thompson, Conn.

Gibbs, J. L., Jr. 1960. "The Judicial Implications of Marital Instability Among the Kpelle." Unpublished Ph.D. dissertation, Harvard University.

———. 1963. "Marital Instability Among the Kpelle: Towards a Theory of Epainogamy," *Amer. Anthrop.*, 65: 552–73.

———. 1965. "The Kpelle of Liberia," in J. L. Gibbs, Jr., ed., *Peoples of Africa*. New York.

Gluckman, M. 1941. *Economy of the Central Barotse Plain*. Rhodes-Livingstone Institute Papers, no. 7.

———. 1950. "Kinship and Marriage Among the Lozi of Northern Rhodesia and the Zulu of Natal," in A. R. Radcliffe-Brown and D. Forde, eds., *African Systems of Kinship and Marriage*. London.

———. 1955. *The Judicial Process Among the Barotse of Northern Rhodesia*. Manchester, England.

———. 1965. *Politics, Law and Ritual in Tribal Society*. Chicago.

———. 1972. "Marriage Payments and Social Structure Among the Lozi and Zulu," in J. Goody, ed., *Kinship: Selected Readings*. Harmondsworth, England.

Goffman, E. 1959. *The Presentation of Self in Everyday Life*. New York.

Goodenough, W. H. 1966. "Rethinking 'Status' and 'Role': Toward a General Model of the Cultural Organization of Social Relationships," in M. Banton, ed., *The Relevance of Models for Social Anthropology*. New York.

Goody, E. N. 1973. *Contexts of Kinship: An Essay in the Family Sociology of the Gonja of Northern Ghana*. Cambridge, England.

———. 1975. "Delegation of Parental Roles in West Africa and the West Indies," in J. Goody, ed., *Changing Social Structure in Ghana: Essays in the Comparative Sociology of a New State and an Old Tradition*. London.

Goody, J. 1962. *Death, Property, and the Ancestors*. Stanford, Calif.

———. 1967. *The Social Organization of the LoWiilli*. London.

————. 1969. "Inheritance, Property, and Marriage in Africa and Eurasia," *Sociol.*, 3: 55–76.

————. 1971. "Class and Marriage in Africa and Eurasia," *Amer. J. Sociol.*, 76: 585–603.

————. 1973. "Bridewealth and Dowry in Africa and Eurasia," in J. Goody and S. J. Tambiah, *Bridewealth and Dowry*. Cambridge, England.

Gough, E. K. 1971. "Nuer Kinship: A Re-examination," in T. O. Beidelman, ed., *The Translation of Culture*. London.

Grace, J. 1975. *Domestic Slavery in West Africa, with Particular Reference to the Sierra Leone Protectorate, 1896–1927*. London.

Green, M. M. 1947. *Ibo Village Affairs*. London.

Greenberg, J. H. 1966. *The Languages of Africa*, 2d ed. The Hague.

Greene, G. 1936. *Journey Without Maps*. London.

Gulliver, P. H. 1964. "The Arusha Family," in R. F. Gray and P. H. Gulliver, eds., *The Family Estate in Africa: Studies in the Role of Property in Family Structure and Lineage Continuity*. London.

————. 1969. "Dispute Settlement Without Courts: The Ndendeuli of Southern Tanzania," in L. Nader, ed., *Law in Culture and Society*. Chicago.

Hafkin, N. J., and E. G. Bay. 1976. "Introduction," in N. J. Hafkin and E. G. Bay, eds., *Women in Africa: Studies in Social and Economic Change*. Stanford, Calif.

Hamnett, I. 1977. "Introduction," in I. Hamnett, ed., *Social Anthropology and Law*. London.

Handwerker, W. P. 1972–74. "Entrepreneurship in Liberia," *Liberian Stud. J.*, 5: 113–47.

————. 1973. "Technology and Household Configuration in Urban Africa: The Bassa of Monrovia," *Amer. Sociol. Rev.*, 38: 182–97.

————. 1977. "Family, Fertility, and Economics," *Current Anthrop.*, 18: 259–87.

Harley, G. W. 1941. *Notes on the Poro in Liberia*. Papers of the Peabody Museum, vol. 19, no. 2. Cambridge, Mass.

Harrell-Bond, B. E. 1976. *Modern Marriage in Sierra Leone: A Study of the Professional Group*. The Hague.

Harris, G. 1962. "Taita Bridewealth and Affinal Relationships," in M. Fortes, ed., *Marriage in Tribal Societies*. Cambridge, England.

Hay, M. J. 1976. "Luo Women and Economic Change During the Colonial Period," in N. J. Hafkin and E. G. Bay, eds., *Women in Africa: Studies in Social and Economic Change*. Stanford, Calif.

Herskovits, M. J. 1937. "A Note on 'Woman Marriage' in Dahomey," *Africa*, 10: 335–41.

Hoffer, C. P. 1972a. "Bundu Society: Female Solidarity in a Political Context." Paper presented at the Annual Meeting of the American Anthropological Association, Toronto.

———. 1972b. "Mende and Sherbro Women in High Office," *Canad. J. Afr. Stud.,* 6: 151–64.

———. 1974. "Madam Yoko: Ruler of the Kpa Mende Confederacy," in M. Z. Rosaldo and L. Lamphere, eds., *Woman, Culture, and Society.* Stanford, Calif.

Holsoe, S. 1974. "The Manipulation of Traditional Political Structures Among Coastal Peoples in Western Liberia during the Nineteenth Century," *Ethnohistory,* 21: 158–67.

Hopkins, A. G. 1973. *An Economic History of West Africa.* London.

Horton, R. 1972. "Stateless Societies in the History of West Africa, in J. F. A. Ajayi and M. Crowder, eds., *History of West Africa.* New York.

Howard, A. M. 1972. "Big Men, Traders, and Chiefs: Power, Commerce, and Spatial Change in the Sierra Leone–Guinea Plain, 1865–1895." Unpublished Ph.D. dissertation, University of Wisconsin.

Hunter, M. M. 1933. "Effects of Contact with Europeans on the Status of Pondo Women," *Africa,* 6: 259–76.

———. 1936. *Reaction to Conquest: Effects of Contact with Europeans on the Pondo of South Africa.* London.

Huntington, S. 1975. "Issues in Woman's Role in Economic Development: Critique and Alternatives," *J. Marriage and Family,* 37: 1001–12.

Kopytoff, I., and S. Miers. 1977. "Introduction," in S. Miers and I. Kopytoff, eds., *Slavery in Africa: Historical and Anthropological Perspectives.* Madison, Wisc.

Krige, E. J. 1974. "Woman Marriage with Special Reference to the Lovedu—Its Significance for the Definition of Marriage," *Africa,* 44: 11–37.

Krige, E. J., and J. D. Krige. 1943. *The Realm of a Rain-Queen.* London.

Kup, A. P. 1960. "An Account of the Tribal Distribution of Sierra Leone, *Man,* 60: 116–19.

Kuper, A. 1970. "The Kgalagari and the Jural Consequences of Marriage," *Man,* n.s. 5: 466–82.

Kuper, H. 1950. "Kinship Among the Swazi," in A. R. Radcliffe-Brown and D. Forde, eds., *African Systems of Kinship and Marriage.* London.

La Fontaine, J. S. 1962. "Gisu Marriage and Affinal Relations," in M. Fortes, ed., *Marriage in Tribal Societies.* Cambridge, England.

Lamphere, L. 1974. "Love and Hate Begin at Home: Women's Strategies, Cooperation, and Conflict in Domestic Groups," in M. Z. Rosaldo and L. Lamphere, eds., *Woman, Culture, and Society.* Stanford, Calif.

Leach, E. R. 1957. "Aspects of Bridewealth and Marriage Stability Among the Kachin and Lakher," *Man,* 57: 50–55.

————. 1961. Rethinking Anthropology. London School of Economics Monographs, no. 22. London.

Leis, N. B. 1974. "Women in Groups: Ijaw Women's Associations," in M. Z. Rosaldo and L. Lamphere, eds., *Woman, Culture, and Society.* Stanford, Calif.

Leith-Ross, S. 1939. *African Women: A Study of the Ibo of Nigeria.* London.

Leslie, J. A. K. 1963. *A Social Survey of Dar es Salaam.* London.

Lévi-Strauss, C. 1969. *The Elementary Structures of Kinship.* Boston.

Levin, R. 1947. *Marriage in a Langa Native Location.* Cape Town.

Lewis, B. C. 1976. "The Limitations of Group Action Among Entrepreneurs: The Market Women of Abidjan, Ivory Coast," in N. J. Hafkin and E. G. Bay, eds., *Women in Africa: Studies in Social and Economic Change.* Stanford, Calif.

Lewis, I. M. 1962. *Marriage and the Family in Northern Somaliland.* East African Institute Studies, no. 15. Kampala, Uganda.

Liebenow, J. G. 1969. *Liberia: The Evolution of Privilege.* Ithaca, N.Y.

Little, K. L. 1948. "The Changing Position of Women in the Sierra Leone Protectorate," *Africa,* 18: 1–17.

————. 1949. "The Role of the Secret Society in Cultural Specialization," *Amer. Anthrop.,* 51: 199–212.

————. 1951. *The Mende of Sierra Leone: A West African People in Transition.* London.

————. 1965–66. "The Political Function of the Poro," Parts I and II, *Africa,* 35: 349–65; 36: 62–72.

————. 1967. "The Mende Chiefdoms of Sierra Leone," in D. Forde and P. M. Kaberry, eds., *West African Kingdoms in the Nineteenth Century.* London.

————. 1973. *African Women in Towns: An Aspect of Africa's Social Revolution.* London.

Lloyd, P. C. 1965. "The Yoruba of Nigeria," in J. L. Gibbs, Jr., ed., *Peoples of Africa.* New York.

Lowenkopf, M. 1976. *Politics in Liberia: The Conservative Road to Development.* Stanford, Calif.

Maine, H. S. 1910. *Ancient Law: Its Connection with the Early History of Society and Its Relation to Modern Ideas.* London. 14th ed.

Mair, L. 1953. "African Marriage and Social Change," in Arthur Phillips, ed., *Survey of African Marriage and Family Life.* London.

————. 1961. "Clientship in East Africa," *Cahiers d'Etudes Africaines,* 11: 315–25.

Maquet, J. J. 1961. *The Premise of Inequality in Ruanda.* London.

Meek, C. K. 1931. *Tribal Studies in Northern Nigeria.* London.

Meillassoux, C. 1964. *L'Anthropologie économique des Gouro de Côte d'Ivoire.* The Hague.

———. 1972. "From Reproduction to Production," *Economy and Society,* 1: 93–105.

Mitchell, J. C. 1949. "The Yao of Southern Nyasaland," *Africa,* 19: 94–100.

———. 1961. "Social Change and the Stability of African Marriage in Northern Rhodesia," in A. Southall, ed., *Social Change in Modern Africa.* London.

Moore, S. F. 1978. *Law as Process: An Anthropological Approach.* London.

Morgan, W. B., and J. C. Pugh. 1969. *West Africa.* London.

Murphy, W. P. Forthcoming. "Secret Knowledge as Property and Power in Kpelle Society: Elders Versus Youth," *Africa.*

Murray, C. 1976. "Marital Strategy in Lesotho: The Redistribution of Migrant Earnings," *Afr. Stud.,* 35: 99–121.

———. 1977. "High Bridewealth, Migrant Labour and the Position of Women in Lesotho," *J. Afr. Law,* 21: 79–96.

Myrdal, G. 1957. *Rich Lands and Poor.* New York.

Nadel, S. G. 1942. *A Black Byzantium.* London.

Nieboer, H. J. 1900. *Slavery as an Industrial System: Ethnological Researches.* The Hague.

Oberg, K. 1938. "Kinship Organization of the Banyankole," *Africa,* 11: 129–59.

O'Brien, D. 1972. "Female Husbands in African Societies." Paper presented at the Annual Meeting of the American Anthropological Association, Toronto.

Oppong, C. 1974. *Marriage Among a Matrilineal Elite: A Family Study of Ghanaian Senior Civil Servants.* London.

Ottenberg, P. V. 1959. "The Changing Economic Position of Women Among the Afikpo Ibo," in W. R. Bascom and M. J. Herskovits, eds., *Continuity and Change in African Cultures.* Chicago.

Ottenberg, S. 1973. "Secrecy and Secret Society Initiation Rites." Unpublished manuscript.

Parsons, T. 1967. *Sociological Theory and Modern Society.* New York.

Paulme, D., ed. 1963. *Women of Tropical Africa.* Berkeley, Calif.

Pellow, D. 1977. *Women in Accra: Options for Autonomy.* Algonac, Mich.

Person, Y. 1961. "Les Kissi et leurs statuettes de pierre dans le cadre de l'histoire ouest-africaine," *Bull. Inst. fr. Afr. noire,* 23: 1–59.

Radcliffe-Brown, A. R. 1950. "Introduction," in A. R. Radcliffe-Brown and D. Forde, eds., *African Systems of Kinship and Marriage.* London.

————. 1952. *Structure and Function in Primitive Society.* New York.

Rattray, R. S. 1929. *Ashanti Law and Constitution.* Oxford.

Reyburn, W. D. 1959. "Polygamy, Economy and Christianity in the Eastern Cameroun," *Prac. Anthrop.,* 6: 1–19.

Richards, A. I. 1960. "Conclusion," in A. I. Richards, ed., *East African Chiefs: A Study of Political Development in Some Uganda and Tanganyika Tribes.* London.

Roberts, S. A. 1977. "The Kgatla Marriage: Concepts of Validity," in S. A. Roberts, ed., *Law and the Family in Africa.* The Hague.

Rodney, W. 1970. *A History of the Upper Guinea Coast, 1545–1800.* London.

Rosaldo, M. Z. 1974. "Woman, Culture, and Society: A Theoretical Overview," in M. Z. Rosaldo and L. Lamphere, eds., *Woman, Culture, and Society.* Stanford, Calif.

Rosaldo, M. Z., and L. Lamphere, eds. 1974. *Woman, Culture, and Society.* Stanford, Calif.

Sahlins, M. D. 1963. "Poor Man, Rich Man, Big-Man, Chief: Political Types in Melanesia and Polynesia," *Comp. Stud. Soc. and Hist.,* 5: 285–303.

Schapera, I. 1940. *Married Life in an African Tribe.* London.

Schneider, H. K. 1968. "People as Wealth in Turu Society," *Sthwest. J. Anthrop.,* 24: 375–95.

————. 1970. *The Wahi Wanyaturu: Economics in an African Society.* New York. Viking Fund Publications in Anthropology, no. 48.

Schulze, W. 1973. *A New Geography of Liberia.* London.

Schwab, G. 1947. *Tribes of the Liberian Hinterland.* Cambridge, Mass. Peabody Museum Papers, vol. 31.

Sibley, J. L., and D. H. Westermann. 1928. *Liberia—Old and New; A Study of Its Social and Economic Background with Possibilities of Development.* Garden City, N.Y.

Stack, C. B. 1974. "Sex Roles and Survival Strategies in an Urban Black Community," in M. Z. Rosaldo and L. Lamphere, eds., *Woman, Culture, and Society.* Stanford, Calif.

Stauder, J. 1972. "Anarchy and Ecology: Political Society Among the Majangir," *Sthwest. J. Anthrop.,* 28: 153–68.

Steady, F. C. 1976. "Protestant Women's Associations in Freetown, Sierra Leone," in N. J. Hafkin and E. G. Bay, eds., *Women in Africa: Studies in Social and Economic Change.* Stanford, Calif.

Sudarkasa, N. 1976. "Female Employment and Family Organization in West Africa," in D. McGuigan, ed., *New Research on Women and Sex Roles at the University of Michigan.* Ann Arbor, Mich.

————. n.d. "Understanding the Status and Roles of Black Women in Africa and in the U.S.A.," in B. Awe and F. C. Steady, eds., *The Black Woman in Cross-Cultural Perspective.*

Terray, E. 1972. *Marxism and "Primitive" Societies: Two Studies.* New York.

Uchendu, V. C. 1965. *The Igbo of Southeast Nigeria.* New York.

Van Santen, C. E. 1974. Farm Management and Production Economy. Monrovia, Liberia.

Van Velsen, J. 1964. *The Politics of Kinship: A Study in Social Manipulation Among the Lakeside Tonga of Nyasaland.* Manchester, England.

Van Wing, J. 1947. "La Polygamie au Congo Belge," *Africa,* 17: 93–102.

Vincent, J. 1971. *African Elite: The Big Men of a Small Town.* New York.

Wallerstein, I. 1974. *The Modern World System.* New York.

Watkins, M. H. 1943. "The West African 'Bush' School," *Amer. J. Sociol.,* 48: 666–75.

Welmers, W. E. 1949. "Secret Medicines, Magic, and Rites of the Kpelle Tribe in Liberia," *Sthwest. J. Anthrop.,* 5: 208–43.

———. 1962. "The Phonology of Kpelle," *J. Afr. Lang.,* 1: 69–93.

———. 1971. "The First Course in Kpelle," in J. Gay and W. E. Welmers, eds., *Mathematics and Logic in the Kpelle Language.* Ibadan, Nigeria.

Westermann, D. H. 1921. *Die Kpelle: Ein Negerstamm in Liberia.* Göttingen.

Whitten, N. E., Jr., and D. S. Whitten. 1972. "Social Strategies and Social Relationships," in B. J. Siegel, ed., *Annual Review of Anthropology.* Palo Alto, Calif.

Wilson, G. 1941. *An Essay on the Economics of Detribalization in Northern Rhodesia.* Rhodes-Livingstone Institute Papers, No. 6.

Wilson, M. 1977. *For Men and Elders: Change in the Relations of Generations and of Men and Women Among the Nyakyusa-Ngonde People, 1875–1971.* London.

Wolf, E. 1957. "Closed Corporate Peasant Communities in Mesoamerica and Central Java," *Sthwest. J. Anthrop.,* 13: 1–18.

INDEX